THE LOST SYNAGOGUES OF LONDON

In Memoriam

This book, *The Lost Synagogues of London*, which was originally published in 2000, is reprinted in loving memory of my dear brother, its author, Dr Peter Renton, who tragically and prematurely passed away in December 2003 at the age of 59.

Peter Renton, Pesach ben Avrahom, had a distinguished medical career and was, for many years, Consultant Radiologist at University College Hospital, London and at the Royal Orthopaedic Hospitals, and an Honorary Senior Lecturer at University College, London. Peter's speciality was orthopaedic radiology and he is the author of a number of seminal textbooks on the subject, the last of which is due to be published posthumously.

Peter had an abiding and deep love of Judaism, passed on from our parents, Alfred and Berta Reichenbaum, who, with me, fled from Czechoslovakia in May 1939. Peter's genuine commitment to his religion led him to undertake many charitable acts, particularly in his own field, where he worked tirelessly to provide treatment to the disadvantaged at home, in Israel and elsewhere; there are very many who have cause to be grateful for his help.

This edition is a lasting testimony to his religious belief and his love of Jewish culture. It also speaks to us of his wider scholarship and broad-based knowledge. It is a wonderful keepsake so that we may be reminded of his high ideals and the lofty principles by which he conducted his life.

Dr George Renton

THE
LOST
SYNAGOGUES
OF
LONDON
PETER RENTON

First published in Great Britain in 2000 by Tymsder Publishing,
P.O. Box 16039, London NW3 6WL
E-mail tymsder@aol.com

This commemorative edition published 2004 by Tymsder Publishing
Reprinted 2005

British Library Cataloguing in Publication Data
A catalogue record for this book is available from the British Library.

ISBN 0-9531104-7-8

Printed in Great Britain by Cromwell Press

Typeset by Arc Design Associates

Produced by The Studio Publishing Services Ltd, Exeter EX4 8JN

This book is dedicated, with deep love and gratitude, to the memory of my late father, *Baumeister* Alfred Reichenbaum, who worked on the Synagogue in Zilina, Czechoslovakia, while employed in an architectural practice there, and to my late uncle *Ingenieur* Erich Rosh, who designed a synagogue in Tel Aviv, and their brothers Kurt, Hermann and Leopold.

PREFACE

O Lord, I love the House wherein Thou dwellest

There were many reasons for writing this history. I feel a great sense of loss that once-flourishing communities remain as only a memory to an older generation, and that areas of London, once a home to important synagogues and the many activities associated with them, are now devoid of Jews and their children. Thankfully this is not due to persecution but in the main to prosperity, though in part also to a steady decline in the Jewish population.

Many books of London local history ignore the synagogues and their thriving Jewish communities that once formed part of daily life within these London boroughs. I seek to preserve the memory of these buildings and of 'those who form synagogues and gather therein to pray'.

I have not dealt in any great length with the numerous small synagogues that existed in the East End (these have been described in the many books written by Aumie Shapiro), or in the West End (see Dr. Gerry Black's *Living Up West*,[1] which is still in print).

The devotion of congregants to their communities and the effort put into their foundation and maintenance stands out in many communal histories which I consulted. It was sorrowful to read of their decline and closure, when not even a quorum for prayer could be found. "Verily to hear of it makes our soul sad" (on the destruction of the Temple).

Acknowledgements

Much of what I have written is to be found in numerous congregational histories, many of which are deposited in the excellent Libraries at University College London and Jews' College, London (now the London School of Jewish Studies). I am most grateful to the Librarians, Mrs. Dalia Tracz and Mr. Ezra Kahn, respectively, for their great help and encouragement, willingly given, as well as to the staff of the Manuscript Room, University College London.

Friends and colleagues, who kindly loaned me histories and photographs of communities with which they or their families had been associated, are acknowledged in the text. As these congregations are by definition defunct, and the authors of the histories in the main no longer alive, I sought and was willingly given permission of the parent body to reproduce the contained illustrations. I am particularly grateful to Mr. Elkan Levy, President of the United Synagogue. Some of the illustrations used, and articles quoted, came from Mr. S. Breuer, the late Mr. Hirschler, Mr. Benjamin Meyer and Mr. John Trotter; I am in their debt.

The *Jewish Chronicle*, founded in 1841 and the oldest surviving Jewish newspaper in the world, makes fascinating reading and is a mine of information for the historian. I thankfully acknowledge the permission of the Editor to reproduce illustrations, which are named in the text, and similarly to the National Monuments Record, Islington Public Library, Southwark Public Library and Greenwich Public Library. The *Transactions of the Jewish Historical Society of England* are a rich source of material for the student of communal history and I thank the President of the Society for permission to reproduce illustrations from the *Transactions*. The statistics for the male membership for the United Synagogue came from the Centenary history written by Aubrey Newman.[2] The dates for the opening and closing of the synagogues are *approximate* when based on the *Jewish Year Books*.

Finally, my *most* deep thanks to my long standing and long suffering friends and colleagues: Veronika Aurens, for her diligent editorial assistance; Dirk de Camp, for his meticulous photography and patient treks around London; and Keith Ruggles for the beautifully detailed drawings, often taken from almost indecipherable sources; and to David Roberts who has designed the layout of this book. To them all I am, as always, thankful.

Dr. Gerry Black, President of the Jewish Historical Society of England, kindly read the manuscript and made many helpful suggestions and corrections. If there are any errors, they are entirely my responsibility.

TABLE OF CONTENTS

Jews in London 17
    Pre-expulsion synagogues 17
    Readmission and the first synagogue 21
Population movement at the end of the nineteenth century 24

THE SYNAGOGUES
The Great Synagogue, Duke's Place, EC3 30
    The Rabbinate of the Great Synagogue 35
    The Cantorate of the Great Synagogue..37
The Hambro Synagogue, Fenchurch Street, EC3, later Adler Street, E1 39
    The Revd. Rabbi Samuel Marcus Gollancz 42
The New Synagogue, Leadenhall Street, EC3, later Great St. Helens, EC3,
later Egerton Road, N16 44
The Western Synagogue, Great Pulteney Street, W1, later Denmark Court, Strand, WC2,
later St. Alban's Place, SW1, later Alfred Place, WC1, later Crawford Place, W1 48
    The first synagogue – in Westminster 48
    The second synagogue – in Denmark Court 48
    The third synagogue – the Sans Souci 50
    Relationships with the City synagogues 51
    The secession of Maiden Lane 51
    The Westminster Jews' Free School 52
    The move to St. Albans Place 54
The Beth Hamedrash, Bookers Gardens, EC3, later Leadenhall Street, EC3,
later Duke's Place, EC3, later Mulberry Street, E1 58
    The Revd. Dayan Bernard Spiers 62
The Borough New Synagogue, Heygate Street, SE17, later Wansey Street, SE17 63
    The Borough Jewish School 67
    The first minister, Simeon Singer 68
    Rabbi Francis Lyon Cohen 68
    The Revd. Morris Rosenbaum 69
The West London Synagogue of British Jews, Burton Street, WC1, later Margaret Street, W1,
later Upper Berkeley Street, W1 70
    The Revd. Professor David Woolf Marks 71
The Central Synagogue, Great Portland Street W1 73
    The Revd. Aaron Levy Green 75
The Bayswater Synagogue, Chichester Place, W2, later Andover Place, W2 79
    Rabbi Dr. Hermann Adler 80
    Rabbi Professor Sir Hermann Gollancz 84
The North London Synagogue, Lofting Road, N1 85
    The Revd. Morris Joseph 86
    The Revd. Haim Wasserzug 87
The East London Synagogue, Rectory Square, E1 90
    The Revd. Joseph Frederick Stern 93
    The Revd. Mendel Zeffertt 94
The Dalston Synagogue, Poet's Road, N5 95
    A secession 96
    The Revd. David Wasserzug 97
The Adass Yisroel, Ferntower Road, N5, later Green Lanes, N16 100

Contents

The Jewish Secondary Schools movement 102

RabbiVictor Schönfeld 102

Rabbi Solomon Schönfeld 103

The New Dalston Synagogue, Birkbeck Road, E8 104

The Stoke Newington Synagogue, Shacklewell Lane, E8 104

The South East London Synagogue, New Cross Road, SE14, later Lausanne Road, SE15, later New Cross Road, SE14 108

The Liberal Jewish Synagogue, Hill Street, NW1, later St. John's Wood Road, NW8 112

Claude Goldsmid Montefiore 115

Lily Montagu 116

Rabbi Israel Isadore Mattuck 116

The North West London Synagogue,York Road, NW5, later Caversham Road, NW5 117

The first synagogue at Kentish Town, atYork Road 117

The second synagogue at Kentish Town, at Caversham Road 118

The ministers 119

The Woolwich and Plumstead Synagogue, Anglesea Road, SE18 123

The Revd. Gottlieb Rosenberg 125

The West Ham (Associate) Synagogue, Earlham Grove E7 126

The Revd., later Rabbi, later Dayan Louis Mendelsohn 128

The East Ham and Manor Park Synagogue, Carlyle Road, E12 130

The Brondesbury Synagogue, Chevening Road, NW6 131

The ministers 133

The Brixton Synagogue, Effra Road, SW2 134

The ministers 137

Rabbi, later Dayan Morris Swift 137

Rabbi, later Dayan Meyer Steinberg 137

The Bermondsey and Rotherhithe Synagogue, Jamaica Road, SE16, later Rouel Road, SE16 138

The Hornsey and Wood Green Synagogue, Green Lanes, N8, later Wightman Road, N8 139

The Muswell Hill Synagogue, Fortis Green Road, N10 140

The South West London Synagogue, 104 Bolingbroke Grove, SW11 142

The Upton Park Synagogue, Tudor Road, E6 144

The Richmond Synagogue, Parkshot, later Sheen Road, Richmond 145

The Chelsea Synagogue (the Victoria and Chelsea Synagogue), Smith Terrace, SW3 147

The Settlement Synagogue, Betts Street, E1, later Berners (Henriques) Street, E1 148

The Cricklewood Synagogue, Walm Lane, NW2 151

The Willesden (District) Synagogue, College Road, NW10 155

The Mile End and Bow United Synagogue, Harley Grove, E3 157

The West Central Liberal Synagogue, Alfred Place, WC1, later Whitfield Street, W1 158

The Harrow Synagogue (formerly Harrow (Kenton and District) Hebrew Congregation) Sheepcote Road, later Vaughan Road, Harrow 160

The Dollis Hill Synagogue, Parkside, NW2 162

The Highgate Synagogue, Archway Road, N6 164

The Pinner Synagogue, Cecil Park, Pinner 165

The Streatham Synagogue, Mitcham Lane, SW16, Estreham Road, SW16 166

The Elm Park Synagogue, Elm Park, Essex 167

Other synagogues for Essex men 168

The Federation of Synagogues and the East End closures 169

The Machzike Adass Synagogue, Brick Lane, E1 171

The Princelet Street Synagogue, 19 Princelet Street, E1 172

The Shepherd's Bush Synagogue, Poplar Grove ,W6 174

The Neasden Federation Synagogue, Clifford Way, NW10 176

Renaming of the constituent synagogues 177

Shomrei Adass Synagogue, Finchley Road, NW3 177
Rabbi Kopul Rosen 178
The East End Synagogues after the Second World War 179
Appendix 1
Architects of the synagogues in London 181
Appendix 2
The basic design of a synagogue 184
The movement to Reform 185
Appendix 3
Letter from John Greenhalgh to Thomas Crampton 188
Appendix 4
Another "Battle of Talking" 190
Appendix 5
Photographs of the Conference of Anglo-Jewish ministers 193
Appendix 6
(a) Map of London showing the geographical position of the synagogues. 195
(b) Table to show the date of foundation of the congregation and final closure of the synagogue. 196
References 198
Glossary 201
Index 205

List of illustrations

Fig.

1. Jacobs' map of the London Jewry, 1290.
2. Aggas' map showing the synagogue in Cateaton Street.
3. Burford's map of the medieval City of London.
4. Elevation of the south facade of the synagogue in Creechurch Lane.
5. Ground plan of the synagogue in Creechurch Lane.
6. Ground plan of the synagogue in Creechurch Lane following enlargement.
7. Pages from *Vallentine's Jewish Almanack,* 1875.
8. Map showing the location of the City synagogues.
9. Pages from the *Jewish Year Book,* 1937.
10. Plaque in memory of Moses Hart at the Great Synagogue.
11. Exterior of the Great Synagogue.
12. "A Visit to the Synagogue" – cartoon by Thomas Rowlandson.
13. Bomb damage to the Great Synagogue.
14. Open-air service in the ruins of the Great Synagogue.
15. Temporary building erected in the cleared ruins of the Great Synagogue.
16. Interior of the Great Synagogue shown on a New Year's greeting card.
17. Ark of the Great Synagogue.
18. Hazzan Kusevitsky at the ark of the Great Synagogue.
19. Chief Rabbi Hart Lyon
20. Chief Rabbi David Tevele Schiff.
21. Chief Rabbi Solomon Hirshel.
22. Chief Rabbi Nathan Marcus Adler.
23. Chief Rabbi Hermann Adler.
24. Chief Rabbi Joseph Hermann Hertz.
25. Hazzan Isaac Polak.
26. Hazzanim of the Great Synagogue.
27. Hazzan Forscher.
28. Hambro Synagogue, Magpie Alley. The interior.
29. Hambro Synagogue, Adler Street. Drawing of the exterior.
30. Hambro Synagogue, Adler Street. The interior.
31. Revd. Samuel Marcus Gollancz as a young man.
32. Revd. Samuel Marcus Gollancz as an old man.
33. Memorial plaque to the Revd. Samuel Marcus Gollancz.
34. New Synagogue at the Bricklayers Hall.
35. Interior of the Cheltenham Synagogue.
36. New Synagogue, Great St. Helens, Bishopsgate. The interior (engraving).
37. New Synagogue, Great St. Helens, Bishopsgate. The exterior.
38. Revd. S. Levy.
39. Map showing the location of Denmark Court.
40. Sketch of the interior of the Sans Souci Theatre.
41. Site of the Maiden Lane Synagogue.
42. The reconsecration of the Western Synagogue, St Alban's Place (engraving).
43. Western Synagogue, St. Alban's Place. The interior.
44. Western Synagogue, Alfred Place. Drawing of the exterior.

45.   Western Synagogue, Alfred place. Drawing of the interior.
46.   (a) Prayer hall of the Western Synagogue Cemetery in Montagu Road, Edmonton. (b) Door to the prayer hall.
47.   The Chapelle francaise.
48.   Western Synagogue, Crawford Place. The exterior.
49.   Western Synagogue, Crawford Place. The interior.
50.   Western Marble Arch Synagogue. The ark in the small synagogue.
51.   Beth Hamedrash. The exterior.
52.   Beth Hamedrash. The interior.
53.   Dayan Bernard Spiers.
54.   Borough Synagogue, Albion Place (Heygate Street). The interior.
55.   Borough Synagogue, Albion Place (Heygate Street). The interior.
56.   Borough Synagogue, Wansey Street (The Surrey Tabernacle).
57.   Borough Synagogue, Wansey Street. The interior.
58.   Borough Synagogue. Bulletin cover.
59.   Borough Synagogue, Wansey Street. The ark in the hall.
60.   Rabbi Simeon Singer.
61.   Rabbi Francis Lyon Cohen.
62.   Revd. Morris Rosenbaum.
63.   Revd. Professor D. W. Marks.
64.   Central Synagogue, 120 Great Portland Street. The interior.
65.   Central Synagogue, 133 Great Portland Street. The exterior.
66.   Central Synagogue. The interior.
67.   Central Synagogue. The interior.
68.   Central Synagogue. Memorial candleholder.
69.   Central Synagogue. The Almemar.
70.   Central Synagogue. The interior following bombing.
71.   Central Synagogue. Drawing of the interior of the temporary building.
72.   Revd. A. L. Green.
73.   Bayswater Synagogue. Engraving of the interior.
74.   Bayswater Synagogue. The interior.
75.   Bayswater Synagogue, Chichester Place. The exterior.
76.   Bayswater Synagogue, Andover Place. The exterior.
77.   Rabbi Professor Sir Hermann Gollancz.
78.   North London Synagogue, John Street West (Lofting Road). The exterior.
79.   North London Synagogue. The Feast of Tabernacles, with the Revd. H. Wasserzug (engraving).
80.   North London Synagogue. The interior.
81.   North London Synagogue. The pulpit.
82.   Revd. Morris Joseph.
83.   East London Synagogue. The exterior.
84.   East London Synagogue. The interior.
85.   East London Synagogue. The interior.
86.   East London Synagogue. The interior.
87.   East London Synagogue. Chief Rabbi Lord Jakobovits preaching.
88.   East London Synagogue. Bookplate.
89.   East London Synagogue. The exterior.
90.   Revd. Mendel Zeffertt.
91.   Dalston Synagogue, Poet's Road. The exterior.
92.   Dalston Synagogue. Cover of pamphlet showing the interior.

93.   Dalston Synagogue. Order of Service at the consecration.
94.   Past and present officers of the Dalston Synagogue.
95.   Adass Yisroel Synagogue, Green Lanes. The exterior.
96.   Hazzan Soffe.
97.   Adass Yisroel Synagogue, Burma Road. The Tahara House.
98.   Rabbi Dr. Victor Schönfeld.
99.   Rabbi Dr. Solomon Schönfeld.
100.   Revd. A. Feldman.
101.   New Dalston Synagogue. Order or Service at the consecration.
102.   Revd. S. Manné.
103.   Stoke Newington Synagogue, Shacklewell Lane. The exterior.
104.   Stoke Newington Synagogue. The interior.
105.   Stoke Newington Synagogue. Ground floor plan.
106.   Rabbi Harris Cohen and Revd. Coleman Davies.
107.   Stoke Newington Synagogue. The interior.
108.   Officers of the Stoke Newington Synagogue.
109.   Stoke Newington Synagogue. The exterior.
110.   South East London Synagogue. Order of Service at the consecration of the synagogue in Lausanne Road..
111.   Cover of *The Jewish World* showing the exterior and interior of the South East London Synagogue and its officers, New Cross Road.
112.   South East London Synagogue . The exterior.
113.   South East London Synagogue. The interior.
114.   South East London Synagogue. The exterior.
115.   South East London Synagogue. Plan of the interior.
116.   Liberal Jewish Synagogue, Hill Street. The exterior.
117.   Liberal Jewish Synagogue, Hill Street. The interior.
118.   Liberal Jewish Synagogue, St. John's Wood Road. The exterior.
119.   Liberal Jewish Synagogue, St. John's Wood Road. The interior.
120.   Liberal Jewish Synagogue, St. John's Wood Road. The interior.
121.   Rabbi Dr. Israel Mattuck.
122.   Site of the first North West London Synagogue, York Way.
123.   North West London Synagogue. Order of Service at the consecration of the first synagogue.
124.   Revd. Woolf Esterson.
125.   North West London Synagogue. (a) Order of Service at the consecration of the second synagogue. (b) An Appeal for funds.
126.   North West London Synagogue, Caversham Road. The exterior.
127.   North West London Synagogue, Caversham Road. The interior.
128.   Revd. Walter Levin.
129.   Revds. S. Lipson and Mendel Brown.
130.   Revd. E. Drukker.
131.   Revd. H. Bornstein.
132.   Rabbi B.D. Klein.
133.   North West London Synagogue. The exterior.
134.   Woolwich Synagogue, Anglesea Road. The exterior.
135.   Woolwich Synagogue, Anglesea Road. The original ark.
136.   Woolwich Synagogue, Anglesea Road. The exterior of the new building.
137.   Woolwich Synagogue, Anglesea Road. The interior of the new building.
138.   Revd. Gottlieb Rosenberg.

139. West Ham Synagogue, Earlham Grove. The exterior.
140. West Ham Synagogue, Earlham Grove. The interior.
141. Past and present officers of the West Ham Synagogue.
142. East Ham and Manor Park Synagogue. The exterior.
143. Brondesbury Synagogue. The exterior.
144. Brondesbury Synagogue. The interior.
145. Brondesbury Synagogue. The exterior.
146. Dayan H.M. Lazarus and Revd. N. Peckar.
147. Brixton Synagogue. The exterior.
148. Brixton Synagogue. The interior.
149. Brixton Synagogue. The Hebrew classes c.1958.
150. Brixton Synagogue. The exterior.
151. Rabbi A. Mishcon.
152. Rabbi, later Dayan, Morris Swift.
153. Rabbi, later Dayan Meyer Steinberg.
154. Bermondsey and Rotherhithe Synagogue, Rouel Road. The exterior.
155. Hornsey and Wood Green Synagogue, Wightman Road. The exterior.
156. The Athenaeum – the Muswell Hill Synagogue. The exterior.
157. Muswell Hill Synagogue. The interior.
158. Balham Synagogue, Boundaries Road. The exterior.
159. South West London Synagogue, Bolingbroke Grove. The exterior.
160. South West London Synagogue, Bolingbroke Grove. The interior.
161. New South London Synagogue, Balham High Road. The exterior.
162. Upton Park Synagogue, Tudor Road. The exterior.
163. Upton Park Synagogue, Tudor Road. The exterior.
164. Richmond Synagogue, Sheen Road. Plan of the exterior.
165. Richmond Synagogue, Sheen Road. Plan of the interior.
166. Oxford and St. George's Settlement, Betts Street. The exterior.
167. Sir Basil Henriques.
168. St. George's Settlement, Bernhard Baron House, Berners Street. The exterior.
169. St. George's Settlement, Bernhard Baron House, Berners Street. The interior.
170. Cricklewood Synagogue, Walm Lane. The exterior.
171. Cricklewood Synagogue, Walm Lane. The interior.
172. Rabbi Dr. Louis Rabinowitz.
173. Rabbi Emil Lichtigfeld.
174. Cricklewood Synagogue. The exterior.
175. Willesden United Synagogue, College Road. The exterior.
176. Willesden Federation Synagogue, Heathfield Park. The exterior and interior.
177. Mile End and Bow United Synagogue, Harley Road. The exterior.
178. West Central Liberal Synagogue, Whitfield Street. The interior.
179. West Central Liberal Synagogue, Whitfield Street. The interior during a service.
180. Site of Harrow Synagogue, Vaughan Road.
181. Dollis Hill Synagogue, Parkside. The exterior.
182. Dollis Hill Synagogue, Parkside. The interior.
183. Highgate Synagogue, Archway Road. The exterior.
184. Highgate Synagogue, Archway Road. The interior. Rabbi Nemeth

conducting a service.

185. Pinner Synagogue, Cecil Park. The exterior.
186. Pinner Synagogue, Cecil Park. The exterior.
187. Pinner Synagogue, Cecil Park. The interior.
188. Streatham Synagogue, Mitcham Road. The exterior.
189. Streatham Synagogue, Estreham Road. The interior.
190. Streatham Synagogue, Estreham Road. The exterior.
191. Elm Park Synagogue. The exterior.
192. Elm Park Syngogue. The interior.
193. Cannon Street Road Synagogue. The exterior.
194. Fulham and Kensington Synagogue, Lillie Road. The exterior.
195. Fulham and Kensington Synagogue, Lillie Road. The interior.
196. Leyton and Walthamstow New Federated Synagogue. The exterior.
197. Ezras Chaim Synagogue, Heneage Street. The exterior.
198. Lambeth Synagogue. The exterior.
199. Yavneh Synagogue. The interior.
200. West Hackney Synagogue. The exterior.
201. Machzike Adass Synagogue. The exterior.
202. Princelet Street Synagogue. The exterior.
203. Princelet Street Synagogue. The interior.
204. Princelet Street Synagogue. The interior.
205. Rabbi Schmuel Melnick.
206. Shepherds Bush Synagogue. The exterior.
207. Shepherds Bush Synagogue. The interior.
208. Rabbi Professor Israel Abrahams.
209. Gladstone Park and Neasden Synagogue. The exterior.
210. Ohel Shem Synagogue, Chamberlain Road. The exterior.
211. Shomrei Adass Synagogue. The exterior.
212. Shomrei Adass Synagogue. The interior.
213. Rabbi Kopul Rosen.
214. Bethnal Green Synagogue. The exterior.
215. New Road Synagogue, Whitechapel. The exterior.
216. Montagu Road Synagogue. The exterior.
217. Montagu Road Synagogue. The interior.

JEWS IN LONDON

According to Elkan Nathan Adler,[3] Jews were to be found in England prior to the Norman conquest. The Venerable Bede (d. 755) apparently studied Hebrew with Jews resident in Mercia, while in 810 Jews fleeing Germany found refuge in England.[3] Alfred the Great's grandson Athelstan (925-940) had the Bible translated from the Hebrew into Anglo-Saxon by local converts. The arrival of the Jews with William the Conqueror brought about the establishment of Jewish communities in many cities, including of course London, where they prospered under William the Conqueror and his son, William Rufus.

In 1158, Abraham Ibn Ezra[*] visited London as apparently the poet felt safer in England than in Paris. At that time, there were nearly 2000 Jewish *families* in London, but only 2000 *Jews* in London in 1241.[3] Clearly, the number of Jews in London declined prior to their expulsion.

Some Jews prospered because they practiced usury, playing an important role in the economy of the land. However, progressively heavier taxation finally eroded their value to the King and the Exchequer. Anti-Jewish riots took place at the Coronation of Richard I on 3rd September, 1189, followed by similar massacres at Bury St. Edmunds, Lincoln and York.

While the majority of the Jews in England were poor, a few were extremely rich, building stone houses, at least one of which - Aaron's in Lincoln - survives today. Aaron had financed the building of Lincoln and Peterborough Cathedrals, while between 1245 and 1272, notes Adler, Henry III spent half a million pounds sterling on rebuilding Westminster Abbey, largely wrung out of the Jews. This so impoverished them that in 1255 the Jews applied to leave the country, but their request was denied.

In 1264, 1500 Jews were said to have been killed in London and, in 1280, Jews were forced to attend conversionist sermons. By 1282 all the synagogues in London, bar one, were closed. In 1287 a fine of £12,000 on the community could not be met and as the Jews, by now impoverished, no longer had an economic function in the state, they were expelled in 1290.

Pre-expulsion synagogues

Chroniclers of the pre-expulsion synagogues in London include John Stow,[5] Joseph Jacobs,[6] Revd. David Wasserzug[7] and, more recently, H.G. Richardson[8] and J. Hillaby.[9] Between them they have identified at least five major synagogues (Fig. 1):

(1) at the north-east corner of Old Jewry;
(2) in Threadneedle Street, opposite the Royal Exchange;
(3) in what is now Gresham Street;
(4) on the west side of Coleman Street, toward the south end;
(5) in Ironmonger Lane.

John Stow's *Survey of London* was first published in 1598 and is still available; his book tells us about the history of medieval London Jewry and describes four synagogues.[5]

(1) **Old Jewry** - *"On the south side of this street* (Lothbury or Lothburie), *amongst the founders* (i.e. foundries), *be some fair houses and large for merchants,*

[*] The *Encyclopaedia Judaica* describes Abraham Ibn Ezra (1089-1164) as a *"poet, grammarian, biblical commentator, philosopher, astronomer and physician."*[4] He was in London between 1158 and 1161 and there he wrote two major works. He was both a secular and religious poet. His biography in the *Encyclopaedia Judaica* fills seven columns.

Fig. 1 A map drawn by Joseph Jacobs showing the sites of the synagogues on properties owned by Jews prior to the Expulsion. (Reproduced from *Papers Read at the Anglo-Jewish Historical Exhibition, 1887.*[6])

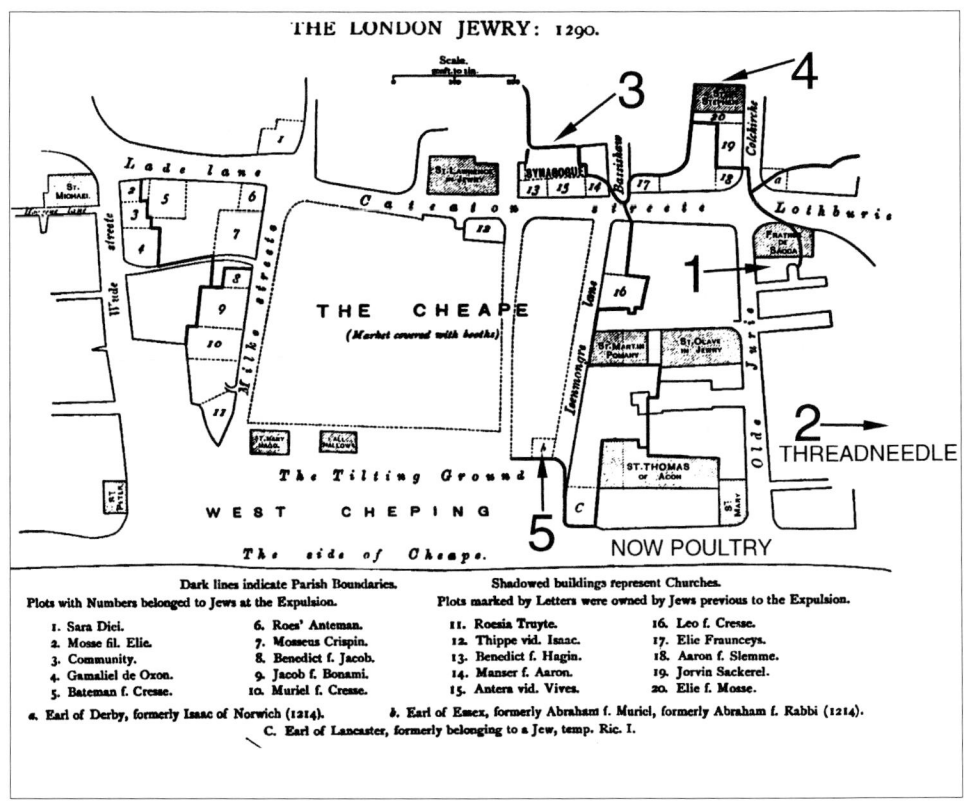

namely, one that of old time was the Jews' synagogue, which was defaced by the citizens of London, after that they had slain 700 Jews, and spoiled the residue of their goods, in the year 1262, the 47th of Henry III. And not long after, in the year 1291, King Edward I banished the remnant of the Jews out of England … The said synagogue being so suppressed, certain friars got possession thereof …"[5]

These were the 'Fratres de Sacca' (Friars of the Sack), so-called because they dressed in sackcloth. They were instituted *"for the benefit of married people who required repentance"*. Wasserzug, in an article in the *Jewish Chronicle*, says the synagogue was originally the house of a Jew, Cresse Fil Moses, and notes that the Friars, who had a small chapel next to the synagogue, had complained to the King that the ululation of the Jews disturbed them; whereupon in 1272 the Jews were ejected.[7]

"Now it followed," Stow continued, *"That in the year 1305, Robert Fitzwalter requested and obtained of the said King Edward I, that the same friars of the Sack might assign to the said Robert their chapel or church, of old time called the Synagogue of the Jews, near adjoining to the then mansion place of the same Robert, which was in place where now standeth the Grocers' Hall;* **and the said Synagogue was at the north corner of the Old Jewry.**"[5] (At the time of Stow *"it is now a tavern, and hath to sign a windmill."*

(2) **Threadneedle Street.** Of the synagogue in Threadneedle Street, Stow wrote that in 1231 *"the Jews in London built a synagogue, but the king demanded it should be dedicated to our Blessed Lady, and after gave it to the brethren of St. Anthony of Vienna, and so was it called* **St. Anthony's Hospital.**"[5] Wasserzug added that the synagogue was opposite where the Royal Exchange now is, and was completed in 1253 and *"surpassed in magnificence all the Christian churches."*[7] Its splendour excited the hatred of the Gentiles who, in the riots of 1263, partially destroyed it. It later became a Greek school at which Sir Thomas More and Dean Colet were educated.*

(3) **Gresham Street (previously Catte or Cateaton Street).** Stow

*Henry III founded a church and house for converted Jews in New Street, by the Temple, which attracted a large number of converts.

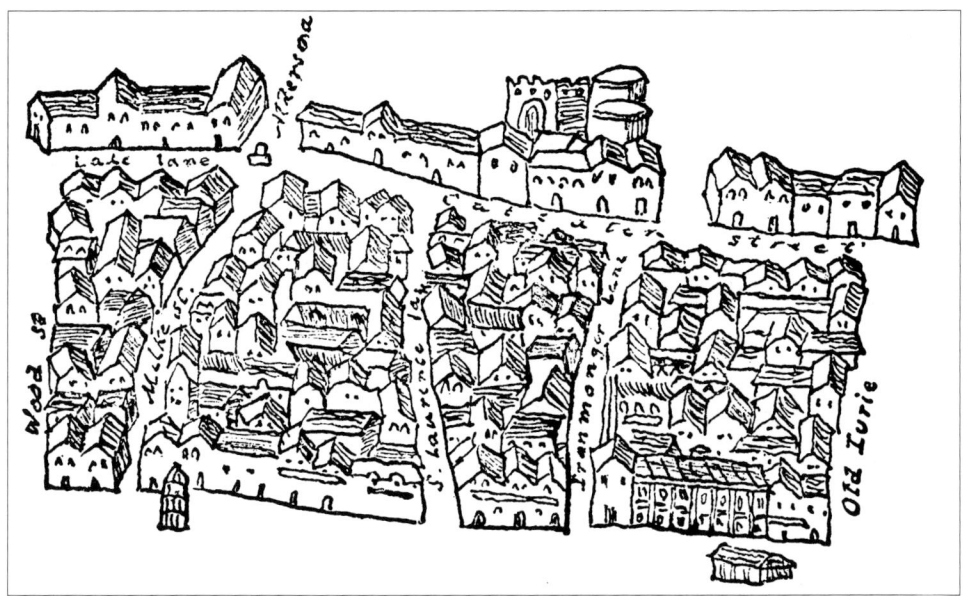

notes that : "*On the west side, almost at the south end thereof, is Bakewell Hall, corruptly called Blackewall Hall, concerning the original whereof I have heard divers opinions, which I overpass as fables without colour of truth … That this house hath been a temple or Jewish synagogue (as some have fantasied) I allow not, seeing that it had no such form of roundness*[*]*or other likeness.*"[5]

In the volume entitled *Papers Read at the Anglo-Jewish Historical Exhibition 1887*[6] published by the *Jewish Chronicle* in 1888, Joseph Jacobs[**] contributed an article entitled 'The London Jewry, 1290', in which he noted that the boundaries of the City parishes were fixed around the time that the Jews were expelled from England, that is, between 1273 and 1294. It seems that the parish boundaries followed the outline of the backs of the houses (Fig. 1), whilst the fronts of the houses give the lines of the streets.

Jacobs quotes from a manuscript in the British Museum: "*In 1227 the same Sampson fil. Isaac pays half a mark for having inscribed on the Great Poll of the Exchequer that he has given to Abraham his son, and the son of Malke his wife, the land which he holds in St. Lawrence Jewry, which land lies between the property which was Abraham's fil. Avegaye, on the east, and Judah of Warwick's on the west, and extends in length from the highway to the* **Synagogue**".[10] This synagogue he believed to be a hitherto unknown synagogue in a street running east to west in what was called Catte or Cateaton Street (now Gresham Street) (Fig. 1).

Stow believed that synagogues were round in form and built of stone, and that "*some have fantasied*" that Bakewell Hall had been a synagogue, though he decried such a view as Bakewell Hall "*had no such form of roundness*". Jacobs, however, believed, despite Stow, that this synagogue in Catte (Cateaton) Street stands out clearly in Aggas' map of London (1560) which, according to Jacobs, has a sketch of what was a medieval Jewish synagogue situated in the back gardens of three houses owned by Jews in what is now Gresham Street. That the houses were owned by Jews is known, as they reverted to the King on the Jewish expulsion, and he issued writs for inquisition into their value and position before passing them on to his friends. Compare Aggas' map (Fig. 2) with that by Joseph Jacobs of the same area (Fig. 1) based on the outlines of the parishes, and on the owners and positions of the houses in manuscripts held in the British Museum.

Wasserzug was also firmly of the belief that Stow was wrong – and

[*] From this Adler deduced that the synagogues of this period were round in form and probably of stone, though it is unsafe to generalise about this.

[**] Joseph Jacobs[6] (1854-1916) was a historian born in Australia who studied in Cambridge and Berlin. He organised (with Lucien Woolf) the Anglo-Jewish Historical Exhibition of 1887, founded the Jewish Year Book in 1896, which is still being published today, and in 1900 went to the United States where he became an editor of the *Jewish Encyclopaedia* and a lecturer at the Jewish Theological Seminary.

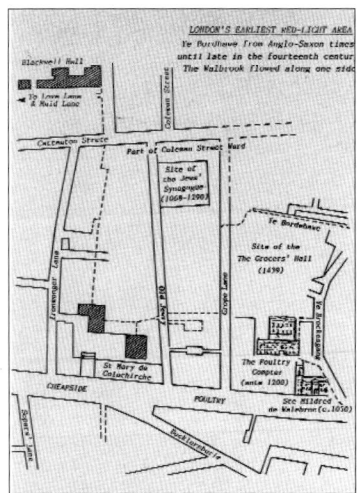

Fig. 3 A map of the area of Jewish settlement in the City, superimposed by E.J. Burford, on the medieval red light district shown within the dotted lines. The street known as Old Jewry is right in the centre of this.

popular belief correct – in that Bakewell Hall had indeed been a synagogue. Following expulsion from Threadneedle Street by the Friars of St Anthony in 1272, a new synagogue had been built on a site owned by Aaron, son of Vives (presumably sites 14 and 15 on Jacobs' map in Fig. 1), which lay on Catte Street (see above), named after *Simon le Chat*, who had property there. Wasserzug quotes the 'Close Roll' of 1256: "*The King gave to John Fitz Geoffrey his Chapel of St Mary **adjacent to the house of said John, where once was a synagogue of the Jews.** The chapel was the Guildhall Chapel.*"[6] He asks what house was it that was once a synagogue, adjacent to the chapel, and finds the answer in a deed dated 1356: the house of John, where once had been a synagogue of the Jews, was then none other than Bakewell Hall, which now belonged to Thomas Bakewell, who was living in it in 1348, i.e. long after the expulsion, and from whom Stow had derived its name. Moreover, Wasserzug cites another document, dated 1292, which mentions that the property of Aaron son of Vives passed to one Alderman John de Banquelle, i.e. the next owner, soon after the expulsion. It may well be that Thomas Bakewell was a descendent of Alderman John de Banquelle, the name having been anglicised.[*] Bakewell (or Blackwell) Hall is also seen on a map drawn by the contemporary historian of medieval London, E.J. Burford (Fig. 3). This, too, is at exactly the same site as the round building of stone in Aggas' map (see Fig. 2). Of interest in Burford's map is the location of the Jewish quarter in the 'red light' district.[11]

Bakewell House was converted to a woolmarket and later destroyed in the Great Fire.

(4) **Coleman Street.** Stow referred to the Coleman Street Synagogue: "*On this north side against the Old Jewry is Coleman Street, so called of Coleman, the first builder and owner thereof; as also of Colechurch … on the west side, towards the south end, is **the parish church of St. Stephen, …This church was sometime a synagogue of the Jews.***"[5] Wasserzug confirms this.[7]

(5) **Ironmonger Lane**. According to Jacobs, there was a synagogue in Ironmonger Lane.[6] It was later taken over by the Earl of Essex because of its proximity to the Tilting Ground, where jousts were held (see the area marked b. in Fig. 1).

H.G. Richardson, in his book *The English Jewry under the Angevin Kings*, notes a 'great' synagogue.[8] Such a title is often given to the first or major synagogue established in any city. Richardson puts the site of the Great Synagogue, according to a contemporary charter, in Ironmonger Lane, but states in a footnote that Joseph Jacobs had placed this synagogue in Gresham Street (see above).

J. Hillaby[9] believes that Richardson has misplaced the 'magna scola' (see his reference 39). There is some confusion as to the meaning and use of the word *scola*. The then Archbishop of Canterbury, John Peckham, wrote that "he understood that a new synagogue was being constructed by the London community under the pretence of a school – *scola*." The use of the Yiddish *shul*, that is, similar to the German *Schule*, is a similar linguistic device.

Contrary to the other authors, Hillaby locates the Gresham Street synagogue on the south side of the street, and not the north as did Jacobs.

Hillaby also mentions the 'Great Synagogue' of Abraham, son of Rabbi Josce, "*the most distinguished member of the London community in the first half of the twelfth century*", and believes that the *magna scola* was Josce's own foundation, the magnates of that time apparently having their own domestic chapels. Hillaby places the *magna scola* on the east side of Colechurch Lane,

[*] Jacobs believed *Bakewell* to be a corruption of *Bathwell*, i.e. a Mikveh, but this seems highly fanciful.

now named Old Jewry; presumably this is the synagogue taken over by the Friars of the Sack,

If there was a synagogue by that name in Ironmonger Lane, it was presumably a domestic chapel. The house at No. 11 is known to have been occupied by Jews. Recently a plaque has been placed in Ironmonger Lane, near Poultry, indicating that, on a site nearby, stood a medieval Great Synagogue.

READMISSION AND THE FIRST SYNAGOGUE

The complex story of the readmission of the Jews to England in 1656 has been well described by, amongst others, Margoliouth,[12] Picciotto,[13] Roth[14] and Hyamson.[15] The readmission was based on English commercial and financial interests, as well as on Puritan study of the 'Old' Testament, allied with a desire for the ultimate conversion and redemption of the Jews.

The movement of New Christian* (Marrano) merchants to London from Spain, Portugal, France, Holland and the West Indies was in part motivated by an intense fear of Spain, Catholicism and the Inquisition. These groups lived in London initially as Catholics but, in 1655, war broke out between England and Spain. The next year all Spanish possessions, including those of the New Christian merchants residing in London, were subject to seizure by the English state. At this point, one Antonio Robles declared himself to be a Jew and not a Spanish Catholic. The Council of State agreed, restored his property to him and, by the end of 1656, on 19th December, the now openly practising Jews in London acquired a house in Creechurch (or Cree Church) Lane for use as a synagogue.

W. Samuel[16] has written a comprehensive history of this building. The synagogue opened early in 1657, at the same time as the cemetery at Mile End.

Proof that the synagogue was located in Creechurch Lane is found in a list of names of Jews settled in London, drawn up in 1660, and including *"Sin (Señor) Moses Eatees (or Attias), Creechurch Lane, a Jewish Rubay,"*[13] the same as *"Sin Moses the Prest wer the Sinagoge is."*[16] By 1674, the synagogue needed to be enlarged; the neighbouring brick-built building, formerly a merchant's house, was used for this purpose.

One of the two brick houses was on a corner site, opposite a great stone gate (demolished in 1816), leading into Duke's Place (named after Thomas Howard, Duke of Norfolk), the gate being initially the entrance to a priory and subsequently to the Duke of Norfolk's mansion. The Creechurch Lane synagogue was used until the new synagogue opened in Bevis Marks. Its buildings then reverted to domestic use and subsequently became the Parish Workhouse until 1857, when they were demolished. The Deeds for the two buildings dating from 1622 show that the buildings on 5 Creechurch Lane, three hundred years later, had exactly the same dimensions as the earlier buildings.

A drawing, dated 1757, exists of the southern facade of the Workhouse, that is, the exterior of the synagogue. It was drawn by the city surveyor because of a legal dispute involving Jeremy Bentham's father, Jeremiah, who owned a neighbouring property (Fig. 4).

The design of the interior of the synagogue was deduced by Samuel from two sources. The first synagogue is described in a letter from John Greenhalgh to Thomas Crampton, dated 22nd April 1662, now in the British Museum, that is, before the original synagogue was enlarged.[15, 16] This

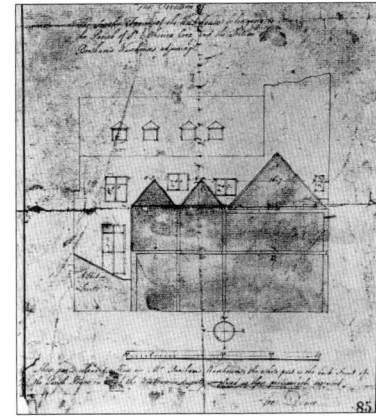

Fig. 4 Elevation of the exterior of the Synagogue in Creechurch Lane after its enlargement. (Reproduced from the article by W. Samuel[14] by kind permission of the Jewish Historical Society of England.)

* 'New Christians' were descendants of Jews who had outwardly converted to Catholicism, but in private practised a form of Judaism, whereas 'Old Christians' were those whose families had always practised Christianity. The distinction between the two groups ended in Spain only in the last century.

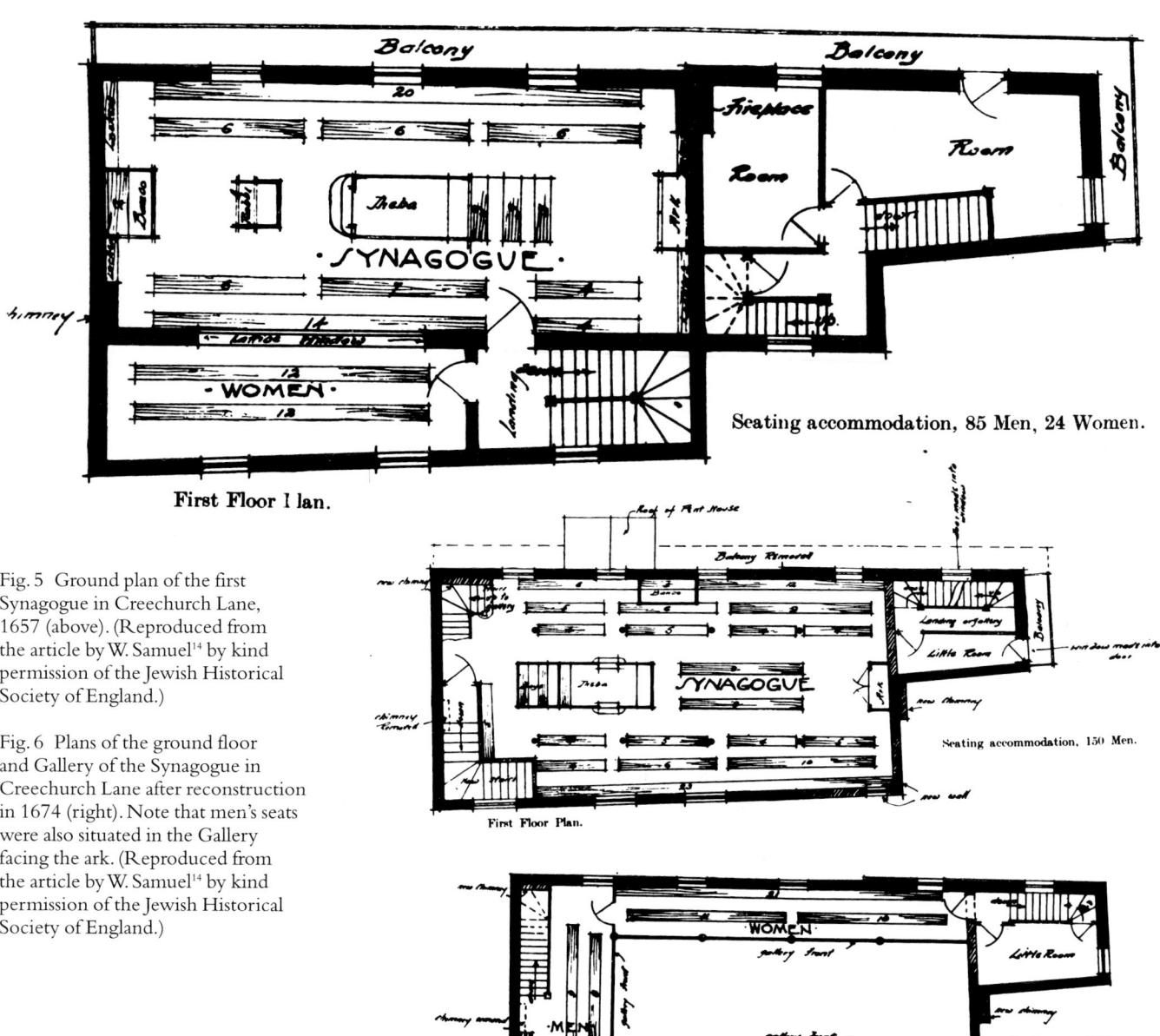

Fig. 5 Ground plan of the first Synagogue in Creechurch Lane, 1657 (above). (Reproduced from the article by W. Samuel[14] by kind permission of the Jewish Historical Society of England.)

Fig. 6 Plans of the ground floor and Gallery of the Synagogue in Creechurch Lane after reconstruction in 1674 (right). Note that men's seats were also situated in the Gallery facing the ark. (Reproduced from the article by W. Samuel[14] by kind permission of the Jewish Historical Society of England.)

is quoted in full in Appendix 3, p. 188.

In the original building, Greenhalgh counted 100 Jewish males, and there was apparently accommodation for 25 females. In the enlarged building, the floor area was much greater and two ladies' galleries were provided on the north and south sides.

A carpenter's agreement dated May 1674 sets out in great detail the building works needed for the enlargement.[16] Samuel wrote: *"The 1674 alterations were on a larger scale: the two houses were combined, and on the ground-floor the yard of the small corner-house was built over. On the first floor all partitions were removed, so that the Synagogue's main floor measured some 1104 square feet — an increase of about 350 square feet. A large portion of the second floor was completely cut away, and two ladies' galleries, measuring 40 feet in length and having double rows of seats, were provided on the north and south sides. There was also a gallery on the western side; this was not enclosed as were the women's galleries, but was provided 'with rails and bannisters leaneing heighth and not with pannells,' and it is highly probable that it was used by male worshippers, as there was a staircase behind leading straight down into the Synagogue. The interior of the building was panelled throughout, the galleries were supported by Doric columns and arches, and the ceiling under the gallery coved. The columns were carried up above the galleries, and there were arches from one capital to the other supporting the main ceiling of the Synagogue, which was also coved. The main entrance to the Synagogue must have been quite impressive: there were double doors 'Hansome and Workmanlike,' with fanlights above them and posts outside them and a pair of benches in the street. The passage was 'between six and seaven foot wide,' and over the doorway was a penthouse having a pediment 'ornamentall and workmanlike' – all in the best traditions of seventeenth-century architecture. On the south end of the passage there was a broad, easy-going staircase which led up to the body of the Synagogue on the first floor. The ladies' northern gallery had a separate entrance from the street, the front door of the corner-house having been appropriated for the purpose. Unfortunately, there was no Greenhalgh to describe to us minutely the seating-arrangements in the enlarged Synagogue, but Mr. Castello, basing himself on the available floor-space and taking into consideration the customary arrangements, assesses the accommodation as follows:*

Men on the main floor	*150*
"in the western gallery	*22*
Women in the northern gallery	*42*
"in the southern gallery	*42*

This gives a total of 172 men and 84 women.

The estimated cost of the 1674 extension-scheme was £222 – a big sum in those days – but in addition Dr. Gaster's history records a number of payments to Jewish workmen – all of whom were German Jews – for work done to the Ark and for helping in the construction of the new reading-desk."[16]

From the descriptions, Mr M.N. Castello, ARIBA, of the Spanish and Portuguese congregation, was able to draw up detailed plans of the building in Creechurch Lane in its original state as the first synagogue in 1657 (Fig. 5) and after its enlargement in 1674 (Fig. 6).

POPULATION MOVEMENT AT THE END OF THE NINETEENTH CENTURY

Before the assassination of Tsar Alexander II in 1881, the Jewish population of London was approximately 47,000.[4] Over the next 25 years this rose to 150,000, of whom 100,000 lived in the East End. The earlier groups of immigrants – Sephardim from the Iberian peninsula, Holland and Italy, and Ashkenazim, mainly from Germany – were dwarfed by an influx of poverty-stricken Jews from Russia and Poland over the next few years, altering the nature of the Jewish community and its institutions, charitable and religious, as well as English history. The established community attempted to halt or even reverse the flow of immigrants by advertising in Yiddish on the Continent, warning would-be immigrants of the difficulties they would face, as well as encouraging immigrants either to return or to look for pastures new, such as South Africa.

The East End was the existing centre of Jewish life and industry, and soon whole streets were entirely Jewish, displacing earlier groups of immigrants – especially the Irish. A smaller centre of Jewish life around Soho and East Bloomsbury existed in an area of great poverty and vice.[1] This too became a Jewish enclave, west of more prosperous Bloomsbury and south of Regent's Park (now called Fitzrovia).

Immigration continued up to the First World War and beyond that, though at a much slower pace, but simultaneous movement of Jews from the City and the East End was already underway by the middle of the nineteenth Century.[17] The wealthier Jews had long had their country houses, but it was with the rise of a prosperous middle class that migration from the City began, first to Islington and Hackney.

A list of subscribers for David Levi's *Machzor* (prayer book) for Pentecost (1824) shows Jews living in Lambeth, Islington, Crawford Street in Marylebone, Holborn, Hackney, Canonbury, Fishmonger Alley in the Borough, Edgware Road, Newington, Soho, New Kent Road, Blackfriars Road, East Lane in Walworth, Holliwell Street, Strand, St. John Street in Clerkenwell, Maiden Lane, Tottenham Court Road, Clapham Road, Mary-le-Bone Lane, Brixton Hill, St. Martin's Lane in Charing Cross, New Bond Street, Poland Street – often two or more families resident in the same street.

Families living in some of these areas in 1824 could walk to work in the City and reside in the newer, less crowded suburbs. Migration from the city began in the middle of the nineteenth century aided by the development of horse bus and, subsequently, by train and tram services.

According to Lipman, 25% of Jews in the 1848 Post Office Directory lived in Bloomsbury (the 1851 census listed thirteen Jewish households in and around Gower Street).[17] This area supported Jewish butchers, publishers and, of course, University College and its School, which attracted Jewish students who lived in Jewish boarding houses. Jews' College and its School in neighbouring Finsbury also attracted some Jewish residents.

Lipman notes that by 1860 Jews were moving to Bayswater. What is now the Metropolitan Line on the Underground opened in 1863, connecting Bayswater to the City. The local Bayswater Synagogue opened in the same year, taking members from the then most westerly congregation – the Central.

Further, wealthy Jewish migration led to the opening of the New West End United Synagogue in 1879. This congregation encouraged a smaller synagogue for artisans to open locally at Notting Hill, under the aegis of the Federation of Synagogues (see p. 169). In 1890 a branch of the United synagogue opened in Hammersmith and in 1912, in Ealing.

Another migration was to Maida Vale, which became the home of middle-class Jews and especially the intelligentsia, along the line of Edgware Road, with its buses into town. By 1880, Lipman estimates that there were possibly 2,000 Jewish residents in Maida Vale, soon to decline in number, albeit slowly, with Jewish migration along the north-west passage. By 1890, following opening of the New West End Synagogue in St. Petersburgh Place, the majority of members of the Bayswater Synagogue now lived in Maida Vale.

Canonbury and Barnsbury too began to attract Jewish residents; by 1861 there were 1,000 Jews in the area, migration encouraged by the development of the North London Railway which reached Broad Street in 1865. The synagogue in Barnsbury opened in 1868, but by 1878 the majority of its members lived in Highbury, stimulating demand for a new synagogue there, built eventually at Poet's Road near Newington Green. This of course depleted the membership of the synagogue in Barnsbury, which in any case had had fewer Jewish residents. Further congregations followed, including the Stoke Newington Synagogue in Dalston, so named to distinguish it from the Dalston Synagogue in Poet's Road, founded earlier at the junction of Stoke Newington and Islington in an area of elegance and affluence, as shown by the mansions in Highbury New Park. Stoke Newington, Kingsland and Barnsbury, while not as affluent, were clearly an improvement on the East End. Hackney at that time seems to have been an upper working-class area. Lipman notes that by 1913 the United Synagogue membership for north and north-east London was around 15,000, that is 10% of the Jewish population of London. With rising prosperity, the migration from the East End was well under way.

In the 1880s, Kilburn became a popular area for Jews,[17] following the opening of the North London railway from 1860 onwards. Subsequently Brondesbury and Willesden showed a large increase in the general population after the extension of the Bakerloo line to Willesden in 1915. Synagogues were founded in Brondesbury (1900), Cricklewood (1923-1931), Willesden (1926) and Dollis Hill (1929).

Lipman also describes an alternative migration – eastwards – again made possible by cheap workmen's fares on the tram lines and railways. Railway lines to Edmonton and Walthamstow were followed by the development of the furniture industry in the Lea Valley, providing employment for Jews who did not then have to commute to the East End.

By 1914 there were 10,000 Jews in west London, 20,000 in the north and north-east, 6-7,000 in the north-west and 5-6,000 south of the Thames.[17] Fewer Jews settled in the south, possibly because the lines of communication to the centre were not as good as from the north. The area around the

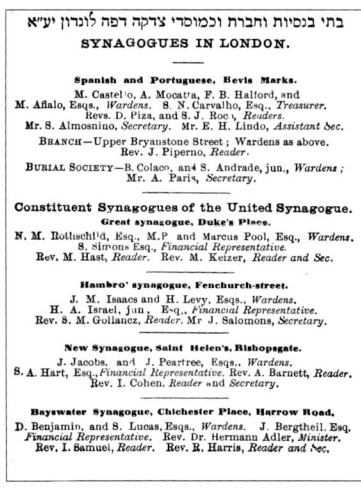

Fig. 7 Synagogues in London from
Vallentine's Almanack, 1875.

Borough and Walworth, however, were not too far away from the City via London, Southwark and Blackfriars Bridges, whilst the underground and tram lines opened up Brixton, Streatham and Clapham to Jewish residents.

By the early twentieth century Street Directories of the East End show, as expected, that in an area with 100,000 Jews, most of the shops were occupied by Jewish traders of all sorts. In particular, Jews seem to have been attracted to certain types of stores, besides tailoring and groceries. In the inner suburbs the average High Street might have had its Jewish doctor, solicitor or optician, delicatessen, tobacconist, tailor, barber or publican – all of whom of necessity might have become involved in the local congregation because they all lived over the shop.

The demise of the inner city and inner suburban congregations in London occurred for a number of reasons. The effect of increasing wealth and the opening up of suburbia between the Wars, due to the new Metropolitan, Northern and Central underground railway lines, meant that a shopkeeper in the Borough could reach Golders Green or Edgware in 30–60 minutes and live in a nice new, reasonably priced, 'moderne' house, fully fitted, with a garden; he no longer had to live 'over the shop'.

The flight from inner London during the Second World War caused many who fled the bombing not to return to the world they had left behind – it no longer existed. The massive post-War slum clearance in the inner city compounded this effect. The more affluent, fit and young moved to the outer suburbs. In addition, there has been a decline in the number of Jews in the United Kingdom, from about 450,000 to around 300,000, with a declining Jewish birth-rate, increasing intermarriage and a general decline in religious observance. There is no longer a pool of poor Jews in Eastern Europe to settle in the inner city; the little immigration here now is from Israel and South Africa. However, a few new Sephardic congregations have been formed in London.

The life span of a Jewish congregation seems to be around fifty to seventy years, from the foundation of a synagogue to its eventual demise. *Vallentine's Jewish Almanac* for 1875 (Fig. 7) lists the following synagogues (see Fig. 8 for their location in the City): the Spanish and Portuguese, Bevis Marks and six

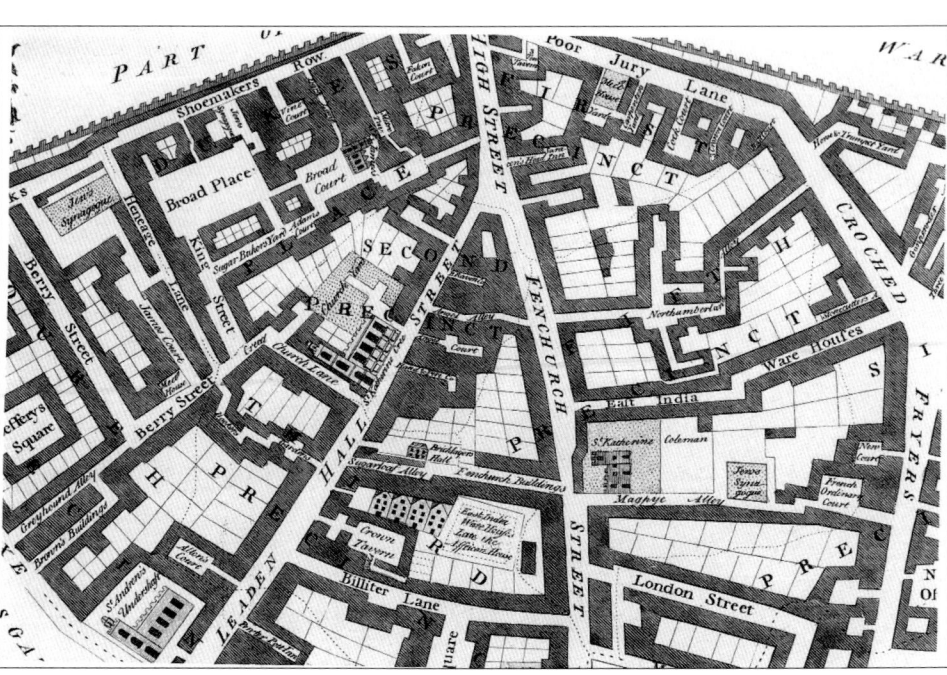

Fig. 8 Jacob Ilive's plan of the Ward of Aldgate (1739), showing the location of City synagogues.

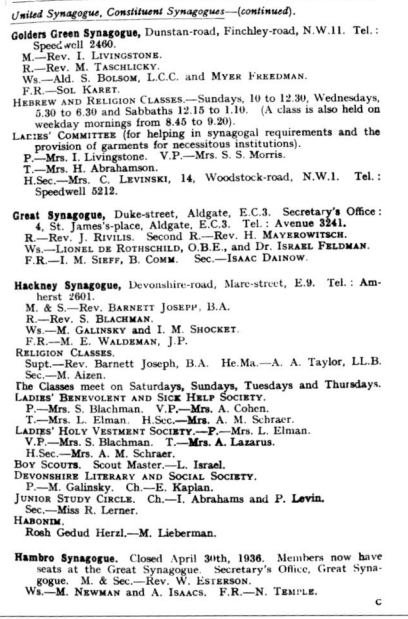

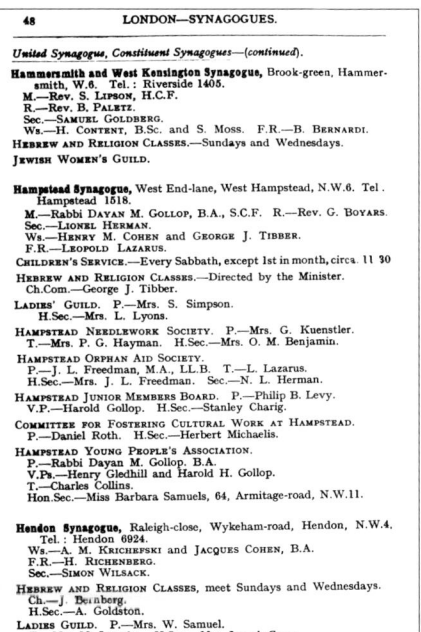

branches of the United Synagogue: the Great Synagogue, Duke's Place; the Hambro Synagogue, Fenchurch Street; the New Synagogue, Great St. Helen's; the Bayswater Synagogue, Chichester Place; the Central Synagogue, Great Portland Street and the Borough New Synagogue, Wansey Street; as well as the West London Synagogue of British Jews (Reform), Upper Berkeley Street; the Western Synagogue, St. Alban's Place; the Maiden Lane Synagogue, Covent Garden; the North London Synagogue (John Street West, later Lofting Road) and seven 'minor' synagogues.

Today, only the Central and the West London still exist on the same site.

The Jewish Year Book for 1937 lists nineteen constituent synagogues of the United Synagogue (Fig. 9), of which only eight of the original buildings remain in use in 1999.

Fig. 9 Constituent synagogues of the United Synagogue from *The Jewish Year Book* for 1937. Most of these are now closed.

THE
SYNAGOGUES

THE GREAT SYNAGOGUE

DUKE'S PLACE, EC3

Fig. 10 A plaque in memory of Moses Hart in the old Great Synagogue, Duke's Place. (Reproduced from *A History of the Jews of Richmond* by Arthur Howitt,[111] with permission).

In the 1690s, an early group of Ashkenazim opened their own cemetery and rented a house in Duke's Place in which to hold services. With increasing Jewish immigration from Germany a need arose for a larger synagogue. A successful stockbroker, Moses Hart, who had won a lottery, used this money to pay for a new building on the same site in Duke's Place (Fig. 10). The Preface from the *Rules of the Congregation, 1827*, reproduced below, elegantly describes the opening:

"The Wardens of the Great Synagogue, Duke's Place, presume that it will neither be deemed irrelevant nor intrusive if they seize the opportunity afforded by the publication and distribution of the newly arranged Code of Laws, to prefix to the same an account of the early establishment of this Congregation, together with a cursory detail of its present arrangement, and of the course pursued by the Officers and Vestry to effect the objects of their anxious care.

It appears from the remnant of an ancient manuscript book of laws and minutes of transactions still existing among the documents lying in the Synagogue Chambers, that a meeting for prayer at least, if not a place specially devoted for Public Worship, must have been established by the German Jews, prior to the year 1692: the Synagogue in Duke's Place, however, was the first Building, excepting that of the Portuguese Congregation, purposely erected for divine service after their settlement in this happy realm in the year 1655. This pious work was effected at the sole expense of Moses Hart, Esq., a wealthy merchant of that time, the consecration of which took place on the Eve of the New Year A.M. 5482 or 1722, and by a codicil to the will of this religious and generous benefactor, bearing date 1756, the property was bequeathed to the Congregation altogether.

In 1767, this Building was repaired, enlarged and consecrated; since that period however, the community having greatly increased, the whole was taken down and the present elegant structure (being twice the size of the former) was erected in 1790, toward the expense of which, Mrs. Judith Levy, the then only surviving daughter of the original founder, subscribed the sum of £4000.

The Synagogue thus renewed, is the oldest and most spacious in London belonging to the German Jews, besides which, as the population has increased, several others have since been erected; but in consequence of its early standing, this of Duke's Place has always been the principal point whereto the poor, both resident and foreign, have looked for, and found relief. At the head of its religious department we have at the present time the happiness to boast of the superintendence of the highly gifted and worthy Dr. Solomon Hirschell, Q.D.C., whose reverend and esteemed father also guided Israel in this place from the year 1757 to 1764; divine worship is, of course, regularly and devoutly attended to under his auspices, while the Honorary Officers and Vestry are zealously employed in the general superintendence, in the dispensation of charity to the poor, the attention to the sick, and burial of the dead. Fixed monthly stipends are allotted to proper objects, as well as casual relief administered as occasions arise, and the sums dispensed among the foreign poor who apply are very considerable, besides a large annual expense incurred for the distribution of matzos for which there always are an immense number of applicants; a Physician, Surgeon and Apothecary are also engaged to attend in their several departments for the benefit of the poor.

Thus are our principal duties, of worship to the Almighty God, and charity to his creatures, attempted to be fulfilled. May we find grace in the sight of the Lord, and may he bless his people. Amen."[18]

Rule 148 provided that the religious direction shall be under the guidance of the *Rav Av Beis Din* (Chief Rabbi). Rule 150 states that he is to deliver two discourses, on the "Great Sabbath" (before Passover) and the "Sabbath of Penitence" (between the New Year and the Day of Atonement) before the Reading of the Law at the morning service; Rule 152, that he should read the prayers for Rain (at the onset of winter), Dew (at the beginning of spring) and Neilah (at the end of the Day of Atonement); Rule 154, that he is by virtue of office obliged to perform the ceremony of marriage to all persons belonging to the congregation; Rule 158, that all persons who on marriage receive a portion not exceeding £100 shall pay to the Chief Rabbi not less than one guinea; Rule 159, that should the marriage portion exceed £100 the party shall pay an additional half guinea for every £100 beyond the first; Rule 165, that the Hazzanim and Shamash (translated in the history as two Readers and a clerk) must at all times be present in the Synagogue *arrayed in their proper costume,* which they must retain during the whole period of the service; Rule 166, that the Hazzan whose appointed duty it is to read prayers and neglects the same, is liable to be fined.

The custom of wearing ministerial garb, even during weekdays, certainly persisted at the Great Synagogue until the Second World War. Cantor Vigoda of New York, who succeeded the legendary Joseph Rosenblatt at the 'First Hungarian Congregation Ohab Zedek' visited the Great Synagogue in the 1930s. He writes, in his *Legendary Voices,*[19]

"At the 'Great' the chief Cantor alternated with the second Cantor in conducting the daily services, mornings and evenings all year round, both Cantors garbed in their ceremonial robes and hats, and the sextons in their 'Prince Alberts' and silk hats, when the services were mostly attended only by the Asoro Batlonim, *the ten idlers who were hired for that purpose. I myself had occasion to witness this strange custom when I dropped in one Wednesday evening at the Duke's Place Synagogue. Clad in their Cantorial vestments, in walked Chief Cantor Rivilis and Assistant Cantor Mayerowitsch; the first recited the Mincha (afternoon service), the second the Maariv (evening service) ritual."* (This custom also persisted for morning services at the Golders Green Synagogue until the 1960s.)

A whole section of *The Rules* is devoted to the Laws regarding Kaddish – again, these customs are not often followed.

Rule 235 stated, following the German custom, that *"a list shall regularly be kept, and posted ... to notify the regular order of each individual's right to Kaddish"*; Rule 236 that *"the person saying Kaddish must place himself near the Teva* (desk);" Rule 237 that *"any person during the 30 days of mourning is entitled to one Kaddish each day"*; Rule 238 that *"any stranger, on Jahrzeit is entitled to one Kaddish, after Mizmor, but persons renting a seat have the preference on this occasion."*

Another custom, originally derived from Alsace, was that of the responsive saying of the Friday night psalms (apparently in order to improve decorum). It had been introduced by Chief Rabbi N.M. Adler and was still in use at Golders Green until the 1960s.

Dr. Cecil Roth has written the comprehensive and definitive *History of the Great Synagogue,*[20] and a full description of its architecture can be found in

Fig. 11 *The Great Synagogue*. The exterior (undated). (Reproduced from *A History of the Jews of Richmond* by Arthur Howitt,[111] with permission).

an article by C. Epstein in *Building Jerusalem*, edited by S. Kadish (1996).[21] This article includes plans of the alterations dating from 1765-6 (these plans can be found at the London Metropolitan Archives and the plans for the ceiling can be found in the Sir John Soane Museum). The alterations were carried out by George Dance, Snr., the City surveyor, and his son, also George, who remodelled the interior. The house next door was purchased and the dividing wall between both removed, resulting in a synagogue larger than Bevis Marks. The plans show an ornate cupboard-like ark surrounded by pillars, with a surrounding metal fence, a central Almemar and traditionally arranged pews. The Almemar was surrounded by two giant columns acting as supports which, according to Epstein, would have obstructed the view along a central axis.

Epstein also describes the second reconstruction in 1788-90, when the entire sanctuary was razed and rebuilt to designs by the Spiller brothers. The exterior remained simple (Fig. 11), whereas the interior was rendered more ornate. It was illustrated in *The Microcosm of London*.[22] The illustrations were by Charles Pugin and Thomas Rowlandson. Pugin was said by Sir John Summerson[23] to be a pompous aristocrat, but he drew the architecture of the "*Microcosm*" with "*photographic accuracy*" and a feeling for subtle lighting. Rowlandson provided the caricatures; he was said to be a genius, absorbed "*by the everyday life of his fellow creatures, their humours, pomposities and antics ... and magical knowledge of what makes an English crowd.*"[23] The characters in his engraving, reproduced on the inside front cover of this book, show rather stereotyped Jews.

In her book *The Architecture of the European Synagogue*, Rachel Wischnitzer describes the interior of the Great Synagogue: "*The broad nave is separated from the aisles by large Ionic columns supporting the galleries. Three levels of windows let in an abundance of light, with lunettes above rounded windows in the Gallery. The Galleries have a grill, later removed.*"[24] (For a fuller description, see Epstein.[21])

The oval Almemar was central and balustraded. The Hazzan and his assistants – the tenor and the bass – are shown wearing tricorn hats (see

Fig. 12 Rowlandson's satire on the visit of the Royal Princes to the Great Synagogue.

inside front cover), a customary practice prior to the adoption of a more Germanic form of clerical garb during the Rabbinate of Dr. N.M. Adler (1845–1890).

The eastern wall was divided into three parts by two large columns. The central part contained the ark in a niche screened off by two pillars.

An oil painting by J. Harwood (1834), reproduced on the outside front cover of this book, shows the building from the western end, at ground level, and without pews. Light streams in through the windows. The Jews here are shown as Orientals – somewhat of a speciality of the artist – rather than poor, old clothes merchants with large noses. (The colour of the *Parokhet* in this painting is of a delicate blue, but in the print by Pugin it is red.)

Thomas Rowlandson satirised the visit to the Great Synagogue of the three Royal princes – sons of George III – the Dukes of Cambridge, Cumberland and Sussex (the Duke of Sussex had a Hebrew tutor, Dr. Loewe) on Friday evening, 14th April, 1809 (Fig. 12). A special Order of

Fig. 13 *The Great Synagogue* destroyed during a bombing raid. (Reproduced from the *Illustrated*, 12th July, 1941.)

Fig. 14 A service of intercession held on 7th September 1941 in the ruins of the Great Synagogue with the Chief Rabbi preaching.

Fig. 15 A simple synagogue erected in 1943 in the cleared grounds of the Great Synagogue, Duke's Place, in use during and after the Second World War. (Photograph courtesy of the *Jewish Chronicle*.)

Service was compiled and printed on silk. As Royalty descended from their carriages, their path was strewn with flowers. The *Parokhet* of crimson, as shown in *The Microcosm*, had been presented by N.M. Rothschild. The 'High Priest', Rabbi Hirschell, was dressed in a robe of white satin of considerable value, that had been ordered expressly for him by Abraham Goldsmid. A space between the pulpit and ark had been appropriated to the Princes and nobility, who stood on a rich platform with four Egyptian chairs. "*The Galleries were crowded with beautiful Jewesses, who attracted much of the attention of the Royal party.*"[20]

On 11th May, 1941, the Great Synagogue was destroyed by bombs (Fig. 13). An open air service was held in the ruins on 7th September of that year to make the vow: "The Great Synagogue will rise again" (Fig. 14). Every section of the community was represented, with hundreds of people standing packed together and amplifiers relaying the service to 300 more standing outside in Creechurch Place. Dr. Hertz officiated with Hazzanim S. Kusevitzsky and H. Mayerowitsch, while aircraft droned overhead. Dr. Hertz prayed for "*the men, women and children of our country – let not their homes become their graves*", and for the Royal family, followed by a memorial prayer for fallen servicemen. The text of his sermon was "*From the depths I cry unto thee*" and ended "*that Victory will crown the righteous cause of Britain, and the Great Synagogue will rise again.*"

Alas, this did not happen.

The City of London suffered severely during the bombing raids, accelerating Jewish migration away from the area. The walls of the ruined synagogue were razed to the ground and a simple structure erected in its place in 1943 (Fig. 15). This building closed on 26th October, 1958, because there were too few members; the congregation, or its remnant, subsequently worshipped in a room in Adler Street, previously used by a Friendly Society, until that, too, eventually ceased on 10th April, 1977.

In *The Jewish East End 1840-1939*[25] there is a most moving account by Maurice Michaels on his childhood memories of the Synagogue. He was at its closing service. The congregation numbered just forty. After nearly three hundred years, he writes, the Great Synagogue went out of existence "*unwept, unhonoured and unsung.*"

Michaels had been a chorister there from 1932 until 1940. Mr. David Levine, once choirmaster (who also appears in the history of the Brondesbury Synagogue) later became choirmaster at the Golders Green Synagogue, where he brought much of the musical tradition from the Great Synagogue. But the *Minhagim* (customs) mentioned by Michaels are either now forgotten or even frowned upon. Michaels remembers the children walking in file to the Great Synagogue from the Jews' Free School, annual military services, as well as policemen controlling the entrance (see below, under Hazzan Kusevitsky). On Simchas Torah he counted the Scrolls – there were thirty six! He also remembers there were fifteen different tunes for Adon Olam.

Michaels writes "*I have taken what the old Great Synagogue implanted in me to synagogues around the world hoping to find somewhere, someday, services of such beauty. But nothing will ever replace the Great Synagogue.*"[25] (Figs. 16, 17 and 18).

The Rabbinate of the Great Synagogue

The Rabbis listed by Roth[20,26] were:

Judah Loeb Cohen (1696–1700);

Fig. 16   Fig. 17   Fig. 18

Fig. 19   Fig. 20   Fig. 21   Fig. 22   Fig. 23   Fig. 24

Fig. 16 *The Great Synagogue*. A New Year's greeting showing the interior; the architectural detail is good.

Fig. 17 The ark of the Great Synagogue. One of the Wardens was a Rothschild. (Reproduced from the *Illustrated*, 12th July 1941.)

Fig. 18 Hazzan Kusevitsky at the ark of the Great Synagogue. (Reproduced from the *Illustrated*, 12th July, 1941.)

Fig. 19 *Chief Rabbi Hart Lyon*. The engraving dates from his Rabbinate in Berlin.

Fig. 20 *Chief Rabbi David Tevele Schiff*. (Reproduced from Cecil Roth's *History of the Great Synagogue*.[20])

Fig. 21 *Chief Rabbi Solomon Hirschell*, son of Hart Lyon.

Fig. 22 *Chief Rabbi Nathan Marcus Adler*.

Fig. 23 *Chief Rabbi Hermann Adler*.

Fig. 24 *Chief Rabbi Joseph Hermann Hertz*.

Aaron the Scribe of Dublin, acting Rabbi (1700-1704);

Aaron Hart (1704-1757) – according to Hermann Adler,[27] the first of the post-Expulsion Chief Rabbis;

Hart Lyon (1758-1764) (Fig. 19) – accepted as Rabbinical Authority by the Hambro Synagogue;

David Tevele Schiff (1765-1792) (Fig. 20) – "High Priest of the Great Jews' Synagogue";

Moses Myers, of the New, acting Rabbi (1792-1802)

Solomon Hirschell (1802-1842) (Fig. 21) – the first unquestioned holder of the office of Chief Rabbi;

Nathan Adler (1845-1890) (Fig. 22) – Chief Rabbi;

Hermann Adler (1891-1911) (Fig. 23) – Chief Rabbi;

Joseph Hertz (1913-1946) (Fig. 24) – Chief Rabbi;

Rabbi I. Jakobovits (1947) (see Fig. 85) – later Chief Rabbi.

The interested reader can find the biographical details of these in the *Encyclopaedia Judaica*; see also the biography of Solomon Hirschell by the late Hyman Symons.[27] In addition, various books have been written on the subject. *The Rabbinate of the Great Synagogue from 1756-1842* by Dr. C. Duschinsky,[28] originally published in Oxford in 1921, was reprinted in 1971. Dr. Cecil Roth also contributed a chapter entitled "The Chief Rabbinate of England" in *Essays Presented to J.H. Hertz*[26] and, as a filial duty as well as an interest, Dr. Hermann Adler published an article on the Chief Rabbinate in *Papers Read at the Anglo-Jewish Historical Exhibition, 1887*.[29] This latter article deals with 'Chief Rabbis' both before the Expulsion and after the Readmission. Hart Lyon (Hirsch Loebel, the Berliner Rav) was the father of

Rabbi Solomon Hirschell, who was born in England in 1762, while David Tevele Schiff married the sister of a Rabbi Beer Adler, the grandfather of Rabbi N.M. Adler. Schiff therefore was the grand uncle of N.M. Adler.

The Cantorate of the Great Synagogue

Less well known than the Chief Rabbis are the Hazzanim of the Great Synagogue. Fortunately, one of the latter, Hazzan Mayerowitsch, has left a memoir, which was first published in 1942 in *Miscellanies of the Jewish Historical Society of England* [30] and subsequently in Roth's *History of the Great Synagogue, London, 1600-1940.* [20] The Hazzanim are listed as follows:

Jehuda Leib ben Moses of Lissa (1690-1706)

Menachem Mendel (1706- ?)

Joseph — (? -1722)

Samuel Hertz of Schwersenz (1730- ?)

Isaac Polak of Holland (1746-1802) (Fig. 25). There is a engraving of him, showing him to be clean-shaven, wearing a wig and a tricorn, indicating that he must have adopted fashionable English ways very rapidly. His two assistants were Myer Leoni and the famous tenor John Braham, composer of *The Death of Nelson*, who later sang at Covent Garden; Braham's daughter became Countess Waldegrave and his son a Church of England clergyman.

Myer Metz of Offenbach (1814-1827)

Nathan Solomon of Groningen (1815-1817). The unsuccessful candidate when Myer Metz was appointed, he was made Second Reader.

Binom Elias of Darmstadt (1827). Another German, who could not tolerate the London weather. He brought with him as boy soprano J.L. Mombach, later choirmaster and composer.

Simon Ascher of Groningen (1832-1871). A fine tenor, he instituted a choir at the Great Synagogue. He had three musical children – two

Fig. 25 *Hazzan Isaac Polak.*
(Reproduced from Cecil Roth's *History of the Great Synagogue.* [20])

Hast

Gordon

Katz

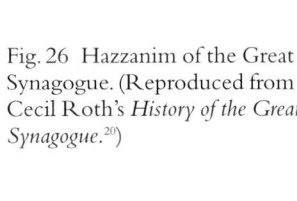

Fig. 26 Hazzanim of the Great Synagogue. (Reproduced from Cecil Roth's *History of the Great Synagogue.* [20])

Mayerowitsch

Rivilis

Kusevitsky

Fig. 27 *Hazzan Forscher.*
(Photograph courtesy of
Mrs. Forscher.)

daughters and a son. The latter became conductor to Empress Eugenie and was the composer of *Alice, where art thou?*

Aaron Levy Green (1851-1854) (see Fig.70), who later became Reader and Preacher at the Central Synagogue (see p. 75).

Moses Keizer of the Hague (1857-1876), who also became the first Superintendent of the Jewish Board of Guardians.)

Marcus Hast of Breslau (originally of Warsaw) (1872-1911) (Fig. 26). According to Vigoda, Hast, born in 1841, was a great Talmudic scholar, known as the *Praga'er Ilui* (teenage prodigy) and possessed of a beautiful voice.[19] After much study he became a fine pianist. Initially Hazzan in Warsaw, he later served at Breslau before coming to London. His anthology *Seder Hoavodah* was an anthology of synagogue music in use in England. He also composed two oratorios and a cantata.

Abraham Gordon (1888-1919) (Fig. 26), *"a cultured Hazzan of the German style with an unbounded passion for music, and a worker for charitable causes."*[30]

Abraham Katz (1913-1930) (Fig. 26). Apparently the other candidate at this time, D. Steinberg of Odessa, exemplified the Eastern European style and was technically remarkable, but too Eastern for the members of Great Synagogue. Hazzan Katz's style was more Western, and he blended in so well with the choir under S. Alman that the services reached a standard never heard anywhere else. Mayerowitsch describes him as *"an outstanding tenor, free of fuss, never pompous, with devotion and dignity."*[30]

Jacob Rivilis (1932-1937) (Fig. 26), had a *"pleasant and flexible voice."*[30] He came from a small congregation in Romania, but could not cope with the exacting nature of his position at the Great Synagogue. Apparently his voice always gave way on the High Holy days. He returned to Romania.

Simcha Kusevitsky (1937-1947) (Figs. 14 and 18; see also Fig. 108). Born in Poland, he was one of four brothers, all Hazzanim. Having served as a Hazzan in Rovno, Poland, he went to Glasgow and from there to the Stoke Newington Synagogue in Shacklewell Lane (see p. 104) before being appointed to the Great Synagogue. So popular were his services, that policemen had to control the crowd at the gates, and the Ladies' Gallery was given over in part to the men. In 1947 he moved to South Africa and died there, in 1998, at the age of 93 years.

He was succeeded by Hazzan **Forscher** (Fig. 27), whose twin brother was Hazzan at the Hammersmith Synagogue. My father knew their father, who was also a Hazzan in an orthodox congregation in Maehrisch Ostrau, Czechoslovakia.

THE HAMBRO SYNAGOGUE

FENCHURCH STREET, EC3,

LATER ADLER STREET, E1

The history of the Synagogue was written in 1925 by the Revd. W. Esterson on the occasion of the 200th Anniversary of its foundation.[31] It is also described in Elkan Adler's *London*[3] and in Cecil Roth's *History of the Great Synagogue*.[20] There is, in addition, a helpful letter by Wilfred S. Samuel in the *Jewish Guardian* in 1925.[32]

The name 'Hambro' may well be a corruption of 'Hamburg'. The Synagogue had no connection with the banking family of the same name who, although originally Jewish, coming to London from Copenhagen via Hamburg, seem to have had no connection with the London community and rapidly converted to the dominant faith.[4]

Marcus Hamburger (*Hebrew*: Mordecai, the son of Moses Libush, one of the founders of the Hamburg community) married Freudiche, the daughter of Glueckel of Hameln (called the German-Jewish Pepys by Samuel and Roth). In 1704, while living in Whitechapel, he sought to establish a Beth Hamedrash and Synagogue in a house in St. Mary Axe. The Court of Aldermen, urged on no doubt by Moses Hart (brother of Aaron, the Rabbi at Duke's Place), managed to stop the scheme.

In 1706 Aaron Hart, the Rabbi of the Great Synagogue, granted a conditional divorce in secret to one Asher Cohen who wished to leave for the West Indies. Such conditional divorces were granted in case the husband did not return, or vanished, leaving the wife in limbo without the divorce. Hamburger publicly protested against the divorce, which he said was irregular because it had not been publicised and the assessors (*Dayanim*) were not Rabbinical scholars.[29] As a result, he was excommunicated.

Because of this *Herem*, Marcus Hamburger could take no part in communal life, nor use the Four Species on Tabernacles. As can be seen in Fig. 35 – the engraving of the New Synagogue – few individuals could afford to buy their own. In addition, that year only the Sephardim had obtained them, from Italy, and they lent only one set to the Synagogue in Duke's Place. Also, Hamburger could not be called up to the Reading of the Law, nor to the great distress of his wife, could their recently born daughter have a naming ceremony in the Synagogue.

According to Roth,[20] in 1707 Hamburger, with some friends from Hamburg, established a synagogue in his own house in Magpie Alley, Fenchurch Street, using the Hamburg rite.* R. Jochanan Holleschau, previously of the Beth Din, was appointed as the Rabbi of the small congregation; he had taken the side of Hamburger in the matter of the divorce. Hamburger also purchased a burial ground at Hoxton on 25th March, 1707, on a 150 year lease at ten shillings per annum. It is, according to W. Samuel, "*the oldest possession of any Ashkenazi community in the British Empire. It contains the graves of the Hamburger, Gompertz, Amschel and Salomons families.*"[32] Their second cemetery in Hackney became disused in 1872; it

★ The laws of the congregation, dated 5605 (1845) state however that "the form of prayer throughout the year shall be conformably to Minhag Polin as already established by the congregation from the earliest period (Law 1). Law 112 states that "the Shamas, Hazzanim and Secretary must at all times be present in the Synagogue previous to the commencement of prayers". Law 113 instructs "the Readers and the Shamas shall enter the Synagogue arrayed in their proper costume at all times of prayer at least five minutes before the time appointed, and if they do not strictly conform they shall be liable to a fine of five shillings for each neglect". Law 119: "The First Reader shall perform the marriage ceremony attired in his official dress unless a member shall make choice of the Chief Rabbi to solemnize the same who shall have a claim to a sum of not less than one guinea; in this case the usual fees shall be paid to our Chazanim". Law 120: "If it at any time should so occur that any prejudicial report be attached to the reputation of the bride or to the character of the bridegroom ..... the Second Reader shall perform the ceremony".

Fig. 28 *Hambro Synagogue*. The interior of the building in Magpie Alley, Fenchurch Street, still lit by candlelight. This early photograph gives an air of mystery to this Georgian Synagogue. The benches were without upholstery and the pillars supporting the Ladies Gallery led directly onto the second row of benches. The box between the ark and the Almemar was presumably for the Wardens. There seems to have been an apse above the ark and perhaps an urn surmounting the ark.

★ These sources do not all give the same dates for the events described above.

★★ Hart Lyon - Hirschel Loebel

lies near Lauriston Road.

However, the excommunication ruined Hamburger financially and, in 1711, he went to the West Indies (according to Samuel[32]), or in 1717 went to India (according to Adler[3] and Roth[20]), or to the East Indies (according to Esterson[31]). In any case, after several years abroad, he returned in 1721 (according to Samuel and Roth) with gems, including the largest diamond ever seen in Europe.[3] Services had continued in the house in his absence.

In 1718 the government had decided that English-born Jews would be allowed to own land and, according to Adler, Hamburger acquired the freehold of his house (even though he was foreign-born). In its garden was built the next Hambro Synagogue, in 1721 according to Adler[3], but the foundation stone being laid in 1725, according to Roth[20] and Esterson[31], by Wolf Prager (of Bohemia), his son-in-law.★

The interior is shown in Fig. 28. There are three rows of men's pews with a central box (presumably for the Wardens) situated between the ark and the Almemar. At the time of the photograph the building was candlelit with large candles upon the Almemar, which is of wood and curved. The ark is built into the eastern wall, with two columns on either side continuing up to the ceiling. The ark appears to have an urn above. A large skylight can be seen in the roof.

In 1756 Hirsch Lewin★★ (Fig. 19), father of Solomon Hirschell, was appointed Rav and, in 1765, Schlomo Emden, grandson of the Chacham Zevi.

In 1752 the three congregations, the Spanish and Portuguese, the Great and the Hambro Synagogues, united in order to prevent unauthorised conversions but, even so, Lord George Gordon converted in 1787 in Birmingham. He visited the Hambro Synagogue and made an offering of £100.

In 1803 Mr. E.Y. Salomons, who by then owned the property, presented it to the Synagogue in perpetuity.

Membership of the Hambro was never large – in 1880, 162 members and in 1890, 102. Perhaps it was in the wrong place, even for the City. There were numerous schemes for closure and amalgamation with the Great Synagogue, proposed by the Hambro, one being in 1863. As part of the proposed amalgamation, the Hambro wished the Great Synagogue to engage its Reader (Rabbi Gollancz), its Secretary, and its *Shamus* (sic) at their existing salaries, or to give them compensation. The Great Synagogue, however, declined to re-engage the ministers and, for whatever reason, the amalgamation did not then proceed.

In 1893 the Hambro Synagogue in Magpie Alley, Fenchurch Street was closed. (Its foundation stone was discovered by Delissa Joseph when the building was being demolished in that year). For the next six years, the congregation held its services in the vestry room of the Great Synagogue. The Hambro's property and books had been deposited in the basement of the synagogue in Great Portland Street but, when later reclaimed, many of the valuables were missing.

Fig. 29 *Hambro Synagogue*. The exterior of the second Synagogue building in Adler Street. (Redrawn by Keith Ruggles from a photograph by courtesy of Dr. A. Goldberg.)

Fig. 30 *Hambro Synagogue*. The interior of the second Synagogue. Stairs on either side of the forward-situated Almemar led to the men's part of the Ladies Gallery. There does appear to have been a partition in one Gallery to the side of the ark. Altogether, a most peculiar design. There still seem to have been gaslights on the walls of the Synagogue. The pulpit presumably was at the top of the stairs and centrally situated; the seats immediately below it may well have been for the Wardens. (Photograph courtesy of Dr. A. Goldberg, the grandson of the Revd. W. Esterson (see Fig. 124), the long-serving minister of the Hambro Synagogue.)

In 1899 a new Synagogue in Adler Street – a more easterly situation – was consecrated, the building having been designed by Lewis Solomon. The Revd. W. Esterson* was appointed as minister.

The exterior of the new Hambro was of unremitting ordinariness (Fig. 29), while the interior, in contrast with the tranquillity of the previous synagogue, was really of little beauty. As well as the ground floor seating for men, the eastern half of the galleries were also used by men and were screened off by seven feet high wooden partitions. Access to these parts of the galleries were by steps running up the sides of the ark. The *Almemar* and *Omed* were up against the eastern wall. There was a large apse with a gallery above the ark (Fig. 30).

Membership remained at about 200, but the Synagogue was eventually closed and amalgamated with the Great Synagogue in 1936. On this occasion, the ministers were retained in service at the Great, but the situation was not a happy one and Mr. Esterson resigned shortly after.

The Reverend Rabbi Samuel Marcus Gollancz,
Rabbi of the Hambro Synagogue from 1854-1899 (Fig. 31).

His most enjoyable autobiography was published in 1930, some 30 years after his death, translated from the German by his eldest son, Rabbi Professor Sir Hermann Gollancz, as a *"token of filial love and respect"*.[33] It provides an excellent insight into Jewish life in Poland and Germany in the early and mid 19th century.

Rabbi S.M. Gollancz had taken his name from his father's birthplace – Gollancz, in the province of Posen, western Poland. His father was called Israel, as was one of his sons.

His Preface to the book shows us that he was a man of piety and of great and simple faith. He writes *"with fervent thankfulness to G-d, whose Fatherly hand has hitherto guided us, who has created us in his own image and given us the world, this earth to cultivate, beautify and illuminate with the light of wisdom in order to have dominion over it, we contemplate the world and turn our thoughts to human life."*

Life in the village revolved around the synagogue, its Rebbe and its Hazzan. The young Gollancz, as was the custom, began to study the Talmud at an early age, and also accompanied the Hazzan in the synagogue service.

As a child he had been taken to the Rebbe, who reached for a large tome: *"See, my son, this passage of Gemara, this Rashi, this Tosephot. Look them over, then I will examine you."* His answers were obviously good. *"My good father could scarcely speak for joy."*

The lad studied both *Hazzanut* and Talmud with the local Hazzan, who was invited to sing in Posen. There he met and was blessed by the great R. Akiba Eger of Posen.

"One day a splendid carriage was sent to take him (Rabbi Eger) *to the ceremony of circumcision at which he was to assist. A student and I escorted our reverend master down the steps; he got into the carriage, but it was some time before he would sit down. He insisted on the cushions being removed (because of the Law of mixed stuff)* (Deut. xxii 11)*, then the great man took his seat on the bare boards, and drove away."*[33]

As seems to have been the custom, the young Gollancz left the family home and travelled from community to community, learning here, singing there – Berlin, Hamburg, Altona, Bremen, the Hague. In Bremen he heard of a vacancy at the Hambro Synagogue and, despite knowing nobody in London, wrote to Dr. Adler applying for the post which, after some delay, he

* see under North West London Synagogue, Caversham Road, p.118.

42

obtained.

In his book he tells of his friendship with Dr. Adler and Sir Moses Montefiore. His eldest son, Rabbi Hermann Gollancz, entered University College (Baroness Mayer de Rothschild sent a letter of congratulation). His daughter attended Queens College, Harley Street, and later Newnham College, Cambridge. Israel, the younger son, attended the City of London School.

Rabbi Gollancz was, according to his son, "*a fine writer in Hebrew and German, a man of musical talent, an artistic designer, a carver in ivory and amber. He had a broad heart without the least tinge of fanaticism. He helped to found the Board of Guardians and the Soup Kitchen for the Jewish Poor. He was in addition an accomplished poet.*"[33]

"*I read the prayers on the Sabbath and Feast days without the aid of glasses, and recite them clearly and distinctly. I am proud of it; and as long as I am granted this favour I will praise the everlasting God with all my soul and with all my might,*" wrote Rabbi Gollancz to one of his sisters in 1892.

A photograph, taken in his latter years, shows an old man with a kindly face (Fig. 32). He served his congregation for 45 years, retiring in 1899, dying in 1900 (Fig. 33).

Fig. 31 *Rabbi Samuel Marcus Gollancz* (left) upon his appointment to the Hambro Synagogue. Rabbi Gollancz is wearing clerical bands. There may be a rosette on the front of his top hat. (Reproduced by kind permission of Oxford University Press.)

Fig. 32 *Rabbi Gollancz* (right) as an old man, in his study. He is robed and wearing bands. (Reproduced by kind permission of Oxford University Press.)

Fig. 33 A memorial plaque to Rabbi S.M. Gollancz from the Hambro Synagogue. (Reproduced by kind permission of Oxford University Press.)

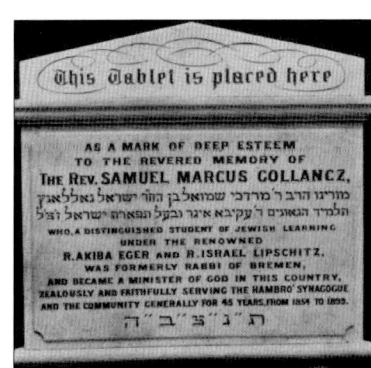

THE NEW SYNAGOGUE

LEADENHALL STREET, EC3,

LATER GREAT ST. HELENS EC3,

LATER EGERTON ROAD, N16

Fig. 34 *New Synagogue*. The Synagogue at the Bricklayers (or Bucklers) Hall. The symbols of the craft are seen outside the door to the side of the inn. The gentleman emerging from door wears a tricorn hat - presumably he is Jewish.

James Picciotto[13] notes that, by 1761, the two German Synagogues then open – the Great and the Hambro – were too small for the rapidly increasing number of worshippers. Members from these two Synagogues, together with some new immigrants, united to form a new congregation – the New Synagogue.

The instigator was Moses Jacob, a silversmith of Little Duke's Place. The new congregation worshipped at the Bricklayers' (or Bucklers') Hall in Leadenhall Street. This upset the remaining members of the Great and Hambro Synagogues and, at a meeting held at the Great Synagogue on 16th August, 1761, they passed the following resolution:

"*Whereas certain persons unworthy of our countenance and protection have formed themselves into a society calling themselves a congregation at Bucklers' Hall; we do hereby strictly charge our Priest, now and hereafter, that he does not directly or indirectly, or other in his name or with his knowledge or permission, officiate either publicly or privately in the service of marriages, burials, circumcisions, or other acts of priesthood, for any persons whatever belonging to the said society. And to prevent any persons from unwarily joining with that Society, we order that this resolution be read publicly two Sabbaths successively in our synagogues, that none may plead ignorance thereof. And we further order that a copy of this resolution be forthwith delivered to the Mahamad of this Portuguese Synagogue, desiring their concurrence in supporting and maintaining with us the good order of our respective communities.*"[34]

The Hall, in which the New Synagogue was situated, was opposite Cree Church in Leadenhall Street. The engraving reproduced in Fig. 34 shows the door, decorated with builders' symbols, adjacent to a tavern. Beneath the Synagogue, according to A.B. Levy,[34] was a wine cellar, prompting the couplet: "The spirits above are spirits divine; the spirits below are spirits of wine."

The secessionists also purchased their own burial ground in what today is Brady Street. The relationship between the congregations was strained. It seems that in 1790 a pauper's body lay in a coffin outside in the middle of Duke's Place. Neither Synagogue would give it a burial, each saying it was the other's turn. A Portuguese Jew informed the Wardens at Bevis Marks, who finally persuaded the New Synagogue to bury the body.

Relations improved, writes Levy, when the principal member of the New Synagogue, Nathan Solomons, married the daughter of Asher Goldsmid, the founder of Goldsmid & Mocatta, bullion brokers to the Bank of England, of the Great Synagogue, Duke's Place.

The Rabbi of the New Synagogue, Dutch-born Moses Myers, also acted as Dayan of the Great Synagogue in the ten-year interregnum between the death of David Tevele Schiff and the appointment of Solomon Hirschell in 1802. He should be listed as a 'Chief Rabbi'.

In 1837 the congregation built a new Synagogue in Great St. Helens in Bishopsgate, which was consecrated on 13th September, 1838. The original

Fig. 35a The interior of the Cheltenham Synagogue currently contains the ark, Almemar, pews and prayers for the Royal Family from the New Synagogue in the Bricklayer's Hall, Leadenhall Street. This photograph is reproduced from *The Hebrew Community of Cheltenham, Gloucester and Stroud*, 2nd edition (1999) by Revd. B. Torode, with the kind permission of the author.

Fig. 35b Cheltenham Synagogue interior, looking towards the rear. (Courtesy Dr. Simon Cohen.)

Fig. 36 *New Synagogue*. The interior of the Synagogue in Great St. Helen's, Bishopsgate, at the Feast of Tabernacles. The scene must be just after Hallel. There seems to be only one set of the four species. Two scrolls of the Law have been removed and the curtain is being drawn before the ark. There is a choir of men and sweetly dressed little boys. The Officiants are still wearing tricorn hats, but have clerical bands at their necks. (Steel engraving by H. Melville, after T.H. Shepherd. From *London Interiors*, 1841.)

synagogue was later occupied by the Jewish Literary and Scientific Institution.

The *Jewish Chronicle* of 21st May, 1999, reporting on the 160th anniversary of the Cheltenham Synagogue, noted that the "*light oak Ark, bimah, benches and reading desk, now over 230 years old* (Fig. 35)*, were a gift from the New Synagogue, when it moved, in 1837, from Leadenhall Street to Bishopsgate.*" In addition, two plaques, one for the Royal Family, were reconsecrated during this anniversary service. During their restoration the names of George II, George III and William IV were uncovered beneath that of Queen Victoria. These plaques, made in 1827-30, started life at the Great Synagogue, were taken to the New in 1761 and donated to the Cheltenham Synagogue seventy eight years later.

Some confusion exists as to the identity of the architect of the synagogue in Great St. Helens. Helen Rosenau[35] names two different people – George Basevi, who had already converted to Christianity, and J. Davies, architect to the Rothschilds, who is mentioned in the communal history[34] as being the only architect. Rachel Wischnitzer[24] however believes that the architect was David Mocatta (who designed the railway station in Brighton, which still stands today).

The beautiful interior has been preserved for posterity in the steel engraving of 1841 in *London Interiors* by H. Melville from a drawing by T.H. Shepherd (Fig. 36). The engraving depicts the Feast of Tabernacles. A solitary set of *Arba Minim* — the four species — is being taken round. The *Parokhet* is being drawn. A choir of three men and two boys are to the left of the Hazzan, who is wearing a tricorn hat. The built-in ark lies flush with the wall of the semi-domed apse. Wischnitzer[24] notes the "*dominance of the ark, with every line converging to the focal point. The double beams of the ceiling echo the twin columns of the framework of the apse. The large stained-glass windows in the apse direct the eye toward the ark.*" Elaborate railings of metal line the Ladies Gallery. Two large plaques, presumably prayers for Queen Victoria, lie to the side of the apse.

The street facade had a length of 110 feet (Fig. 37). Elegant iron gates can be seen, with a forecourt, three arches for the doors and stairs in recessed lateral wings; residences were on either side. The Vestry Room lay above the foyer.

The Revd. Solomon Levy (Fig. 38 and Appendix 5a) was appointed as the Synagogue's first minister in 1895 (previously, as elsewhere, the officiant was the Reader). By the turn of the century the congregation was in decline, the wealthier members of the congregation having moved to the West End. In 1885 there had been 390 seatholders, but by 1906, at a time when the Jewish population of the East End was near its peak, there were only 280 as the Synagogue lay in the City, rather than in Stepney or Whitechapel.

The United Synagogue determined to close down the building – the site being valued at £70,000 in 1897 – and relocate the Synagogue. Lord Swaythling cleared the financial deficit of the congregation, protesting against the closure of "*the most beautiful building of its kind in the United Kingdom.*"[34] Unfortunately, he was opposed by Lord Rothschild, who voted for closure and relocation.

The New Synagogue closed in 1911. Various proposals for a new situation were mooted. The congregation itself wished to moved to Commercial Road, but the Hambro objected to this. The United Synagogue favoured Egerton Road in Stamford Hill, but this was objected to by the Stoke Newington Synagogue. Both South Tottenham and Bromley-by-Bow pressed their claim, but Egerton Road prevailed.

When the Synagogue did move to Stamford Hill, there was a move to dismiss Mr. Levy, and he carried on only as temporary minister, despite having been twenty years in post.

The site at Great St. Helens was eventually sold to Marcus Samuel & Co. (the Shell Petroleum Co.) for £135,000 and the new building of the New Synagogue opened in Egerton Road in 1915.

Its interior matched as far as possible that of the old, but the choir was situated on top of the ark and the three large windows were no longer present. A large pulpit was placed in front of the ark, though much of the detail in the new building was similar to that in the old.

In the 1960s the congregation had over 1,000 members, but the neighbourhood has since altered and few Anglo-Jewish congregations survive in the vicinity. In 1984 there had been 324 male members but, by 1989, there were only 211. This number had declined still further by 1997, to 107 male members, less than 10% of the membership at its peak in 1960. The Synagogue was sold to Chasidim, the only Jews remaining in Stamford Hill in any great number. The greatly reduced congregation now worships in a local hall.

Fig. 37 *New Synagogue*. Illustration from *Synagogue Review* of May 1929 of the exterior of the building in Great St. Helens, Bishopsgate.

Fig. 38 *The Revd. S. Levy*, who served at the New Synagogue, both at Great St. Helens, Bishopsgate, and at Egerton Road. (Reproduced by kind permission of the Jewish Historical Society of England.)

THE WESTERN SYNAGOGUE

GREAT PULTENEY STREET, W1,

LATER DENMARK COURT, STRAND, WC2,

LATER ST. ALBAN'S PLACE, SW1,

LATER ALFRED PLACE WC1

LATER CRAWFORD PLACE, W1

The main sources for the study of the history of this congregation are:

The *Takkanos* or rule book for 1832 which contain an abridged history;

A history published in 1897 written by Mathias Levy;

A fuller history written in 1932 by Dr. Cecil Roth.[36] This volume had the benefit of much original material subsequently lost by the Synagogue when Alfred Place was bombed in 1941.

The definitive history written by the longstanding minister of the congregation, the Revd. Arthur Barnett, Honorary Chaplain to the Forces (see Appendix 5a), published in 1961 on the occasion of the Bicentenary of the congregation.[37]

Westminster was a settlement of antiquity with Royal Palaces, its Abbey, and Schools. In 1762 the 'Westminster Paving Act' was passed, so that instead of each householder being responsible for the pavement outside his house, a 'Paving Commission' took over responsibility for pavements and gutters. The resulting attractiveness of the area made Westminster a desirable area of residence for the wealthy, who attracted tradesmen, tailors, jewellers, opticians and embroiderers. According to Piciotto,[13] within a short time, over 100 Jewish families had settled there.

The first synagogue – in Westminster

These families would all have been members of the City congregations, but the trek on Sabbaths and Festivals to the City must have been tiresome. The first *Minyan* seems to have been established in Great Pulteney Street, in the house of Wolf Liepman, who had been born in Berlin but had settled in the City of London in 1749.

The first available document relating to the "Holy congregation of the Keneseth Israel of Westminster in London" is the Law Book of the Burial Society (*Hebra Kadisha*) drawn up by Philip Abraham, embroiderer, of 13 Denmark Court, Strand, in 1767. This book also contains accounts which refer to an "old ledger", which led Barnett to believe that the congregation must have been in existence by 1765.

The second synagogue – in Denmark Court

J.J. Smith's *Ancient Topography of London* (1815) states that a synagogue existed in Back Alley, Denmark Court, Strand, in 1765, in a single hired room.[38] This suggests that the *Minyan* had transferred to the Strand before the death of Wolf Liepman in 1773.

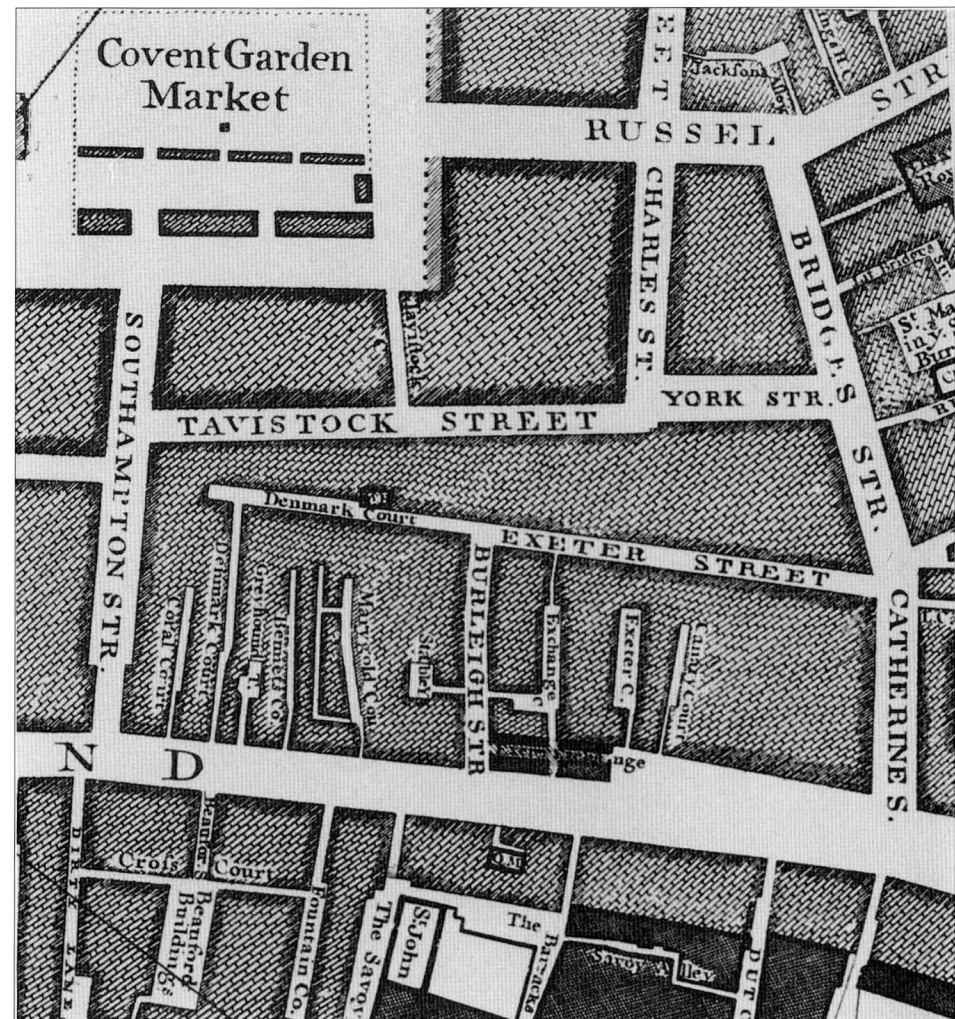

Fig. 39 A map showing the Strand at Covent Garden and Denmark Court. (Detail from *The A to Z of Georgian London*, 1982. London Topographical Society Publication No. 126. Reproduced with permission.)

By 1768 the already well-established congregation engaged a *shochet* (slaughterer), who acted as *shomer* (supervisor of food) and also gave a *shiur* (talmudic discourse). There was also, according to Mr. Barnett, who had access to the Minute Books, a lay *Hazzan* (Reader) and *Baal Koré* (Reader from the Scroll of the Law), a *Shammes* (beadle), a caretaker, cleaner and a '*Shabbes goy*' (a gentile employed to light fires on the Sabbath) – all cheaply had, no doubt, for the congregation had also engaged a 'teacher' whose annual stipend was £3 – for which each member paid ½d (about one-fifth of 1p today) per week.

Drury Lane at that time was an area of substantial immorality. Gordon, in his book *Old Time Aldwych, Kingsway, and Neighbourhood* quotes Steele, in the *Tatler* of 26th July 1709, who wrote: "*There is near Covent Garden a street known by the name of Drury, which, before the days of Christianity, was purchased by the Queen of Paphos, and is the only part of Great Britain where the tenure of vassalage is still in being. All that long course of building is under particular districts or ladyships, after the manner of lordships in other parts, over which matrons of known abilities preside, and have, for the support of their age and infirmities, certain taxes paid out of the rewards of the amorous labours of the young. This seraglio of Great Britain is disposed into convenient alleys and apartments, and every house, from the cellar to the garret, inhabited by nymphs of different orders, that persons of every rank may be accommodated.*"[39]

Denmark Court (see Fig. 39) was demolished in 1830[40] and is now apparently the site of the Strand Palace Hotel.

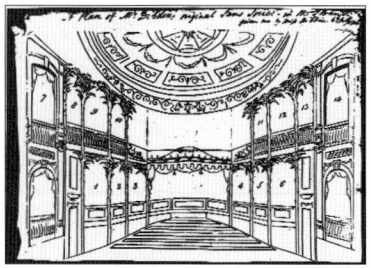

Fig. 40 The interior of the Sans Souci Theatre in the Strand, looking towards the stage. (Reproduced with kind permission of the Harvard Theatre Museum.)

The third synagogue – the Sans Souci

A theatre existed in Denmark Court – the 'Sans Souci' – at which the renowned actor, author and composer Charles Dibdin (1745-1815) staged his plays. Mr. Barnett states that the theatre was probably unprofitable and had to close but, according to Dibdin's biographer,[41] his leaving the Sans Souci was due to the inconveniences caused him and his patrons by another tenant of the building, a wine merchant who occupied the cellar in which he did his bottling. The merchant and his assistants, no doubt inebriated, would insult and assault the theatre audience. Wine barrels would block the theatre entrance and customers stayed away rather than approach a place *"so forbidding in its appearance."* In any case, the theatre moved to Leicester Square, a much better theatrical location, retaining its name.

An engraving still exists of the interior of the first Sans Souci Theatre, which was soon to become the third synagogue of the 'Holy Congregation of the Assembly of Israel of Westminster in London'. The auditorium was described as bell-shaped, with palm trees giving the effect of gothic arches, making two tiers of 'cabins' (Fig. 40).[42] The 'Royal Pavilion' near the stage *"formed an elegant accommodation for promiscuous company."* The house, with a rural motif, was decorated with foliage and silver, the stage with marble and gold. There was a large painting above the stage.

The lease for the building was signed in 1797, no doubt by the more prosperous members of the congregation. This also gives their addresses and occupations:

Jacob Hart, jeweller, Strand
Aaron Lazarus, button dealer, Carnaby Market
Jacob Lazarus, mercer, Gerrard Street
Hyam Hart, auctioneer, Strand
Israel Isaacs, salesman, Holywell Street
Moses Jonas, salesman, Covent Garden
Lyon Benjamin, sealing wax maker, Strand
Philip Phillips, embroiderer, Denmark Court

Clearly, these were merchants and tradesmen of a better sort, far removed

Fig 41 *Maiden Lane*. The stage door of the Adelphi Theatre is in the foreground. The building next to it was stated by the Revd. Barnett to be the site of the Maiden Lane Synagogue. (Photograph courtesy of National Monuments Record.)

from the immigrant peddler, rather well settled, and catering to a middle-class clientele.

The main hall of the synagogue measured 50' x 36', and there was also an office and vestry . The conversion of the theatre cost £645.11.0d, a not inconsiderable sum in those days.

The Rabbi or preacher at Denmark Court was Tobias Goodman, the first to preach in the English language. The text of his sermon on the death of Charlotte, Princess of Wales, was published in 1817 and another, on the death of King George III, in 1820. It appears that the Western Synagogue engaged him for regular discourses, unlike the usual practice of twice-yearly *Derashot* (sermons) in Yiddish.

A dress injunction existed in the *Takkanos* (Rule Book) of the Western Synagogue in 1809 – 'no flunkey in livery' could have a *Mitzvah* (say a blessing over the Scroll of the Law), from which Barnett assumes there were at that time many Jewish coachmen and footmen, butlers and valets. Also noted was the requirement for the *Hazzan* (Reader) and Shammes (beadle) to be capped and gowned in the synagogue, a custom in use in the Great Synagogue; they were fined if they were not present at services (a half-crown on Mondays and Thursdays, but five shillings on the Sabbath!). The Shammes was Simon Kisch, son of Zevi Kisch, Hazzan at Gröningen in Prussia. His descendants included Royalton Kisch, the conductor, and Sir Cecil Kisch of the India Office. A later Shammes, Lewis Raphael, would precede the Scrolls on the Sabbath "*in dress clothes, wearing a gold-ribboned silk hat and white gloves, and carrying a silver wand.*"

Relationships with the City synagogues

In view of later events that led to the foundation of the West London Synagogue of British Jews, it is surprising that the congregation in Westminster was tolerated. Membership of the Western Synagogue was allowed by the City synagogues only for those who resided *within* six miles *west* of the Temple Bar, that is, neither City nor country residents could join the Westminster congregation whose members had to pay dues to the City congregations. As the latter owned the cemeteries then in use, they clearly had the upper hand. All these, and other draconian ordinances, were set out in a document signed by the two parties in 1808.

The secession of Maiden Lane

As not infrequently happens, a schism occurred in the Denmark Court congregation and a new *Minyan* and congregation formed in the West End, first in Dean Street, then in Brewer Street, Golden Square. Many members were engaged in the fruit trade in neighbouring Covent Garden – a traditional Jewish occupation, as at Duke's Place (see p. 30) – but also were manufacturers of quills, umbrellas, watches and cigars (another 'Jewish' trade), and jewellers and engravers. The Hebrew name of the congregation was 'Pillars of the Upright'.

The Synagogue eventually closed due to lack of interest in 1827 but re-opened in 1829 in Maiden Lane, finally closing in 1907. Mr. E. Jamilly, in a lecture given at the Jewish Museum, recalled seeing the bare walls of this sanctuary long after it had closed. Mr. Barnett visited it around 1930; the building was small, with a Ladies' Gallery, and was then in use as a dress-pattern manufactory. He noted that it was next to the stage door of the Adelphi Theatre (Fig. 41).

Fig. 42 *Western Synagogue*, St. Alban's Place. The reconsecration service. I wonder if the small gentleman in the procession is Dayan Aaron Levy. (Reproduced from the *Illustrated London News*, 19th April, 1851.)

According to Barnett, the Synagogue was of little significance, but the Reader between 1846 and 1869, who lived in a flat above the synagogue, was David Joseph. One of his children, Morris Joseph (see p. 86), subsequently became the minister of the North London Synagogue and, later, of the West London Synagogue.

The members of this small secessionist congregation urgently needed their own cemetery, land for which they eventually purchased in Bancroft Road, Mile End. As the City synagogues had taken no action against the new congregation at Maiden Lane, despite the treaty, the Western Synagogue also felt free to open its own cemetery, which it did, in Brompton, in 1815.

The cemetery in Bancroft Road eventually became disused; funds for its repair were raised in response to a letter in the *Jewish Chronicle* signed jointly by Chief Rabbi Dr. Hertz and Morris Joseph of the West London Synagogue.[43]

The Westminster Jews' Free School (Hebrath Talmud Torah Ve'-derech Hayashar B'Westminster)

The congregation had its own day school which was established as early as 1819 and was founded by Solomon Graeditz, its first teacher. Funding, as was often the case with voluntary institutions, was by subscription; the subscribers had the right to nominate children. Education was given to children between the ages of 5 and 13, and they were clothed by a separate Benevolent Society.

After 1837 funds were regularly raised by an annual concert held at the

Fig. 43 *Western Synagogue* (opposite), St. Alban's Place. The interior. (Reproduced from Cecil Roth's *Records of the Western Synagogue*.[36])

Fig. 44 *Western Synagogue*, Alfred Place. The exterior. (Photograph reproduced from *The Western Synagogue Through Two Centuries*, by the Revd. A. Barnett.[37])

Fig. 45 *Western Synagogue*, Alfred Place. The interior.

Theatre Royal, Covent Garden. Barnett notes that the children, who attended the Sabbath service with their Jewish teacher, were marched in file afterwards to Trafalgar Square, from whence they could disperse to their homes. The School moved to Hanway Place, off Tottenham Court Road, in 1883, at its peak, having 700 pupils. It closed as a result of the Second World War, but the building survived until recently.

The move to St. Alban's Place

By the time the lease on the Sans Souci expired, the Jewish population of the West End had greatly increased and now included not only artisans and shopkeepers, but also the affluent, who found it a more convenient, shorter walk to the Strand than to the City. A ninety-year lease was taken on a site in St. Alban's Place, off the Haymarket, and a new Synagogue opened in 1826. This building served the congregation the whole length of the lease, until 1917. It seems curious today that there were enough Jews residing around the Haymarket to support a congregation, but even now there are still many shops around the Strand and Covent Garden with flats above. The Jews, however, have long decamped.

Despite being newly built, the synagogue seems to have fallen rapidly into disrepair, so that it was necessary to rebuild and reconsecrate it in 1836.

By 1850 the congregation was in financial difficulties and the building again in disrepair. Further rebuilding took place and the Synagogue was again reconsecrated on 13th April 1851. On this occasion, its interior was recorded for posterity in the *Illustrated London News* of 19th April (Fig. 42). Present at the ceremony were the Chief Rabbi, Dr. Adler, the Dayanim, as well as the Revd. Professor D. W. Marks of the Reform Synagogue, who had been *Baal Koré* of the Synagogue many years previously, when it was at Denmark Court.

Further rebuilding and reconsecrations of the Synagogue in St. Alban's Place took place with regularity, again in 1857, on this occasion supervised by the Jewish architect, H. H. Collins (see Appendix 1, p. 181), the grandson of an earlier President of the congregation (Fig. 43).

Another minister to the Synagogue, the Revd. Marcus Haines (1874-1879), subsequently went to the New West End Synagogue.

Barnett discusses the effect on the Western Synagogue of the establishment of the Central Synagogue in Great Portland Street, which opened in 1855. The building of new, large synagogues in London always harmed the pre-existing local ones. The City synagogues had long resisted further expansion westwards, which was one of the reasons for the establishment of the West London Synagogue by the Reform movement. The new Branch Synagogue in Great Portland Street threatened not only the viability of the Western but also, especially, of the Maiden Lane Synagogue, both of which entered yet again a period of decline.

In addition, the area around the Haymarket was becoming less residential and, towards the end of the nineteenth century, the Jews began migrating to the new suburbs. Approaches made to the newly formed United Synagogue with a view to establishing some sort of association were rebuffed. Finally, the Chief Rabbi himself suggested that the Synagogue should move to Soho, where many recently arrived immigrants had settled.

As the lease was about to expire, and its renewal would have been expensive, the last service in the old Synagogue was held on 20th June, 1914. A new site was obtained in Alfred Place, off the Tottenham Court Road, and

(a)

(b)

a temporary sanctuary erected at 40, Whitfield Street, in a hall with a gallery (unfortunately no photograph could be found). The First World War delayed the completion of the Synagogue. The ark and Almemar from St. Alban's Place were placed in the basement of the new building in Alfred Place, which opened for worship in an incomplete state in 1918.

As can be seen from Fig. 44, the exterior of the building was imposing. It is described as having a marble stepped entrance with wrought iron and glass gates surmounted by tablets with the decalogue; above, a huge arched window. Stars of David surrounded the Hebrew words of Isiah: "*For my house shall be a house of prayer for all nations.*" The exterior, entirely of stone, was said to be "*lacking in strength, due probably to the flatness of treatment of the main facade, very possibly dictated by planning exigencies requiring every inch of space and therefore not allowing any deep break on the elevation.*"[44]

The foyer was marble-floored and oak-panelled. The interior had a circular domed skylight and, from the drawing, the Omed is seen on the Almemar at the eastern end, with the pulpit central facing transversely aligned seats (Fig. 45). The ark and its gates are straight against the curve of the eastern wall; the choir was probably above it. A stained glass window was placed each side of the ark, divided into six, each containing a Jewish symbol, a Lion, Tablets and a Paschal lamb. The galleries covered half the area of the ground floor, on the western, northern and southern walls, with no pillars to obstruct the view of the east wall. The whole synagogue was furnished in oak. A notable feature was the pipe organ, which the Chief Rabbi, Dr. Hertz, refused to allow to be played on the Sabbath – much to the annoyance of the donor, who promptly left the congregation.

Unfortunately, states Barnett, the synagogue was in the wrong place – the Jewish population having deserted Bloomsbury. Before the Second World War there were still many working-class Jews in Soho and north of Oxford Street, around Cleveland Street. The Western Synagogue did not cater for them; they attended smaller, cheaper and more traditional conventicles in the neighbourhood, in Lambs Conduit Street, Manette Street and in Soho Square.[37,45] Presumably neither the Western nor the Central Synagogues held much attraction for them. The Western Synagogue was deserted apart from

Fig. 46 (a) The prayer hall of the Western Synagogue Cemetery in Montagu Road, Edmonton. The cemetery is still in use and lies adjacent to the Federation of Synagogues cemetery. (b) The door to the prayer hall comes from the old Western Synagogue in Alfred Place.

Fig. 47 The Chapelle francaise in use by the Western Synagogue until 1957 (above). (Photograph courtesy of National Monuments Record.)

Fig. 48 *Western Synagogue*, Crawford Place - the exterior of the penultimate Western Synagogue (centre). (Photograph reproduced from *The Western Synagogue Through Two Centuries*, by the Revd. A. Barnett.[37])

Fig. 49 *Western Synagogue*, Crawford Place (above right). The interior. (Photograph reproduced from *The Western Synagogue Through Two Centuries*, by the Revd. A. Barnett.[37])

the High Holy days. Mr. Barnett called it 'heartbreaking'. The Revd. Gerald Friedlander was minister from 1897, dying in office in 1923, and so had served both in the Haymarket and at Alfred Place. He edited *Vallentine's Pocket Almanac* and wrote *The Jewish Sources of the Sermon on the Mount* – a robust defence of Judaism and incidentally a denial of the views of C.G. Montefiore – as well as a four-volume English edition of the *Laws and Customs of Israel*.

It all came to an end in 1941, when the building received a direct hit during a bombing raid. No-one was killed in the Synagogue, but the adjacent Jewish Girls' Club was also destroyed with much loss of life. All that remained of the building were the front gates and the decalogue on stone tablets. One of these gates now guards the prayer hall at their cemetery in Edmonton (Fig. 46).

After the bombing the congregation moved to the Central Synagogue in Great Portland Street until that too was similarly destroyed. The congregation moved yet again, to the Grotian Hall in Wigmore Street, but within six months that too had been bombed, although the ark and Scrolls were saved. The congregation were able to use a large shop next door until it had found its next home, in the old French Chapel Royal off Portman Square (Fig. 47). The ark used was that salvaged from the basement of Alfred Place, which had previously been in the Haymarket and possibly even earlier in Denmark Court. The building seated only 250 people but contained a little gallery which had once supported the throne of French kings in exile.

In 1957 the congregation moved yet again, this time to occupy a former non-Conformist Chapel in Crawford Place, W1, (founded by a Jewish convert who led the British Society for Propagating the Gospel Among the Jews). Both the exterior and interior, as can be seen from Figs. 48 and 49, were simple and dignified, yet of large dimensions, accommodating 800. The Almemar was again in front of the ark, which was of wood surrounded by marble, with the choir above. Below, in the basement, was a communal hall with kitchens, as well as classrooms.

The Western Synagogue always had a good musical tradition – in the 1920s Hazzan G. Boyers (later at Hampstead) was there and, just prior to the Second World War, Hazzan J. Dollinger, previously of Antwerp and subsequently of Belsize Square, who has left behind a wonderful recording made with the London Jewish Male Voice Choir. He was a superb musician. In the 1960s, Hazzanim I. Roeg and P. Copperman were both outstanding and sang to a packed synagogue.

For reasons which today seem inexplicable, the United Synagogue built a new synagogue at Marble Arch – in direct competition with the Central, New West End, Bayswater and Western Synagogues, and the independent synagogue in Dean Street. Moreover, the Jewish population of the area was in decline. The large mansion blocks in the West End, once occupied by mainly elderly Jews, became settled by new arrivals from the Middle East, and the area which was once Jewish is now much less so.

The Western Synagogue vacated its premises and moved into the Marble Arch Synagogue in 1991. The Dean Street Synagogue also eventually closed and its congregation too moved there, holding separate services in the building.

The ark of the current weekday synagogue at Marble Arch (now called the Western Marble Arch), came from the Western Synagogue, replacing the previous ark which had come from the Borough Synagogue. Thus moved the ark, as in the wilderness, resting for a short time, then moving to a new location (Fig. 50).

Fig. 50 The ark of the Western Synagogue at Crawford Place, now in the weekday synagogue at Marble Arch, together with some of the stained glass windows.

THE BETH HAMEDRASH

BOOKERS GARDENS, EC3,

LATER LEADENHALL STREET, EC3,

LATER DUKE'S PLACE, EC3,

LATER MULBERRY STREET, E1

There is a historical sketch of the Beth Hamedrash, or 'House of Study', written in 1905 by Philip Ornstien,[46] secretary of the United Synagogue at that time, and a later manuscript written by Arnold Hertzberg,[47] a Trustee of the Beth Hamedrash, who was also associated with the Finsbury Park, Dalston and Hampstead Synagogues

The institution of the Beth Hamedrash is ancient, existing at least from the time of Hillel (first century of the Common Era). More than a synagogue, it is also a place of study for Bible and Talmud and was deemed a necessity for every major community.

The functions of the Beth Hamedrash were defined by Ornstien[46] as:

    (1) a synagogue

    (2) a court of Jewish religious law

    (3) a library

    (4) a place of study

According to Hermann Adler, there was evidence of a Beth Hamedrash in pre-expulsion days.[48] In the Common Pleas of the 17th year of the reign of Edward II,* mention is made of a dwelling in the parish of St. Mary Creechurch next to the house which was formerly the **great school** of the Jews, belonging to Abraham Fil Raby,[48] but this presumably refers to a magna scola (see Hillaby[9]).

The Sephardim in London established their first Beth Hamedrash in 1664, calling it *Etz Chaim*.[15] It is still in existence at Lauderdale Road.

In 1704, some members of the Great Synagogue attempted to form their own Beth Hamedrash in St. Mary Axe. After an appeal by the Wardens of Duke's Place to the Lord Mayor, the scheme was forbidden. The Ashkenazim subsequently established their own Beth Hamedrash at some time before 1782 in a small house in Booker's Gardens (later known as Sussex Place), a small road on the north side of Leadenhall Street leading to Bury Street. It was not attached to any one synagogue but was for the use of members of all three City congregations. Hertzberg[47] writes that Solomon Hirschell, who resided at Bury Street, would no doubt have found it convenient to have the Beth Hamedrash close at hand for study and to sit at his court (Beth Din), thus uniting both teaching and judicial functions.

Many years after Dr. Hirschell's death, the *Jewish Chronicle* of 1876 noted: "*The old Beth Hamedrash miserable as was its locale, there was an element of life, an earnestness. Every evening without exception might be seen between afternoon and evening prayers a crowd of scholars ... Dr. Hirschell in their midst, pursuing a study of the Talmud.*"[49]

* Edward II was born in 1284 and reigned from 1307 to 1327.

In 1829 Solomon Arnold bequeathed £1,000 so that land could be purchased for the erection of a library. At the time, a theological college was to have been set up, but nothing came of the proposal. With the bequest and other monies raised, the Beth Hamedrash moved, in 1841, to No. 1, Smiths Buildings in Leadenhall Street. There, it had a library, a synagogue seating sixty, and residential accommodation. After Rabbi Hirschell's death, his library of 4,000 books and 148 manuscripts was purchased for £300 by the Trustees of the Beth Hamedrash.

According to Hertzberg,[47] Chief Rabbi N.M. Adler was less interested in the Beth Hamedrash, though the Beth Din still met there and he gave his Shabbat Hagadol (before Passover) and Shabbat Shuva (before the Day of Atonement) lectures there. Rabbi Adler did however institute a Talmud Study circle there in 1847 and attended himself every Monday and Thursday evening from 8 until 9 o'clock. Around thirty people would study with him.

In 1849 Abraham Moses donated £2,000 in shares, the resulting income being used to employ a librarian. The first such was Aaron Levy (1794-1876). Levy was also scribe to the Beth Din and Dayan. He is probably present in the scene describing the reconsecration of the Western Synagogue, which is shown in Fig. 42. In 1828 he travelled all the way to Australia to effect a Jewish divorce. He lived in the building and, in the summertime, would open up at 3 or 4 o'clock in the morning to admit students. Since that time, a Dayan has always been in charge of the books, one way or another. In 1852 it had been proposed that the Library be moved to Jews' College, but unfortunately nothing came of the scheme.

Even in those days the Beth Hamedrash was insolvent; in 1872 it made an application to the United Synagogue to be taken over and this duly happened in 1875.

The United Synagogue erected a building for the Beth Hamedrash adjacent to the Great Synagogue, but without accommodation for Dayan Levy, now 80 years old. He had lived in Smiths Buildings for 45 years. His salary continued to be paid, however, plus an extra £50 per annum in lieu of accommodation.

In March 1876, upon the opening of the new building, the Revd. B. Spiers (see below) was appointed as Librarian and Dayan. Alderman[50] states that he was unacceptable as a Judge to the immigrant masses but on what grounds, is not made clear.

The work of the Beth Din increased greatly during the years of the great immigration. While previously the court may have sat for one to two hours twice a week, it now needed to sit for three to four hours, and often in the evenings too.

The synagogue, however, did not flourish. Dr. Hermann Adler gave his addresses to a full house at the Great Synagogue rather than at the Beth Hamedrash. The Library was barely used as the majority of the Jews now lived further east. Proposals were therefore made to move the Beth Hamedrash yet again but, more importantly, that new Dayanim should be appointed – at least one of whom would be Yiddish-speaking, whilst another would have to be an English scholar to manage the other components, educational and cultural of the scheme.

The English-speaking Dayanim appointed, the Reverends Hyamson of the Dalston Synagogue (see Fig. 94) and Feldman of the Stoke Newington Synagogue (see Fig. 102), first had to be given Rabbinical ordination – again

Fig. 51 **Beth Hamedrash**. Exterior view. (Reproduced from *Historical Sketch of the Beth Hamedrash*, by P. Ornstein.[46])

Fig. 52 **Beth Hamedrash**. The interior view, leading to the court. (Reproduced from *Historical Sketch of the Beth Hamedrash*, by P. Ornstein.[46])

a fairly recent innovation in England.

In 1894 the United Synagogue purchased land in Adler Street and in adjacent Mulberry Street. The Hambro Synagogue moved from Fenchurch Street onto part of this plot in Adler Street and, on the adjoining land in Mulberry Street, a new building for the Beth Din was built. This contained a library, reading room and court, with a permanent residence for a Dayan, who would be available for consultation at all times. The first such resident Dayan was Dr. Feldman, who was followed subsequently by Dayanim Hillman, Abramsky, Jakobovits (who was the father of a later Chief Rabbi) and Grosnass. Because the building was sited next door to the Hambro, a synagogue was not needed, but services were held there on festivals (Figs. 51 and 52).

The new Beth Hamedrash was opened in 1905. The *Jewish Chronicle* reported: "*On Tuesday last the premises of the new Beth Hamedrash and Library, Mulberry Street, Commercial Road … was consecrated and opened. The Chief Rabbi, who was assisted by Dayanim M. Hyamson and A. Feldman, performed the ceremony of consecration, and the building was declared open by Lord Rothschild. The large attendance included the majority of the Jewish clergy and lay representatives of nearly all the congregations of London and members of various other communal bodies…*

"*The proceedings, which took place in the beautiful lecture hall, commenced with the recital of Psalm xxx by Dayan Hyamson, after which Dayan Feldman read the Evening Service. Dayan Hyamson next read the some appropriate Biblical passages.*

"*The Chief Rabbi then delivered the following Address:*

"'*Thus speaketh the Lord of hosts, saying execute true judgement, and show mercy and compassion every man to his brother.' Zachariah vii, 9.*

"*My dear friends, on this day, the twelfth of December, 250 years ago, the third sitting was held of the Conference of statesmen, divines, and judges which met at Whitehall under the presidency of the Lord Protector. At this Conference it was decided that there was no law which forbade the Jews' return to England − a decision which enabled the members of the house of Israel to take up their abode again in this country. We had hoped to celebrate this memorable event in Anglo-Jewish history by a service of thanksgiving and a festive gathering, but we felt that, in the face of the calamity that has befallen our brethren in Russia, any manifestation of joy would be discordant and incongruous. It is not meet to sing songs with a heavy heart. And thus 'Our harp was turned to mourning and our rejoicing into the voice of them that weep.'*

"… *How greatly have the scope and purpose of a Beth Hamedrash been extended since those (pre-Expulsion) days. But I hope that this house will always be devoted to its original purpose, and that eager and conscientious teachers and learners will gather here to study Bible and Talmud. And in connection herewith I may mention that in the opinion of several learned historians the city of Madras received its name from the fact that a university or high school existed in the seventeenth century called in Arabic Medrash. We hope that this fine library will be fully utilised, and that some of the contents of this valuable collection of manuscripts will be given to the world.*

"*And within these walls the Beth Din will hold its periodical sittings, where we shall exert our utmost efforts to facilitate and to safeguard the due and adequate observance of our religious precepts. We shall here endeavour to obey the Divine bidding 'Execute true judgement.' We shall, to the best of our ability, adjust disputes between litigants, between employers and workmen, between landlords and tenants, between buyers and sellers. It will be our duty to seek and restore peace to a distracted household, to lend a willing ear to tales of woe − sad recitals in miniature of Israel's tragedies. And it will be our most anxious care to protect the widow and the fatherless,*

REV. DAYAN B. SPIERS,
JULY 12, 1901—TAMUS 25, 5661.
WHO TO-MORROW COMPLETES HIS SILVER JUBILEE.

Fig. 53 *Dayan Spiers*, who died shortly after this photograph was taken.

the stranger and the poor, the deserted wife, the waif and stray, left forlorn and desolate in this huge wilderness."[51]

The building was damaged during an air-raid in September 1940. The Beth Din was sitting, but fortunately no-one was killed. The library had already been moved out.

From 1948 until 1958 the Beth Din sat at Adler House in Adler Street, and from then until 1996 at Woburn House, where the library was also situated. The Beth Din now sits in North Finchley and the library is auctioned off. *Sic transit gloria mundi.*

The Reverend Dayan Bernard Spiers (Fig. 53)

Dayan Spiers was born in Schleschim, Poland, and was ordained at the age of 20.[52] He was a Rabbi in Posen before coming to England around 1855. His appointment as Dayan was made in 1876, and he was said to have raised the position to a quality never before obtained. He was fully occupied in the Beth Din in St. James Place – either as a judge, or as a teacher or as a librarian. He catalogued the collection of books, published a Haggadah and wrote *The School System of the Talmud*, which for some reason was subsequently translated into Marathi.

He was the first person to hold Talmud Shiurim in English, both at the Beth Hamedrash and at the Bayswater Synagogue. He was a fluent preacher in English, German and Yiddish.

When Dr. N.M. Adler retired to Brighton, Dayan Spiers took his place at the Great Synagogue. He died on New Year's Day, 1901. The *Jewish Chronicle* reported that: "*The funeral took place on Thursday morning, and long before ten o'clock, the hour fixed for the removal of the body, a crowd of between two and three hundred persons, mostly belonging to the humbler class of the community, had assembled in Christopher Street, and by pressing in front of the house made it difficult for those who had been invited to enter. It would be impossible to give a list of all who were present. They included nearly the whole of the Clergy of both sections of the Orthodox Community ...*

"*About thirty coaches and broughams had been provided, but these proved insufficient to accommodate all who wished to proceed to the Cemetery, and as the last few broughams were drawing up, there was somewhat of a scrimmage to obtain seats, but the firmness of Mr. G. Friedlander, Sexton of the United Synagogue (who efficiently carried out all the arrangements), prevented any invited persons being ousted.*"[52]

THE BOROUGH NEW SYNAGOGUE

HEYGATE STREET, SE17

LATER WANSEY STREET, SE17

There is a long history of Jewish settlement, or at least involvement, in south London and, in particular, the historic area of Southwark, which from Roman and medieval times was the settlement on the south side of London Bridge on the road from the ports.

Roman and medieval Southwark was for centuries a place of licence – including brothels ('Stewes').[53] These were on land owned by the Prior of Bermondsey Abbey who, of course, could not be seen to be aiding sexual licence – so the houses were listed as being owned by Jews! Burford notes: *"The hypocritical part of the matter is that the king, through his hidden nominees, the Jews, owned brothel properties in Southwark."*[53] There was in addition a *domus Conversorum* (a House of Converts for the proselytising of the few remaining Jews into Christianity) in medieval Southwark.

Jews must have settled in the area in more recent times because of its proximity to the City via London Bridge. In addition the Borough fruit market and other local street markets, such as East Street Walworth, provided employment for market traders, fruit especially being a Jewish trade, originally centred in Duke's Place.

The history of the Borough New Synagogue was written in 1917 to commemorate the 50th Anniversary of the opening of its Synagogue in Heygate Street.[54] The author was the then minister, the Revd. Morris Rosenbaum (see below).

The presence of Jews around Walworth has already been noted in the lists of subscribers to early English prayer books. There is a well known coaching print dated 1826, showing the Elephant and Castle public house; the very large building next to it is Levy's clothes shop.

Local residents are said to have held services in the local Debtors' prison, the unfortunates making up the quorum, and a Captain Lewis reading the Law.*

Subsequently, a Mr. Nathan Henry, born in 1764, established a *Minyan* in his house at No. 2, Market Street, or Dantzic Street, off Newington Causeway. He roofed over his yard and, at his own expense, fitted out the enclosed space as a synagogue. The entrance was through the front of his shop – an old-iron store – while women went upstairs, through a bedroom, to a tiny Ladies Gallery.

Mr. Henry seems to have been an autocrat and a secessionist synagogue was formed in Prospect Place, St. George's Road, in 1823 – this congregation lasting until the New Synagogue opened in 1867. Mr. Aaron Cohen was its Treasurer for 50 years. His children were still members of the Borough Synagogue in 1917, to tell the story of its foundation. This so-called 'Borough New Minyan' was held in stables, converted at a cost of £40 and subsequently rebuilt in 1831 for £230 and, again, in 1841. Another

* Rosenbaum[54] notes that there was a 'Tents of Righteousness' Friendly Society, established in 1812, which provided benefit in times of need, and a *"Surrey Jewish Philanthropic Association for the Relief of Distressed Israelites who reside in Southwark"*, established in 1825.

Fig. 54 *Borough Synagogue.* An illustration of the first Synagogue at the time of its opening, taken from the *Illustrated London News* of 4th May, 1867. The address is given as Vowler Street, Walworth Road.

prominent local family were the Levys, perhaps of the huge clothes emporium nearby. This Synagogue appointed an official, Nathan Ornstien, from Nymegen in Holland. His son, Philip, became the Secretary of the United Synagogue and author of the history of the Beth Hamedrash (see p. 58).

When Nathan Henry died in 1853, aged 88 years, his Synagogue closed and members transferred to Prospect Place, although Nathan Henry himself had never set foot in it. His nephew, H.A. Henry, was the minister at the Western Synagogue in St. Alban's Place. When Dr. Adler visited the Borough, he would go only to Mr. Henry's Synagogue.

From 1853, the small synagogue in Prospect Place was the only one in the district. The lease expired in 1866 and the usual public meetings were held to obtain funds for a new building.

Prospect Place Synagogue was described in the Jewish press as "*a place of worship which for dinginess and insalubrity we do not believe had an equal*".[54] It had room for 110 men and 36 women, and was too small to accommodate the local Jewish population. Rosenbaum notes that the old building was dilapidated and unsightly, and the roof let in the rain, so that umbrellas sometimes had to be raised during services. Even the Public Appeal, held in the Synagogue, had to be curtailed because of rain.

The meeting resolved to build a synagogue and a new Jewish school, as there was already one in the vicinity run by the Second Reader, Mr. Harris, but apparently not very good, and most of the local children walked to the Jews' Free School in the East End of London.[54]

The Appeal was not very successful, despite Messrs. Rothschild donating £250, as the City congregations were not willing to help out, despite – or because of – large sums having been spent on new synagogues in the west of London. Members of the Borough were also members of the City synagogues, if only because of the need for burial.

Fig. 55 *Borough Synagogue.* The interior of the first Synagogue during the feast of Hannukah; the Revd. Francis Lyon Cohen conducts a special service for Jewish soldiers and volunteers. The pulpit is draped with the Union flag. (Reproduced from the *Graphic*, 23rd December, 1893.)

A plot of land in Heygate Street, then called Albion Place, was acquired from the Fishmongers Company through Mr. A. Harris, already at that time a member of the Camberwell Vestry. Because of lack of funds, no minister's house could be built, nor was a ceremony of laying the foundation stone held.

The consecration of the new building took place on 7th April, 1867, and the synagogue was called the Borough New Synagogue (Fig. 54). As was the custom, the ministers of most London synagogues were present, including those of the Reform Synagogue. In the evening a dinner was held at Radley's Hotel in Bridge Street.

According to the *Illustrated London News* of 4th May 1867 the architect was Mr. H. H. Collins. Although the site was irregular, both the Synagogue and the school – the Borough Jewish School (see below) – were built on it.

The Synagogue was 60' long, 40' wide and 35' high. There were ornamental gates before a Doric portico leading to a spacious vestibule lined with tiles. The Ladies' Galleries were supported on red and bronzed twisted iron shafts. The Ladies' Gallery too and the Almemar also had "*graceful iron scrollwork*".[55] The ceiling was divided by ornamental bands. Pillars on each side of the ark led to a semidome of amber yellow glass. Above the ark were, unusually, two tablets of stained glass bearing the Decalogue.

The paintwork was white, relieved by blue, and the iron scrollwork had "*touches of blue*". The curtain to the ark was blue, bearing the inscription

Fig. 56 **Borough Synagogue** (right).
In 1928 the Synagogue moved to the
former Surrey Tabernacle in Wansey
Street, Walworth. (Photograph
courtesy of National Monuments
Record.)

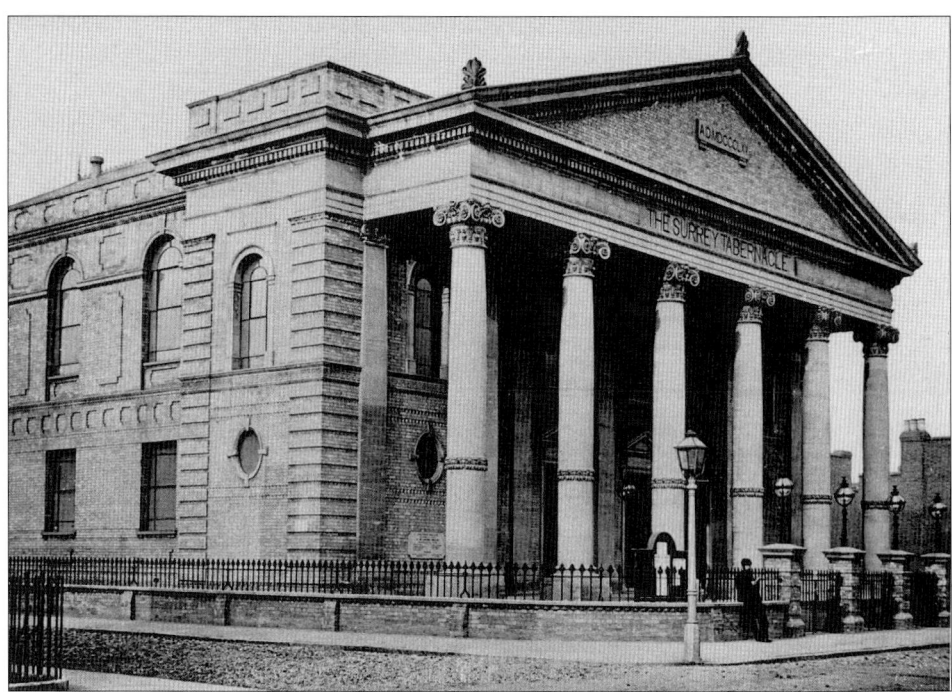

Fig. 57 **Borough Synagogue** (above).
The interior of the Synagogue in
Wansey Street; the Reader's desk is
situated at the eastern end.
(Photograph courtesy of the Revd. A.
Greenbat).

Fig. 58 **Borough Synagogue** (above).
The congregation was a very active
one, with a regular programme
available for members. This one gives
details of a special civic service for the
coronation of King George VI.
Regular socials were held too.
(Photograph courtesy of the Revd. A.
Greenbat.)

'Hearken unto the prayers of Thy people Israel'. The cost was £6,000.

A further view of the handsome interior is provided in the *Graphic* of
23rd December, 1893 (Fig. 55). Here, the second of the Synagogue's
ministers, Francis Lyon Cohen, who was also Chaplain at Aldershot, is seen
on the Almemar before the imposing and pillared apse containing the ark.
The occasion was a special service for Jewish soldiers. Around 100 assembled
"at the bugle call in Mr. Cohen's Synagogue, gaily decorated for the occasion."[56]
Much detail is shown in this engraving.

Alas, in 1869, only two years after the opening, one of the walls caved in
and part of the ceiling collapsed – during the service. It was then found that
the construction was faulty. The Synagogue had to close for the entire
winter while being strengthened. Meanwhile, an explosion occurred next
door, in Paines' fireworks factory, further damaging the Synagogue and
School!

The Synagogue house too was poorly built. There was trouble with the
drains, the house was damp and the garden a swamp. It had to be
demolished.

The United Synagogue was confirmed by Act of Parliament in 1870 and
the Borough New Synagogue acceded, not without difficulty, in 1873.

In 1907 services were held for the first time in Brixton and, since two-
thirds of the Borough Synagogue's members resided in Brixton or Clapham,
the question re-arose of moving the Borough New Synagogue nearer to
Brixton. This proposed amalgamation never took place and the two
synagogues continued separately. Indeed, there was new migration from the
East End to Walworth, so that by 1909 most members now lived locally.

In 1917, in the year of the Jubilee history, Revd. Rosenbaum noted that
the membership was of a floating character, as the area was not residential or
for the well-to-do. There was a continuous stream of newcomers who
believed that south London offered excellent business opportunities – but
disillusionment followed and they returned from whence they had come.

Thus, while between 1909 and 1917 there were 244 *new* male
seatholders, in 1917 there were only 202 male members, and the Synagogue
was always in deficit.

A further history was unfortunately not written but, in a fit of *folie de grandeur*, the congregation moved in 1927 to a new, large and vacated Non-conformist building – the Surrey Tabernacle (Fig. 56). (One such establishment, the famous Metropolitan Tabernacle, still survives at the Elephant and Castle, while there was a further one in Camberwell.)

According to the Revd. A. Greenbat, the fixtures and fittings of the original Synagogue (in Heygate Street) went to the then recently opened South West London Synagogue (see p. 142). The interior and exterior of the newer, larger building is shown, certainly handsome on the outside, with a large portico, though the interior looks a little plain, as befits the Non-conformist chapel that it was (Figs. 56 and 57).

The community had always been active socially (Fig. 58), but membership reached a peak in 1930, with over 300 male members, and then rapidly declined. One of the reasons given to me was the opening of the Northern line extension to Edgware. 'Living over the shop' was no longer a practical necessity. For a relatively small sum, a new house with a garden in a leafy suburb could be purchased, only 30-45 minutes away from the Borough. No doubt the Second World War further accelerated Jewish migration from an area which had never been as densely populated with Jews as the East End, but which was heavily bombed.

After the War the smaller congregation vacated its now overlarge Synagogue and moved the furnishings to the adjacent Barnett Raingold Communal Hall (Fig. 59), where services continued until closure in 1961 and amalgamation with the Brixton congregation (by which time there were only 131 male members). Even with these newcomers, however, membership at Brixton declined by one hundred over the next ten years.

On closure of the Borough Synagogue, after nearly 200 years of Jewish worship locally, the ark and Almemar were installed in the weekday synagogue at Marble Arch. These have been subsequently replaced by those from the last Western Synagogue in Crawford Street.

The Borough Jewish School

The Synagogue at Heygate Street had a school attached and the two buildings were put up together. Although communal funding was not forthcoming for the Synagogue, it seems to have been for the School.

There were four classrooms in a two-storey building, which stood until fairly recently and was visible from the Walworth Road. There was

Fig. 59 *Borough Synagogue.* When the local Jewish population declined, the Synagogue moved into the previous communal hall, taking with it the ark, the Reader's desk, the pews and the prayer boards on either side of the ark. Note the World War I memorial on the side of the ark - with a candle for each fallen soldier. (Photograph courtesy of the Revd. A. Greenbat.)

Fig. 60 *Rabbi Simeon Singer.*

Fig. 61 *Rabbi Francis Lyon Cohen.*

★The major synagogal organisation in Victorian London – the United Synagogue – was established by Act of Parliament in 1870. Its two successive spiritual heads in Victorian and Edwardian England, Nathan Adler and his son Hermann, for many years would not allow other Jewish ministers under their jurisdiction to use the title 'Rabbi', there being only one Rabbi in England – the Chief Rabbi. All other religious officiants were then given the English title "Reverend". These men dressed like Anglican clergymen, preached like Anglican clergymen and, to the stricter immigrant Jewish community, behaved like Anglican clergymen.

accommodation for 150 children. Payment was by fee, with free education for the needy.

The first headmaster, Mr. Berliner, was later minister at St. John's Wood. The School seems to have ceased functioning around the Second World War.

The first minister, Simeon Singer (Fig. 60)

His name is immortalised through his prayer book, first published in 1890, and now in its third edition. It is his permanent memorial.

Rabbi Singer was born in London in 1848, the son of a clothier of Watling Street. His family were originally from Bohemia, direct descendants of R. Jehoneson Eybeschutz. He was one of the earliest pupils at Jews' College and its School.

The Borough New Synagogue, then not yet part of the United Synagogue, wanted a minister who was more than a singer (the custom at that time) but who was also learned. Mr. Singer was appointed to his first congregation at 19 years of age. His salary was inadequate and he had to teach all day at Jews College School, where he was headmaster for some time.

His marriage in 1868 to Charlotte Pyke was the first to be held in the Synagogue. Mrs. Singer later presented a *Chupah* for the use of the congregation – where is it now? She also acted as his secretary.

Rabbi Singer had received his Rabbinical Ordination in Vienna, but was not allowed to use the title 'Rabbi' – the Chief Rabbi was the only Rabbi.★ Even today, he is 'the Reverend S. Singer' in the prayer book.

While at the Borough Synagogue he was Chaplain to the local prisons and attended two executions. He was also an advocate of the 'Volunteer Movement' (today's Territorial Army) and, indeed, two of his sons joined it.

Rabbi Singer left after 11 years for the New West End Synagogue. At his farewell service many, we are told, were in tears.

He came to be regarded as one of the most eloquent of preachers. His voice could "*command or whisper*" and he had "*a keen sense of humour in the pulpit.*"[57] He was a religious progressive, preaching at the Reform Synagogue in Manchester and at the early services of the Jewish Religious Union, but also in Yiddish at working men's services in the East End. He was also an active campaigner against the white slave trade, and was the chaplain to the Jews' Free School Company of the Jewish Lads' Brigade.

Rabbi Francis Lyon Cohen (Fig.61)

Rabbi Singer was succeeded at the Borough Synagogue by the Revd. F.L. Cohen. Mr. Cohen (as he was at the Borough Synagogue) was born at Aldershot in 1862. His father was amongst the earliest settlers there, when the garrison was founded after the Crimean War.

He was educated at Jews' College School, Jews' College and University College, London. He was a man of many talents, matriculating from UCL in music,[58] and was for a short time Second Reader at the Great Synagogue (see p. 30).

He then went to Dublin, staying for only one year, before going to the Borough Synagogue. His obituary[58] states quite clearly that this was a poor and crowded area and that Mr. Cohen was active in social work.

He was chaplain to Brixton Prison, to the Asylum at Darenth and its training ship at Grays, and examined Jewish lads in many state schools.

Because of his association with Aldershot, he was appointed Honorary

Chaplain to the Forces. Regular religious services were held at Aldershot. He instituted the Chanukah Military Service, first at the Borough Synagogue, then at the Great Synagogue.[59] He advocated the formation of, and was chaplain to, the Jewish Lads' Brigade.

Perhaps his greatest contribution to Anglo-Jewry before he left for Sydney, Australia, in 1904 was as a musicologist. He had a fine voice and studied under J.L. Mombach and Hazzan Hast; indeed, he married the latter's daughter – herself apparently possessed of a 'sympathetic' voice. Early *Transactions of the Jewish Historical Society* contain the texts of talks given by F.L. Cohen with musical accompaniment by his wife and daughter; Harriet Cohen, the pianist, was his niece.

Mr. Cohen was a prolific writer on Jewish music. He made a great contribution to the history of Jewish music as part of the Anglo-Jewish Historical Exhibition of 1887 and contributed to the *Jewish Chronicle* on musical subjects. His lasting achievement is *The Voice of Prayer and Praise,*[60] a handbook of synagogue music for the whole year – the 'Blue Book'. He also contributed to the *Jewish Encyclopaedia*.

The Reverend Morris Rosenbaum (Fig. 62)

Revd. Rosenbaum was the successor to F.L. Cohen and if perhaps less well remembered that his predecessors, does not deserve to be, for he too was a scholar.

He was a Londoner by birth and was educated at the Jewish Orphanage, and later studied at Jews' College and University College, where he was awarded a Hebrew Scholarship.

His first ministerial post was at Poplar, then at Hanley in Staffordshire. In 1894 he went to Newcastle, where he became interested in Freemasonry. In later years, he contributed articles on Jews and Freemasonry to the *Transactions of the Jewish Historical Society*.

He was the minister at the Borough Synagogue from 1905 to 1935. An authority on the Jewish calendar, he edited that section of the *Jewish Year Book*. The most noted of his works, however, was the English translation of Rashi's commentary on the Pentateuch, together with M. Silbermann. Though this has recently been reprinted, Mr. Rosenbaum does not get the acknowledgement he deserves in the new reprint.

He was also archivist to the United Synagogue and a historian of note.

His successor, the Revd. M. Bloch, is shown in Appendix 5a.

Fig. 62 *The Revd. Morris Rosenbaum.* (Reproduced from *The Jewish Communities of North East England* by Lewis Olsover (1980), published by Ashley Mark Publishing Co., Gateshead.)

THE WEST LONDON SYNAGOGUE OF BRITISH JEWS

BURTON STREET, WC1,

LATER MARGARET STREET, W1,

LATER UPPER BERKELEY STREET, W1

The history of this congregation is dealt with at length by Picciotto,[13] Philipson,[61] Roth,[14] Rayner[62] and Kershen & Romain.[63] Congregants of the Spanish and Portuguese and of the German synagogues in London began to express their dissatisfaction with the nature and length of synagogue services, with their lack of decorum and the absence of preaching in the vernacular. Moreover, the Elders of the two congregations were unwilling to allow services to be held in the West End of London, where the wealthier members of the community lived, a long irksome walk to the City on Sabbaths and Festivals.

Petitions for minor changes in the services were presented to the Officers of the Great Synagogue in 1821 and to those of the Spanish and Portuguese Synagogue in 1836. By 1839, however, their demands became more radical, including shortening of prayers, a later start to the Sabbath and Festival services, sermons in English, a choir, and the abolition of the second days of Festivals, as well as a branch synagogue in the West End. These demands being rejected by the Elders of the Spanish and Portuguese Synagogue, eighteen Sephardim and six Ashkenazim organised a 'Reform' congregation at a meeting held on 15th April, 1840, when they issued a founding declaration:

"We, the undersigned, regarding public worship as highly conducive to the interests of religion, consider it a matter of deep regret that it is not more frequently attended by members of our religious persuasion. We are perfectly sure that this circumstance is not owing to any want of conviction of the fundamental truths of our religion, but ascribe it to the distance of the existing synagogues from our place of residence, to the length and imperfections of the order of service, to the inconvenient hours at which it is appointed, and to the absence of religious instruction in our synagogue. To these evils we believe that a remedy may be applied by the establishment of a synagogue at the western part of the metropolis, where a revised service may be performed at hours more suited to our habits and in a manner more calculated to inspire feelings of devotion, where religious instruction may be afforded by competent persons, and where, to effect these purposes, Jews generally may form a united congregation under the denomination of British Jews."[61]

The following resolutions were adopted:

"That it is expedient to establish a synagogue in the western part of the metroplis and that it be designated the West London Synagogue of British Jews.

"That a revised service be there performed in the Hebrew language in conformity with the principles of the Jewish religion, and in a manner best calculated to excite feelings of devotion, and that religious discourses be delivered in the English language."[61]

To this, the Elders at Bevis Marks responded by agreeing to a branch synagogue in the West End, using the traditional ritual. This, indeed, did happen, with the establishment of a 'Branch Synagogue' first over a shop in Wigmore Street, W1, subsequently in 1861 in Bryanston Street, W1 and, in 1885, another in a house in Mildmay Road, Islington. The founders of the new congregation wrote to the Elders of the Spanish and Portuguese congregation on 24th August, 1841, of their intention to open a synagogue of 'British Jews' using a reformed ritual. On 24th October a form of excommunication was issued against the new congregation and its prayer book, but not all English congregations accepted this ban.

The first synagogue of the congregation, opening in 1841, was in a former chapel in Burton Street, WC1; the second, in Margaret Street, just north of Oxford Street, W1, opened in 1849. Unfortunately, no significant images of either of these buildings remain, but the third synagogue building still stands in Upper Berkeley Street.

As Rayner[62] notes, the founders of the congregation were in the main long settled and affluent Sephardim – Messrs Montefiore, Henriques, Mocatta and Goldsmid. It was also expensive to be a member – between £3-7 for a seat, and the congregation maintained a certain social exclusivity.

As the congregation could not use the existing communal cemeteries, they had to purchase their own, in the Balls Pond Road, though their initial funeral took place in the cemetery of the Maiden Lane Synagogue. Difficulties followed too with marriages, couples having to undergo two separate ceremonies, civil and religious.

Due to the efforts of two members of the Spanish and Portuguese Synagogue, the Bill of Excommunication was lifted on 9th March, 1849. By the time Picciotto wrote his history (1875): "*To forget and forgive is a pre-eminent virtue in the Jewish code of ethics; and we are happy to think that all traces of past animosities are fast disappearing, nay, perhaps, have already disappeared. Wise men have agreed to differ in matters of opinion. Germans, Portuguese, and British Jews meet together to promote the interests of Judaism, of Jewish education, charity, and moral progress. They exchange together social amenities, they assemble at the same social and festive tables, at the same institutional boards; and if they worship in different Synagogues, and with slightly different forms of prayer, yet they pray to the same God!*"[13]

Revd. Professor David Woolf Marks (1811–1909)

The first minister, he was born in London and attended the Jews' Free School (Fig. 63). Subsequently *Baal Koré* at the Western Synagogue, he later became Second Reader to the Liverpool Hebrew congregation. Even here, he refused to read the Law on second days of Festivals, a situation accepted by the congregation, who found someone else to read it on those days. Appointed to the post of minister to the Reform congregation, he edited its first prayer books; services were read with the Sephardic pronunciation.

Petuchowski[64] notes that, as initially there were more Sephardim than Ashkenazim in the congregation, the prayer book favoured parts of the Sephardic rite. As the founding fathers rejected the Rabbinic Oral Law (as opposed to the written Pentateuchal Law), the synagogue and its prayer book took a very anti-Rabbinical stance, going so far as to change Aramaic prayers into Hebrew. Since the sacrificial cult, the return to Zion and the belief in a personal Messiah all had Biblical origin, these all feature in the 1841 edition of the prayer book, one conspicuous feature of which, notes

REV. PROFESSOR D. W. MARKS
Chief Minister of the West London (Reform)
Synagogue

Fig. 63 *The Revd. Professor D. W. Marks.*

Petuchowski, was its brevity. By 1890 prayers for 'fire offerings' had been omitted.

Professor Marks also held the Chair of Hebrew at University College London from 1844 to 1898 and was also a member of the Marylebone Borough Council. His successor at the West London Synagogue was the Revd. Morris Joseph (see p. 86).

THE CENTRAL SYNAGOGUE

GREAT PORTLAND STREET, W1

There are two main histories of the Central Synagogue, one by the Revd. Simeon Isaacs,[65] probably dated 1948, and one by Rabbi C. Shine[66] published in 1970.

At a meeting of the Great Synagogue in 1848 it was resolved *"that it being considered of the utmost importance that a place of worship in connection with this Synagogue be established at the West End of the Metropolis, this Committee do take the subject into consideration at the next meeting."*[65]

In 1850 the Committee of the Great Synagogue decided to build a new synagogue; £6,000 was voted for the erection of this building. In 1853 a warehouse at 120, Great Portland Street was purchased on a 42 year lease but, because of the delays in construction, the building was not consecrated until March 1855. At the opening ceremony, an announcement was made *"that this building now about to be consecrated is a Branch of the Great Synagogue situated in Dukes Place, in the parish of St. James' Aldgate, in the City of London."*[65] Because of its status, no marriages could be celebrated in it and the management was controlled by the Great Synagogue.

There were 212 seats for men and 144 in the Ladies Gallery (Fig. 64). The Revd. A.L. Green (see below), Second Reader at the Great Synagogue, was elected Reader.

According to Alex M. Jacob,[67] the formation of the Bayswater Synagogue in 1863 led to a large number of members of the Central Synagogue joining the new synagogue in Bayswater, but the vacant seats were filled rapidly and, by 1866, the Branch Synagogue had a larger surplus than Duke's Place. (A list of the original seat-holders at Bayswater Synagogue is given in the 1938 history of that congregation[68] – most resided much nearer Bayswater than Great Portland Street.)

In 1868 the site of the present building at Nos. 133-141 Great Portland Street was purchased on a lease of 80 years. Mr. N.S. Joseph was appointed architect. The cost of this new building was £37,284.

In 1870 the United Synagogue came into being, bringing together the Great, Hambro, New and Bayswater Synagogues. The Central Synagogue was its fifth constituent and was consecrated the same year, the ark being opened by the 85-year-old Sir Moses Montefiore, of Park Lane. A note on the consecration is contained in the *Graphic* of 16th April, 1870.

In her recent book (in German) on the Islamic architectural style of nineteenth and early twentieth century synagogues, Künzl comments that *"the new Synagogue was built according to the old, that is, orthodox pattern. Inside the edifice with three naves and galleries for women at the long side, benches have been put in a longitudinal direction with a view to the central Bima (Almemar). Islamic and Gothic forms are mixed together in this Synagogue, just as in Sümeg (in Hungary).* The Gothic elements can only be seen in the vault and the tracery of the windows. Undoubtedly, the Islamic elements are pre-eminent and a strong similarity to the Synagogue in Leipzig can be detected, for example, in the relatively low*

* Kunzl writes in the present tense and perhaps believes the building still stands.

Fig. 64 *Central Synagogue*. The first Synagogue at 120 Great Portland Street had a remarkably beautiful interior. The apse was decorated with a traditional star motif, in keeping with the promise: "Look now toward Heaven and count the stars, if thou be able to count them … so shall thy seed be." (*Genesis xv 5*). An elaborate curtain hung before the ark, which had been built into the apse. I cannot say whether the platform at the eastern wall was where the services were read, but it seems unlikely in that day and age. It is likely that the pillars, shown on either side of the platform before the ark, were matched by two behind, at the other end of the dome, in keeping with a central European tradition; the dome seems to have been highly decorated and elaborate, and presumably was situated over the Almemar. Rounded skylights are shown over the low-ceilinged Ladies Galleries. The whole appearance was one of beauty and intimacy.

This photograph was taken towards the end of the nineteenth century, by which time the congregation had transferred to the new building. Presumably this building was kept because the lease had not yet expired, perhaps as an act of piety, or even perhaps for overflow services. (Photograph courtesy of Dr. S. Peltz and the Central Synagogue.)

columns of the basement, in the horseshoe-shaped arcades of the Gallery and in details of, for example, the capitals. A large arch frames the great east alcove containing the Aron-hakodesh (ark). As in the Alhambra, it is supported by two pairs of columns, which are designed in the style of the Alhambra too. The alcove is built completely in the Spanish-Islamic style of the 14th Century. Here, the motif of the arch supported by two double columns is repeated above the Torah curtain, with the tablets in the arch area. The arch, the decoration in the spandrels and the rhomboid pattern in the half-dome – as in Leipzig, broken through from above in order to let through light – represents the style of the Alhambra, as do the ornaments in the rest of the building.

"Apart from the Gothic elements, the building appears unified, because its forms have been taken from a uniform style – the Spanish-Islamic style of the 14th century – instead of using a mixture of forms from different cultures and epochs.

"The London synagogue proves wrong the theory that orthodox communities never used this style.

"By reverting to Islamic forms and by combining these with a medieval building style, the London synagogue is a good example of the tradition of synagogue building, developed especially in Germany since the middle of the last century."[69] (Figs. 65, 66 and 67).*

By 1872 membership included five Members of Parliament, six Barons, two Aldermen of the City of London, the Solicitor-General (Sir George Jessel) and a Royal Academician. Sir Anthony de Rothschild was the Warden.

Chanukah services for the Military commenced in 1892. In 1905 a memorial plaque dedicated to the memory of 116 Jewish soldiers who had died in the Boer War was dedicated and unveiled by Field Marshal Earl Roberts, presumably the same as is now in the prayer hall at Willesden Cemetery. After the First World War, a memorial candelabrum was donated by the father of the one of the fallen; this contained 18 candles – one for each soldier (Fig. 68). Similar candelabra were to be found in the Borough Synagogue and the New Cross Synagogue.

A new Almemar of marble was donated by Lord Bearsted in 1928 (Fig. 69).

In 1934 the Revd. M. Adler, DSO, retired from his ministry at the Synagogue. He had been a chaplain to the Forces in the First World War and was the author of *The Jews of Medieval England*,[70] and served as President of the Jewish Historical Society of England.

He was succeed by the Revd. P. Cohen, who became a Chaplain during the Second World War, but resigned on his return and joined the Liberal Synagogue, ending his career as minister to the North West London Reform Synagogue, Alyth Gardens.

Rabbi E. Nemeth acted as a temporary minister during the Second World War.

The Synagogue was destroyed by bombs on 10th May, 1941 (Fig. 70) but services continued to be held at the Adolph Tuck Hall in Woburn House. A temporary synagogue was built in the basement of the cleared site (Fig. 71), being consecrated in 1948. This lasted until 1956, when rebuilding of the new and current Synagogue commenced. This opened in 1958, the ministers being Rabbi C. Shine, previously of Woodside Park Synagogue, and the renowned Hazzan S. Hass.

The opening of the new Synagogue led to an increase in membership, to a peak of 685 in 1960.

Revd Aaron Levy Green (Fig. 72)

The Revd. Green was born in Petticoat Lane in 1821; his Dutch father was a grocer and matzo-maker. He was educated at the Talmud Torah of the Jews'

Fig. 65 *Central Synagogue* (second building). The exterior of the Great Portland Street site after destruction, but prior to demolition. There are Moorish arches to the upper floor windows and, at street level, two tablets, which could be the memorials to those soldiers lost in the South African War, the unveiling of which was described in volume V of the *Transactions of the Jewish Historical Society*. I believe these tablets are now to be seen in the Prayer Hall at Willesden Cemetery. This exterior, in a simplified form, is still present in Hallam Street – the site of the offices of the present day Synagogue. (Photograph by courtesy of Dr. S. Peltz and the Central Synagogue.)

Fig. 66 *Central Synagogue.* The interior as depicted after opening in *Old and New London*, Vol. IV (Westminster and the Western Suburbs), by Edward Walford, published by Cassell Petter & Galpin, London (1875). The Almemar was later replaced, the gift of Viscount Bearsted.

* Translation from the German provided by Mr. Dirk de Camp.

Free School and had a wide knowledge of English and Classical literature. He had a *"fine and particularly accurate voice."*[67] At the age of fourteen, he was conducting services at the Great Synagogue; by his seventeenth birthday he was a minister in Bristol. At the opening of the then Bristol Synagogue in 1842, he delivered a discourse on prayer. As *The Bristol Gazette* noted: *"Mr. Green was remarkable as one of the first ministers to give a sermon in English."*[71] At that time the Jewish clergyman was called a Reader and undertook little preaching, but Mr. Green *"made it an established institution that an English sermon should form an integral part of Jewish worship."*[72]

In 1851 he was appointed Second Reader of the Great Synagogue and, in 1854, to the new Central Synagogue at 120 Great Portland Street. He would preach for up to one and a half hours, possibly today beyond the ability of the preacher and the patience of congregation. In Mr. Jacob's extremely readable biography[67] an interesting note is made on the services at Great Portland Street. The – then usual – break between the morning service and the Reading of the Law had led to the neglect of the earlier service, which could only be maintained by the use of paid Minyan men.

Revd. Green was a visitor to hospitals, asylums and prisons, and played a leading part in the formation of Jews' College, the Board of Guardians and the Anglo-Jewish Association. He was a prolific writer to the press – both Jewish and non-Jewish – and a bibliophile (he left over 6,000 books to Jews' College in his Will).

Mr. Green wrote columns anonymously in the *Jewish Chronicle* under the pseudonym 'Nemo'. From the letters in his column, Mr. Jacob deduces that the Revd. Green was an advocate of minor prayer book reform – abolition of *Piyutim* and in favour of a triennial cycle of Reading of the Law. He certainly attended services at Upper Berkeley Street, but was critical of their form.

The Revd. A.L. Green died suddenly aged 61 in 1883 and was buried at Willesden Cemetery, where he had years earlier conducted the first burial. His stone bears the verse:

> *"I have preached Righteousness in the great congregation;*
> *Lo, I have not refrained my lips."*[67]

Fig. 67 *Central Synagogue.* The view towards the pulpit and ark. This highly ornate, Moorish building must have been a delight to see. Light streams in through a leaded window in the apse, which is highly decorated, as is the surround of the ark. The Parokhet is heavily embroidered and there seem to have been matching drapes on either side. Prayers for the Sovereign in English and Hebrew are surmounted by crowns. (Photograph courtesy of Dr. S. Peltz and the Central Synagogue.)

Fig. 68

Fig. 69

Fig. 68 *Central Synagogue.* The memorial candleholder, with a candle for each soldier from the congregation lost in the First World War. (Photograph courtesy of Dr. S. Peltz and the Central Synagogue.)

Fig. 69 *Central Synagogue.* The remodelled and highly ornate, and possibly incongruous Almemar donated to the Synagogue by Viscount Bearsted in 1925. (Photograph courtesy of Dr. S. Peltz and the Central Synagogue.)

Fig. 70 *Central Synagogue.* The interior after the bombing during World War II. (Photograph courtesy of Dr. S. Peltz and the Central Synagogue.)

Fig. 70

Fig. 71 *Central Synagogue* (below left). The (third) temporary Synagogue, built in the basement of the old Central Synagogue, prior to the reconstruction of the new and current building. (Photograph courtesy of Dr. S. Peltz and the Central Synagogue.)

Fig. 72 *Revd. A. A. Green* (below right). (Photograph reproduced from *Transactions of the Jewish Historical Society of England,* Vol. XXV (1977) with permission.)

Fig. 71

Fig. 72

THE BAYSWATER SYNAGOGUE

CHICHESTER PLACE, W2

LATER ANDOVER PLACE, W2

The main source for the history of this congregation is *The Bayswater Synagogue, 1863-1963* by Olga Somech Philips and Hyman A. Simons, published to commemorate its centenary.[73] A shorter history had been published in 1938 on its 75th Anniversary.[68]

The Branch Synagogue in Great Portland Street, as Philips & Simons note, was still a long walk from this new area of Jewish migration, around Bayswater, and the Western Synagogue off the Haymarket was even further away.

Though the establishment of the Central Synagogue (see p. 73) had not been without struggle, that of the Bayswater Synagogue seems to have gone more smoothly. The first meeting had been held in July 1860, the foundation stone being laid almost exactly two years later in Chichester Place off the Harrow Road (then described as a pleasant, suburban neighbourhood). Philips and Simons note that the congregation was unusual in never having a temporary building, but they do not describe any earlier service in the area; presumably many members previously had walked to Great Portland Street.

The building was completed in July 1863 at a cost of £15,000. It could hold 341 male members and 334 women. At its opening, *The Illustrated London News* reported: "*The building is the Italian style, freely treated, and partakes of the general decorative character of the Venetian School. It is entered by a handsome porch richly decorated with stone carving of elegant design, leading to a spacious vestibule. The Synagogue is 65' long, 50' wide and 50' high. The roof is framed with arched ribs supported on iron columns having highly enriched capitals. The ceiling is divided into large panels boldly moulded. The Gallery is supported by a lower tier of iron columns which have decorated capitals. The Gallery front is formed of diagonal panelling and is surmounted with an ornamental iron grill.*

An arched opening is formed in the east wall and is surrounded with a bold enriched architrave supported upon ornamental columns.

Over this is the main cornice of the ark and surmounting the whole is a handsome wheel window filled with stained glass supported by scrollwork.

The ark is a recessed niche very richly adorned. Over it a counterlight has been arranged as to concentrate a flood of light upon the ark."

The contemporary engraving (Fig. 73) shows the interior from a different perspective to the photograph (Fig. 74). No pulpit is shown, but as the engraving had been obtained before the actual opening of the Synagogue, probably it had not yet been installed. There is no Gallery over the ark but pews on either side of it, perhaps for the choir, which for some time was mixed. I was told however that in later years the choir was placed in the Gallery opposite the ark.

The exterior of the Synagogue in Chichester Place (Fig. 75) shows it to

Fig. 73 *Bayswater Synagogue*. The interior at its opening (contemporary engraving).

have been rather plain, as too was the interior, though the apse was more elaborate, with ornate detail picked out. Also of note is the rather large 'Chief Rabbi's box'. It is evident that some members of the Bayswater Synagogue felt that their surroundings, too, could do with improvement. There is, in the London School of Jewish Studies Library, a pamphlet, undated and for which no author is given, entitled *Another "Battle of Talking"*. It is reproduced in an abridged form in Appendix 4 on p. 190. The 'cook' was clearly the Preacher – whether Dr. Adler or Sir Hermann Gollancz, it is difficult to say. The 'housemaid' presumably was Mr. Samuel, the long-serving Reader.

The last years of the Synagogue were controversial. As noted in the epilogue to the synagogal history,[73] the neighbourhood had changed and the congregation had declined from 419 male members in 1960 (its greatest ever) to just 191 in 1970.

Finally, the Greater London Council (GLC) placed a compulsory purchase order on the building as a new road was being planned.* A lump sum or a new building was offered by the GLC as compensation. The United Synagogue opted for the former, but were then taken to court by the managers of the Synagogue, who won their case. A new Synagogue was then built in Andover Place, Maida Vale (Fig. 76), in an area with a declining Jewish population and a multitude of synagogues. This new Synagogue did not long survive the tragic demise of the driving force behind the congregation – Harold Aron – and the congregation dispersed to the neighbouring synagogues at St. John's Wood and St. Petersburgh Place. The Jewish community, however, had acquired gratis a new purpose-built complex, which is now the Jewish Preparatory School. The interior of the Synagogue has recently been restructured and a small sanctuary erected within the building (the Saatchi Synagogue) at gallery level.

Rabbi Dr. Hermann Adler

The Rabbi of the Great Synagogue was by convention the pre-eminent Jewish religious functionary in England and its colonies. He was styled the 'Chief Rabbi' and those serving under his authority, even if they had

* The building was eventually demolished by the GLC

Fig. 74 *Bayswater Synagogue*. The interior, looking towards the ark, from a photograph taken at the 50th Anniversary of the consecration of the Synagogue in 1913. Note the Chief Rabbi's chair at the side of the apse.

Fig. 75 *Bayswater Synagogue*. The exterior in Chichester place.

obtained Rabbinical ordination abroad, were dignified by the title 'Reverend' – in Hebrew '*Chaver*'. The Chief Rabbi for much of the Victorian era – from 1845 to 1890 – was Dr. Nathan Marcus Adler. His son Hermann, his successor as Chief Rabbi, was appointed 'Lecturer' at the Bayswater Synagogue at the early age of 25, in 1864. He left in 1891 on his preferment.

The text accompanying the Spy Cartoon* of Hermann Adler (see Fig. 23) starts off by calling him "*the greatest Jew divine in the world*" – something even he probably would not have claimed for himself. He was "*well-grounded at University College School*", which was then situated at the university in Gower Street, and was non-sectarian then, as now, without religious discrimination. Among his contemporaries there were Joseph Chamberlain and John Morley.

Dr. Adler pursued his Rabbinical studies in Prague and Leipzig, receiving ordination in Prague. He was a friend of Cardinal Manning.

The note concludes: "*Being the Chief Rabbi, he lives both in the East and in the West – in Paddington, and in Finsbury Square.*"

Cecil Roth[4] notes that Adler saw himself as the Jewish equivalent of the Anglican or Catholic hierarchy, even adopting Anglican episcopal garb. When shown wearing the cruciform CVO, the lower limb of the cross is tucked into his velvet waistband.

The chapter on Hermann Adler in the history of the Bayswater Synagogue[73] is positively adoring, noting his popularity with his congregation and, indeed, with the Reform congregation, who helped financially with the equipment of his City residence – a cheque "*of magnificent dimensions*" presented in "*a beautiful silver casket.*" It was to Hermann Adler, a source of "*extreme gratification*" that the presentation came "*from those who do not own my immediate pastoral supervision.*"

*From an issue of Vanity Fair, date unknown.

It should be remembered that the community into which Hermann Adler was born was strikingly different to that in his later years. Then it was smaller, relatively prosperous and assimilated – the Jews in Highbury, Bayswater or St. Johns Wood differed little outwardly from their neighbours.

The large immigration after 1881 radically altered the nature of English Jewry. Many immigrants did not accept the Chief Rabbi's authority, his relative religious leniency, his Shechita, his Synagogues, his ministers or his Dayanim.[74]

During his Rabbinate, the number of Jews in London increased from around 47,000 at the beginning of the Russian pogroms to over 135,000 by 1900 – the Jewish population of Stepney alone rose from 15,000 to 54,000 over a period of twenty years.[75]

Part of the Anglo–Jewish establishment of the time was "*in favour of legislation that would result in a stemming of the flow of Jewish immigrants to Britain*",[75] including the synagogue architect N.S. Joseph, who was Hermann Adler's brother-in-law. In truth, Adler was not of 'the east' but firmly in 'the west'.

The two Readers of the Bayswater Synagogue at that time were the Revds Isaac Samuel and Samuel Harris. The (always laudatory) authors of the Centenary history[73] note that Mr. Samuel was an octogenarian when he retired and had become deaf, but that the congregants bore any inconvenience because of love of the ministers. That presumably not everyone felt that way can, I believe, be inferred from a sermon delivered by Sir Hermann Gollancz around the time these two Hazzanim retired. Using a text from *Samuel 1*, Chapter 12: "*I am old and gray-headed … whose ass have I taken? Whom have I oppressed?*" Sir Hermann continued: "*The years of a man's life … should be the strongest argument in favour of continued, even increased respect, as years go on, which members of a community should pay to the public worker who*

Fig. 76 **Bayswater Synagogue**. The last Bayswater Synagogue in Andover Place, Maida Vale. It subsequently became the Jewish Preparatory School and is now home to the Saatchi Synagogue, built on the former Gallery floor.

Fig. 77 *Rabbi Professor Sir Hermann Gollancz*. (Reproduced by kind permission of Victor Gollancz, publishers, and Mrs. Phyllis Simon)

has served them with zeal and devotion. Personally I am astonished at times to hear the impatient, ungrateful terms in which some of the most zealous servants of the community are spoken of when long years of active service have rendered their powers somewhat enfeebled."[76]

Rabbi Professor Sir Hermann Gollancz (Fig. 77)

Sir Hermann was born in Bremen in 1852 but came to England at the age of 18 months. He was one of the two sons of the Revd. (Rabbi) Samuel Gollancz of the Hambro Synagogue, the other being Sir Israel, who had obtained a Chair at Kings College London in 1909.*

He preached his first sermon in the Hambro and later was minister in the 'hut' at St. Johns Wood, before moving to the New Synagogue in Great St. Helens. He subsequently accepted a post in South Manchester, before returning to London, to the Dalston Synagogue in Poet's Road, but his last and most successful ministry was at the Bayswater Synagogue, from 1892 to 1922.

Although possessed of Rabbinical ordination, obtained in Germany, he could not use the title 'Rabbi' until 1908, when Dr. Adler finally allowed it; until then he would not allow himself be called up to the Reading of the Law as he could not use this title.

He was a handsome man when young, and dignified when old. A scholar, he held the Chair of Hebrew at University College London. He was deeply committed to interfaith work and also to work in the general community, being the only Jew on the Committee that obtained Clissold Park for use by the public.

Volumes of his sermons can still be found in second-hand bookshops – who reads such things today? The language, of course, has a Victorian style, but the preacher shows the intense patriotism of his age; there are sermons on the death of Edward VII, on the Coronation of George V, and on the death of Captain Scott (*"the heart of the British Nation, with its keen love of the sea … melts in sorrow at the mournful intelligence that this brave captain and his four companions have perished in the noble discharge of duty."*[76]) His sermons show a love of Jewry, orthodox practice, and of England.

Sir Hermann Gollancz retired in 1922 and was replaced by Dayan Gollop (see Appendix 5a), who was later appointed to the Hampstead Synagogue and was in turn replaced by W. Levin (see Fig. 128), who had been previously at the North West London Synagogue, Caversham Road, and the North London Synagogue in Lofting Road. Revd Levin was followed by Dr Isaac Levy (who also moved to Hampstead later) and who has written two autobiographical accounts of his war service as chaplain, which deserve to be read. Dr Levy took the annual Jewish service at the Cenotaph until recently.

* The statutes of which had to be altered to allow a Jew to occupy this position in an Anglican establishment.

THE NORTH LONDON SYNAGOGUE

LOFTING ROAD, N1

The history of the Synagogue was written, 80 years after it had opened in 1868, by its last minister, the Revd. Nathan Bergerman.[77]

With the migration of the Jews to the district, aided no doubt by the building of the North London Railway (Caledonian Road station opened in 1852 and Broad Street station in 1865), a *Minyan* was established in Upper Street, Islington. By 1863 the small room of the Barnsbury Hall, at 2-4 Barnsbury Street, had to be used for Sabbath services and, on Festivals, the large hall. In 1865 the usual public meeting was held and an Appeal Fund launched; £3,000 was collected by the Revd. A.A. Green. Revd. Bergerman notes that, because the ground landlords were not helpful, the synagogue could not be built in Highbury.[77]

Instead, a site was acquired in John Street West (now Lofting Road) and the Synagogue, designed by H.H. Collins, opened in 1868. Its opening was commemorated in the *Illustrated London News* [78] (Fig. 78) and, five years later, a service at Tabernacles was described in the *Graphic* of 2nd November 1872 (Fig. 79).

Fig. 78 *North London Synagogue*. This drawing of the exterior of the Synagogue in Lofting Road – an ornate Italianate design – was published in the *Illustrated London News,* 3rd October, 1868.

The congregation must have been fairly affluent. Today, the local area still has expensive housing, although there are areas of deprivation. The members were able to raise £16,000 themselves to pay off a loan on the building. Many lived 'over the shop' – Chapel Street market, the Angel and Upper Street are all nearby. The architect of the Synagogue was well known, and the building capacious and ornate.

The Synagogue is described as "*being built in the Italian style: 65 feet long, 45 feet wide and 35 feet high. Floriated iron pillars support three galleries and octagonal coffered ceilings. The east end … is approached by a flight of marble steps, its arches supported by columns of rare marble. The plastering is modelled from examples of vegetable forms in the Botanical Gardens – the fig, vine, olive, palm and corn. Over the ark are tablets of stained glass on which are painted the Ten Commandments. Over the ark is written: "Remember before Whom you stand". The doors of the ark were concealed by curtains of rich crimson velvet, fringed and embroidered with gold* (Fig. 80)." [78]

The first minister at the North London Synagogue, from 1868 to 1874, was the Revd. Morris Joseph (see below) and the Revd. H. Wasserzug was elected as Reader (see below).

Mr. Raphael Tuck (of greeting card fame) joined the Board of Management in 1882. Mr. Adolph Tuck presented the pulpit in 1892 (Fig. 81) and Mr. Hermann Tuck a "*large, handsome, bound Bible for Readings by the Minister.*"[77] Mr. Adolph Tuck was knighted in 1909. His name is frequently mentioned in the histories of other synagogues as a supporter of new synagogue buildings.

In 1903 the Revd. Walter Levin (see Fig. 128) was transplanted to Lofting Road from the North West London Synagogue in Caversham Road. During the First World War he served as a chaplain and left in 1930 for the Bayswater Synagogue, where he served briefly.

The Revd. Woolf Morein served the congregation as minister from 1931 but died during the Second World War, in Aldershot, while serving as a military chaplain. The Revd. Nathan Bergerman served as the congregation's last minister, before moving to the East London Synagogue.

Membership of the North London Synagogue, however, must have been affected by the opening of the nearby Dalston Synagogue in 1874 (Highbury was apparently a better address than Barnsbury). The number of members was never great, reaching a peak of 317 male members in 1930, though even in 1950 there were still 301 members.

The last Choirmaster, Mr. E. Carter, tells me that, by the time the Synagogue closed, there were more people in the choir than in the congregation. After closure in 1958, the members transferred to the Dalston Synagogue. In 1960, the amalgamated total membership of both synagogues was 463 members (together it had been over 700 in 1950).

The building of the North London Synagogue has been demolished.

The Reverend Morris Joseph (Fig. 82)

Morris Joseph was born in 1848, the son of the Revd. David Joseph, of the Maiden Lane Synagogue. He was educated at the Westminster Jews' Free School, Jews' College School and finally at Jews' College. In 1868 he was appointed as the first minister (and secretary) of the newly opened North London Synagogue, but left in 1874 for a post at Princes Road in Liverpool. In 1881 he resigned from there, citing ill health, and returned to London, where, for many years he lived in semi-retirement, occasionally writing for

THE FEAST OF TABERNACLES AT THE NORTH LONDON SYNAGOGUE—THE READER TAKING THE PALM BRANCH

Fig. 79 *North London Synagogue*. Drawing of the interior at the Feast of Tabernacles, reproduced from the *Graphic*, 2nd November, 1872. Hazzan Wasserzug takes the four species. Again, none of the congregation seems to have them.

the *Jewish Chronicle*. In 1890 he commenced Sabbath afternoon services at the Hampstead Town Hall. These services were accompanied by music – and a mixed choir (considered acceptable then). The success of the services led to an invitation that he occupy the pulpit of the newly opened synagogue in Hampstead. He was interviewed for this post by Dr. Adler, but found wanting. "*Mr. Joseph, when questioned by me, stated that he could not conscientiously read any of the prayers in which supplication is offered up for the restoration of the sacrificial rite. I also deemed it advisable to afford him the opportunity of explaining the religious views which he has embodied in various sermons which had been published in the Jewish Chronicle. The explanations that he offered proved that I had been correct in my surmise that his opinions were not in accord with the teachings of traditional Judaism.*"[79]

Mr. Joseph, it seems, was not too downhearted as he did not want "*galling shackles*". "*I would have no-one cast a stone at the kind and humane man who has passed upon me this sentence of minor excommunication. The Chief Rabbi is but the administrator of a system and, so long as the community acquiesces in the existence of that system, it is only the community that is responsible for the procedure, whose logical effect would be to exclude from the pulpit of English synagogues some of the most gifted and renowned Rabbis.*"[79]

He was shortly afterwards appointed to the pulpit of the West London Synagogue at which point he resigned his post as Lecturer in Homiletics (preaching) at Jews' College.

He was a moderate reformer who sought to integrate his synagogue into the wider community; indeed, he seems to have been invited to, and attended, the consecrations of many United Synagogues. He retired in 1922. He was, of course, a Victorian and his sermons, published in two volumes, have an old-fashioned – to our minds – flavour.

In his obituary he is described as "*a forceful and lucid preacher. His sermons were literary gems and a means of education to his hearers.*"[79] His book entitled *Judaism as Creed and Life* went into four editions.[80] He was an ardent pacifist

Fig. 80 *North London Synagogue*. The interior showing the apse and ark; a dignified wedding ceremony takes place with robed ministers. (Photograph courtesy of Mrs. Bergerman.)

(as was a colleague in Liverpool, the Revd. John Harris, who was hounded from his post during the First World War). He was a member of the Jewish Deputation to the King on the accession.

He died in 1930 after surgery, at the age of 82 years, but was not buried for some days as he died on the sixth day of Passover. The funeral service at the Reform cemetery in Hoop Lane was conducted by the minister of the West London Synagogue – the Revd. Reinhart – and the former minister of the East London (United) Synagogue – the Revd. J.F. Stern (see p. 93). It is interesting to note who attended: the Revd. A. Barnett (of the Western Synagogue) and Mrs. Barnett, his niece, the Chief Rabbi Dr. J.H. Hertz, Dayan Feldman, Dayan Lazarus, Dayan Gollop and the *Haham* Dr. Gaster, the Revs. E. Levine, J.F. Stern, H.L. Price, M. Zeffertt, J. Harris, N. Goldston, I. Livingstone and D. Bueno de Mesquita – as well as Rabbis Ginsberg (of Richmond Synagogue), Mishcon (Brixton) and Dr. Mattuck (see p. 116).

The memorial service was held at Upper Berkeley Street in the evening after the funeral. This was also attended by the Chief Rabbi, Dr. J.H. Hertz, and by the Revd. S. Levy of the New Synagogue.

The Reverend Haim Wasserzug (see Fig. 79)

There is a very readable biography of Revd. Wasserzug in an excellent book, *Legendary Voices*, by the illustrious Hazzan, Samuel Vigoda.[19]

It seems that this small anglicised community in Barnsbury had, as its Reader, one of the all-time greats, unfortunately before the age of the phonograph. His work lives on, however, and is to be found in the United Synagogue music handbook, *The Voice of Prayer and Praise,* edited by Rabbi

F.L. Cohen (see p. 68) and D.M. Davis, Choirmaster of the New West End Synagogue. What, in fact, landed him in Barnsbury? How did Reb Chayim, der Lomzer Hazzan, become the Revd. H. Wasserzug?

He was born in 1822, in Shieradzs, in the Governorate of Kalish, western Poland, the son of the local Hazzan; his father ensured that he acquired a thorough grounding in Talmud. He learned to mimic his father in a soprano voice at an early age, and was soon assisting him. At the age of 18 he was appointed Hazzan at Kanin. After two years there he was offered a position at Novidvar, near Warsaw. So great was the dismay of the worthies of Kanin that, when he tried to leave, the populace barricaded his van and the police had to be called (folk were rather keen in those days).

Being near Warsaw he was able to attend the local Conservatory. In 1856, he was appointed Hazzan Rishon (First Reader) in Lomza, a famous seat of Rabbinical learning. Here he introduced, against much opposition (the local Chasidim wished to excommunicate him for this), a four-part choir and composed music for it. He also founded a Cantorial Master Class, from which came many notable Hazzanim.

After five years in Lomza came the plum call – and Chayim Lomzer went to Vilna, the 'Jerusalem' of Lithuania. Dr. Vigoda relates how Reb Chaim held a concert once a year in the Synagogue courtyard, with vocal and instrumental music one hour before the Sabbath on *Shabbat Behaloscho* (the Sabbath on which the portion of the Book of Numbers, commencing at Chapter 8, verse 1, is read). Psalms, beginning with *xcv* ("O come, let us exalt before the Lord") were sung while lads with burning brands surrounded the gathering, in literal interpretation of Behaloscho ('when you kindle the lights'). Dr. Vigoda writes that Reb Chayim Lomzer left this apparently idyllic setting because he had family in London, which they painted in rosy colours. So he came, he saw and he conquered – he was much admired in London for his music and his personality.

In 1876 he was 'taking the cure' in Germany. When the Jews of Vilna heard this, they begged him to return, offering him all he had in London, and seemingly more, but, according to Dr. Vigoda, "*he and his family had already become accustomed to the comfortable, tranquil life and the democratic freedom and security of a civilised and enlightened land.*"

Hazzan Wasserzug died in 1882, aged not quite 60 years, having just returned from singing at the house of the Chief Rabbi.

Further Hazzanim at the North London Synagogue after Mr. Wasserzug were the Revd. S. Munz (1883-1918) and the Revd. A. Slavinsky from 1919.

Fig. 81 *North London Synagogue*. The pulpit donated by Adolph Tuck. (Reproduced from the history of the Synagogue.[77])

Fig. 82 *The Revd. Morris Joseph*, later of the West London Synagogue of British Jews. (Photograph reproduced by kind permission of the *Jewish Chronicle*.)

THE EAST LONDON SYNAGOGUE

RECTORY SQUARE, E1

On the occasion of its 25th anniversary in 1902, the then minister, the Revd.
J.F. Stern, wrote a three-page article in the *Jewish Chronicle* on the history of
the congregation.[81] He noted that, strange as it may seem to us today, 30
years previously (that is, 1860-1870) Mile End, Stepney and Bow were still
regarded as 'suburban'.

In 1873 the Council of the United Synagogue resolved to close the
Hambro, which was in a parlous state with a declining membership, a
financial deficit and in need of substantial repair, and to use the funds from
the sale to build a new synagogue in Stepney, which would also be called the
Hambro (this did eventually happen, but the move was to Aldgate). A
meeting of the seatholders of the Hambro was held in 1873, thirty five of
whom attended and voted 17-15 against closure. At that time, as Stern
pointed out in the *Jewish Chronicle*, whilst the Hambro could provide seating
for 273 men (but only for 10 women), it had only half that number of
seatholders and "*could not even remunerate its officers with common decency*". East
of the City, however, prior to the great immigration, there were 200-300
families with children too "*delicate*" to walk the long distance into the City.
Stern further noted that "*a synagogue is not wanted in Fenchurch Street*".

There were at this time small *Minyanim* in Stepney in private dwellings,
including one in Assembly Passage off the Mile End Road, where Revd.
Stern's father was the unpaid officiant.

Fig. 85 *East London Synagogue* (above). A view towards the rear doors, showing the banded, unadorned brickwork, stained glass windows and Hebrew text running along the Ladies Gallery. There seem to be fruits, presumably Biblical, on the columns supporting the Gallery. (Photograph courtesy of Mrs. Bergerman.)

Fig. 86 *East London Synagogue* (right). The slightly curved, central Almemar. (Photograph courtesy of Mrs. Bergerman.)

A Jewish School with seven pupils opened in 1865 in a small house in Stepney; this grew into the second largest Jewish school in London – the Stepney Jewish School – which only recently transferred to Redbridge. A new building for the school, financially supported by the Rothschild family, was consecrated in 1872, and services were held there. It was pointed out at its consecration that while new synagogues were being built in North and West London, the East was inadequately provided for.

At a public meeting £1500 was raised (£500 from Messrs Rothschild, subsequently raised to £1500). Stern wrote: "*The poor, whose greatest effort cannot raise means to supply an actual and pressing want, should and must be helped … Let the question of new synagogues in the west be shelved until the east be duly supplied.*"[81]

The East London Synagogue became the first to be erected under the auspices of the United Synagogue. A local plot of land was purchased by a well-wisher, Mr. Isaac Davis, and the foundation stone laid in 1873. The bells of the local churches honoured the event!

The building itself, designed by Davis & Emanuel had a rather drab exterior (Fig. 83). The *Jewish Chronicle* of 25th April, 1873 noted: "*This simple synagogue was meant to be a 'pride to its promoters, an honour to the district and a glory to the community of Israel.*" The building was "*of brick inside and outside, so as to save the expense of plaster … the plainest character consistent with propriety.*"

"*The exterior of the Synagogue merges with the housing, making no imposing statement.*"

However, the interior was lively and colourful, of banded brick, with Hebrew texts along the base of the Gallery, as at the New West End Synagogue. The *Almemar* was centrally situated and the steps to the ark had ornamental railings before them; the pulpit was to the side of the ark. Boards for the Prayer for the Royal Family had coats-of-arms above them. The ark stood in a recess, surmounted by the decalogue and, above this, a large circular window (Figs. 84–88).

In a sermon delivered on the 25th Anniversary of the congregation, Mr. Stern commented on Sabbath classes, children's services (apparently the first to be held) and a voluntary choir for men *and* women (this latter caused a schism and led to the formation of the Stepney Orthodox Synagogue). There was a Communal League (for intellectual and social life), an Orphan Aid Society and Mothers' Meetings ("*making the path of life easier for hard-pressed and weary mothers*"), as well as a Burial Society. Mr. Stern pleaded for additional help, for workers, because of "*crowds of poor people awaiting their turn for an interview with the minister.*"[81]

Fig. 87 *East London Synagogue*. Chief Rabbi Lord Jakobovits shown preaching from an elevated position in the beautiful and ornate Synagogue. (Photograph courtesy of Mrs. Bergerman.)

Fig. 88 *East London Synagogue*. A bookplate used in the library donated to the Synagogue in 1927 by Lady Rothschild in memory of her husband. (Courtesy of Mr. Bernard Goldblum.)

Fig. 89 *East London Synagogue*. The building as it is today. It has been converted into flats and the pitched roof now contains dormer windows.

Membership held up well, actually increasing to a peak of 467 males in 1960, presumably as other local synagogues closed, but slowly declined from then on.

The building was finally abandoned and vandalised and, in 1978, even the pulpit stolen! It has since been converted into flats (Fig. 89). The small remaining congregation merged with that at Hackney, ending the connection of the United Synagogue with the East End.

Revd. Joseph Frederick Stern 1865–1934 (see Appendix 5a)
There is a most informative article on this complex figure and his synagogue by Judge Israel Finestein in *The Jewish East End, 1840-1939*.[82]

Mr. Stern joined the Synagogue eleven years after its opening. He was seen to be the archetypal Anglo-Jewish clergyman, an outstanding preacher, a pastor and a servant to his congregants. He had been educated at Jews'

Fig. 90 *The Revd. Mendel Zeffertt* greeting youngsters. A day out to Southend? (Photograph courtesy of Mr. Aumie Shapiro.)

College School, Aria College in Portsmouth, at Jews' College and at University College London. He seems to have been a good Hazzan too and, with D.M. Davis as choirmaster, brought an English style of service to the East End. He also joined the Jewish Religious Union at its beginning, but later withdrew from it, along with Simeon Singer, after Dr. Adler's criticism of it; indeed, his support for it divided East London Jewry, further alienating local orthodox opinion.

According to Judge Finestein, Mr. Stern, so active, was a thoroughly dissatisfied minister, resenting the burden of his secretarial duties (many ministers were also synagogue secretaries).* Not until 1924 was he allowed an assistant, the Revd. I.K. Cosgrove. Apparently Mr. Stern disliked the squalor of the area and, despite trying for posts at Hampstead and Great Portland Street, was never able to leave Stepney Green.

Mr. Stern was a member of the Jewish Board of Guardians and Chairman of the local Parish Board of Guardians, Secretary of Stepney Jewish Schools and Chairman of the Committee of the local London County Council Schools, President of the local Jewish Lads' Club and served on the Visitation Committee of Ministers. He was, in short, overworked, eventually living in Northwest London whilst still working in Stepney.

His son, Leonard, heavily involved in the Settlement movement in the East End, was killed in the First World War.

On his death in 1934 Joseph Stern was cremated at Golders Green following a service conducted by Rabbi Reinhart of the West London Synagogue, and his ashes interred in Palestine.

Revd. Mendel Zeffertt (Fig. 90)

In 1928 Mr. Stern was succeeded at the East London Synagogue by the Revd. Mendel Zeffertt[83] who had previously been at Plymouth. Born in Poland, he came to England as a boy, his family settling in Liverpool. He too studied at Aria College and Jews' College. He was involved in the scouting movement, in the Jewish Lads' Brigade and was also chaplain to the London Jewish Hospital. He died in post at the age of sixty five years.

He was succeeded by the Revd. Nathan Bergerman, who had previously been at the North London Synagogue at Lofting Road as its last minister. He, too, was greatly involved with the London Jewish Hospital, now also closed.

* The *Year Book* for 1913 lists the "*East London Minister's Fund. Object - the increase of the number of ministers in East London. Treasurer and Hon. Secretary - The Rev. J.F. Stern.*"

THE DALSTON SYNAGOGUE

POET'S ROAD, N5

There are two main sources for the history of the Dalston Synagogue. The first in 1910 was written by the Revd. D. Wasserzug to commemorate the 25th Anniversary of the opening of the Synagogue in Poet's Road.[84] Dr. J. Rabbinowitz wrote a second shorter history commemorating its Golden Anniversary in 1935.[85]

By 1874, some 700 Jewish families were said to be living within half-an-hour's walk from Dalston Junction, but still some distance from the North London Synagogue in Barnsbury (see p. 85), which had opened in 1868.

In 1874 a meeting was held to consider the erection of a synagogue for the Jews of the Balls Pond Road, Dalston and Hackney. A large room in Colveston House, Birkbeck Road, was obtained, which had a conservatory at the rear for the use of ladies, and altogether seated 200 congregants. Services were held there before the High Holy days. This congregation was joined by a pre-existing *Minyan* worshipping in a house in Clephane Road, N1 (this runs into St. Paul's Road).

A site for a permanent building was found in Newington Green Road, but this aroused the immediate opposition of the North London Synagogue, whose members pointed out, not unreasonably, that the original plan had been to build a synagogue near Dalston, which would not have made a significant inroad into the North London Synagogue membership; the proposed new building, however, would be in the neighbourhood of the more affluent Highbury New Park, which lay within the catchment of the North London Synagogue. The North London Synagogue had been struggling financially for many years and, just when the liabilities incurred in its building were being settled, a new and threatening situation had arisen.

A subcommittee of the United Synagogue also reported unfavourably on the Newington Green Road scheme.

In 1876, however, the proposers leased ground at 120, Mildmay Road, at a yearly rent of £40, and proceeded to erect a synagogue there. This building, which took only five weeks to complete and cost £500, was of corrugated iron with interior walls of varnished pine. There were four Gothic windows on the north and south walls, and one of coloured glass above the ark. Two hundred worshippers could be accommodated, the women being seated at the back and separated by a small screen. The Synagogue opened for New Year services and was crowded. Membership rose from 268 in 1886 to 365 in 1913.

In 1884 a plot of land in Poet's Road – 138' x 102' – was purchased for £650 and the new Dalston Synagogue (Figs. 91 and 92), designed by Mr. N.S. Joseph, was built together with residences for £7,000 and was consecrated soon after (Fig. 93). (The iron building was later sold to the South Hackney congregation for £80.)

The first minister was the Revd. M. Myers and the Hazzan the Revd. J. Lesser (Fig. 94), who at the age of seven had sung in the choir at the Great

Fig. 91 **Dalston Synagogue**, Poet's Road, N5. The exterior prior to demolition in 1969. The rather r un-down nature of the area is already evident. The building is built of plain brick with horizontal stone bands and has vaguely Moorish features reminiscent of the pre–War Central Synagogue, especially in the Moorish-type arches over the first floor windows. (Photograph courtesy of the Islington Public Libraries.)

Synagogue, Duke's Place, and subsequently at the Western Synagogue, St Alban's Place, where he became Second Reader.

Mr. Myers died shortly after the opening of the new synagogue and two candidates applied for the post – the Revd. (later Sir Hermann) Gollancz and the Revd. Mr. M. Hyamson. Mr. Gollancz was appointed but, when he departed for the Bayswater Synagogue after seven years, Mr. Hyamson succeeded him. He, in turn, served for a decade until his appointment as Dayan (Fig. 94).

In his consecration sermon, Dr. H. Adler of the Bayswater Synagogue sympathised with the misgivings of the North London Synagogue. When the New West End Synagogue had opened, drawing members away from the Bayswater Synagogue, he confessed to sadness at missing so many familiar faces, but he had soon recognised that Judaism had gained.

A secession

Mr. Wasserzug notes that "*one or two slight modifications in the service sanctioned by the Chief Rabbi*" were proposed.[84] I assume these were the, by now, usual break between the morning service and the Reading of the Law, and the abolition of sacrificial portions of the repetition of the additional service.

Perhaps because of this, some members of the congregation left and formed a new Minyan in Sandringham Road, Dalston; this eventually developed into the Stoke Newington Synagogue (see p. 104).

After Mr. Hyamson resigned on his appointment as Dayan, advertisements for his replacement were published not only in the Anglo-Jewish press but also in the Continental press, as it was felt that the ministers trained at Jews' College were not of adequate standard.

Eventually, a Rabbi from Frankfurt was appointed by the Board, but this inspired a revolt amongst the membership. Finally, in 1903, after the resignation of some members of the Board, the Revd. D. Wasserzug (see below) was elected instead of the gentleman from Frankfurt, by the difference of one vote. He died in office, in 1918.

The Revd. (later Rabbi Dr.) J. Rabbinowitz (see Appendix 5a) was

DALSTON SYNAGOGUE.

AN HISTORICAL SKETCH

PREPARED BY

THE REV. D. WASSERZUG,

BY THE DESIRE OF THE

"MEMBERS' PRESENTATION COMMITTEE,"

TO COMMEMORATE THE

25th Anniversary of the Inauguration of the Dalston Synagogue in Poet's Road.

Fig. 92 *Dalston Synagogue*. The strikingly beautiful interior is shown in this photograph taken on the 25th Anniversary of the consecration of the building. (Reproduced from the communal history.[84])

ק״ק כנסת ישראל

זמירות ושירות

לשיר במקהלות

ביום חנכת בית הכנסת דאלסטאן

בלונדון הבירה יע״א

ביום א׳ כ׳ב תמוז שנת

ויזמרו לשמו לפ״ק

UNITED SYNAGOGUE.

ORDER OF SERVICE

AT THE

Consecration of the Dalston Synagogue.

THE DEDICATION CEREMONY

WILL BE SOLEMNISED BY

THE REV. DR. H. ADLER, DELEGATE CHIEF RABBI,

ON SUNDAY, JULY 5th, 5645.

The Service will be conducted by the Revs. M. HAST, H. GOLLANCZ, and J. LESSER, with the Choir of the Great Synagogue.

The Crowning Stone of the Ark will be laid by SAMUEL MONTAGU, Esq.

LONDON:

PRINTED BY WERTHEIMER, LEA & CO.

CIRCUS PLACE, LONDON WALL.

Fig. 93 *Dalston Synagogue*. Frontispiece for the Order of Service at the consecration, 1885. (Courtesy of University College London.)

Fig. 94 *Dalston Synagogue*. Photographs of the past and present Officers, taken from the 25th Anniversary brochure. The Revd. D. Wasserzug was the son of Hazzan Wasserug of the North London Synagogue, Lofting Road. The only people with head coverings are the ministers.

inducted in 1925 and served there until his retirement in 1960. His history of the Synagogue ends on a somewhat sad note.[85] It seems that even then the district was undergoing change for the worse; the Synagogue was finding it difficult to replace those members who had moved away or died.

An amalgamation with the Finsbury Park congregation had been proposed in 1932 and a site provisionally purchased at 216, Green Lanes, N4, with a view to erecting a large synagogue, but the United Synagogue had decided that the scheme was too ambitious and expensive.

In 1958 the North London Synagogue closed and amalgamated with the Dalston congregation. The Dalston Synagogue closed in 1967 and the congregation transferred to the Stoke Newington Synagogue.

I have personal memories of the Poet's Road Synagogue. My family lived near Newington Green and attended the 'Goldblum Synagogue' in Highbury New Park, which was actually a large room in one of the big detached houses in Highbury New Park. By then, in the 1950s, the area was already decaying, but what I remember about it most was the vibrant Jewish life, aided by the large number of Continental refugees who had settled there. My parents often went to Poet's Road to hear two great Hazzanim – J. Kusevitsky – one of four brothers (all cantors), – and Hazzan S. Taube, later of Hendon.

I can remember the foyer of the building and the cracks in the wall, and a notice detailing the extremely complex structure of the United Synagogue into Constituent, District and Associate synagogues, which certainly confused me as a child. I also remember, to my disappointment, noting that the columns supporting the Ladies' Gallery were painted and not of real marble.

The circumstances of the closure were sad, in that the many Jews still living there fought a vigorous battle to keep the Synagogue open. In 1960 there had been 463 male members, yet the closure went ahead in 1967 and the congregation was amalgamated with Stoke Newington Synagogue. The combined membership of both in 1970 was only 343, as against nearly 1,000 in 1960 – an indication of the rapid migration to the outer suburbs in that decade. No doubt there was no long term viability for a synagogue in that area but, as can be seen in Fig. 92, the interior was a beautiful and classical example of Victorian synagogue architecture.

Eventually the building was demolished and a block of flats erected on the site.

The Revd David Wasserzug (Fig. 94)

A keen Zionist, Mr. Wasserzug, the son of the Hazzan at Lofting Road, died in 1918. He had entered Jews' College in 1877, when it was still in Finsbury Square. He graduated from University College London in 1888.

On leaving Jews' College in 1891, he took up his first ministerial post in Cardiff. In 1895 he moved to Port Elizabeth in South Africa. From 1897 until 1889 he worked in Johannesburg, establishing there the Jewish Lads' Brigade, a working men's club and a Shechita Board.

He was said to be an eloquent preacher, well versed in English literature and the Classics. His obituary noted that he had 'quaint mannerisms', but did not specify them. J.F. Stern wrote: "*Selflessness struck the key note of his life.*"[86]

THE ADASS YISROEL

FERNTOWER ROAD, N5,

LATER GREEN LANES, N16

Mention has already been made that many of the new immigrants were unhappy with what was on offer from the Anglo-Jewish establishment. There was such dissatisfaction that the Machzike Adass established its own *Shechita* (see p. 172). Nor were the English Dayanim apparently held in much regard, at least until the appointment of Rabbis Reinowitz and Abramsky.

Similar sentiments spread to the then more affluent area of Highbury, where a Beth Hamedrash was formed at 127 Newington Green Road in August 1886. Its origin and basis was the library of Mr. A. Ansell which was donated by his son. It was stipulated that no person was *"eligible for election as a member of the governing body who openly infringes the Sabbath, or partakes of forbidden food or who is not … a strictly orthodox Jew."*[87]

The Beth Hamedrash was open from morning till night; the Librarian was the Revd. J.M. Cohen, and one of the Committee members the Revd. M. Hyamson (of the local United Synagogue).

The history of the Adass Yisroel, published in 1936 to celebrate its Silver Jubilee, notes that Divine services were held there in which a feeling of common Jewish purpose was bred, and that the early *Baale-Batim* were endowed with Torah and *Derech Eretz* – in true Frankfurt style.[87]

Having amalgamated with another *Chevra* of young people (Chevra Mekor Chayim of 92 Newington Green Road), more space was required and 1, Ferntower Road was purchased. This had space for a synagogue, a Beth Hamedrash and accommodation for a Rabbi. It was felt that the local United Synagogues, although conservative, still left room for an additional centre of religious activity.

In 1905 the community moved to a new building at 125 Green Lanes. Feeling grew in favour of the establishment of a separatist community or *Kehillah*, in the style of Rabbi S.R. Hirsch's *Austrittsgemeinde* in Frankfurt. In 1909 Rabbi Victor Schönfeld was appointed (see below).

An Education Committee was set up and, more importantly, a Kashrut Committee, in conjunction with the Machzike Adass, for Shechita separate from the main community. Similarly, foods for use during the year and during Passover came under their own independent supervision (this situation still exists today).

A *Mikveh* had been established at 367, Essex Road, the author of the history of the synagogue noting that *"the building of the Mikveh had rightly taken precedence over the building of the synagogue and was a guiding sign of the Torah loyalty of the congregation."*[87] The synagogue of the congregation – the Adass Yisroel Synagogue – incorporating the North London Beth Hamedrash, was consecrated on 10th December, 1911 (Fig. 95).

I remember the building well because I went to the Cheder there. The Cheder was in a separate classroom block, separated from the back of the Synagogue by a small courtyard. I can remember the central, dark wooden

Fig. 95 *Adass Yisroel Synagogue*. The exterior (Architect: S. Clifford Tee). (Reproduced from the Silver Jubilee history.[85])

Fig. 96 *Hazzan Soffe*, who served the congregation of the Adass Yisroel Synagogue in the 1950s and 1960s.

Almemar beneath the rather curious domed roof which had internal wooden beams. The whole effect was rather gloomy.

I attended the Hebrew classes there because the small coventicle my parents attended had none. This was the Highbury New Park Beth Hamedrash (Goldblum's synagogue) which met in a large room in one of the huge houses in Highbury New Park (No. 139). The Goldblum family were, and still are, quietly most charitable and devout; they no longer lived in the house, but continued its use as a synagogue. The room had a few benches, a central simple table and ark with a Reader's desk to its side. It was here that I saw my first (but not last) punch-up during a service; no doubt someone offended against some custom or other. I spent most of my time playing in the overgrown garden with another lad who is now the Rabbi of a synagogue in Golders Green. I alas did not follow such a path.

When I was a child, the congregation of the Adass Yisroel was Germanic. The Hazzan, Mr. Soffe (Fig. 96) had previously been a teacher with a similar congregation, Adass Jeschurun in Cologne; he was also my Cheder teacher. Sadly, I learned little from him. He was fairly sparing with the ruler, but not averse to its use. His predecessor as Hazzan, the Revd. Hoffman, had been a composer of cantorial melodies. That generation in the main is no more, but the immigrant orthodox German was a unique being. Absolutely upright and honest, clad in a Western way – no fringes showing – and, if bearded, nicely trimmed. Educated and totally observant, they made their own institutions – cemeteries,* Kashrut, welfare organisations – completely separate from the prevailing English orthodoxy. Later, they seceded even from the Board of Deputies. I suspect, however, that nowadays the Germanic nature of the Adass is diluted by an Eastern element, as has happened in New York.

It is difficult to tell one's own children of the beauty of Jewish life in

* Like many other congregations, burials were initially at the cemetery of the Western Synagogue, where a tablet records the gratitude of the Adass Yisroel to the Western Synagogue.

Fig. 97 *Adass Yisroel Synagogue*.
The Tahara House, the last remnant
of the old Synagogue in Burma
Road. Council housing covers
the rest of the site.

Stoke Newington after the Second World War. On Saturdays and Sundays, Clissold Park was full of Jews, mainly German-speaking immigrants, sitting or walking around the bandstand while a military band played. Population movement to northwest London had already begun by the late 1950s and the congregation moved to a new building in Queen Elizabeth's Walk. Today few Jews or congregations are left in Dalston, Highbury or Islington. All that remains now of the Adass Yisroel Synagogue is a small building approached from Burma Road (Fig. 97), in the style of the original, now used for *Tahara*.

The Jewish Secondary Schools movement

Whilst most definitely not the first of the Jewish Schools in London, these certainly had a more intensively religious bias than the mainstream schools. The first such school was opened at 32, Alexandra Villas in September 1929, with the Rabbi of the community, Victor Schönfeld, as the Headmaster. The schools – the Avigdor in Stoke Newington and the Hasmonean in Hendon – have been conspicuously successful, both in the religious and secular education of their pupils.

Rabbi Victor Schönfeld (1880–1930) (Fig. 98)

An outstanding preacher, he was not German, but Hungarian in origin. Initially a Rabbi in Vienna, from 1911 he became Rabbi at the North London Beth Hamedrash. Shortly after his appointment he founded Kashrut and Education Committees for the congregation and, in the same year, the *"first Anglo-Jewish Youth Society which had the Shiur as its main objective."*[4] Cecil Roth, Bernard Homa, Alice Gestetner and R. Lunzer were early supporters, the latter two being of the founder families of the congregation.

Rabbi Schönfeld instituted the Religious Classes and wrote primers – *"Sephath Moshe"* – for use in the elementary classes, as well as a compilation of sermons.[88] During the First World War he worked for the provision of Kosher food for prisoners in internment camps.

Fig. 98 *Rabbi Dr. Victor Schönfeld*, the first Rabbi of the Adass Yisroel Synagogue. (Reproduced from the Silver Jubilee history.[85])

The Rabbi was an early and ardent Zionist. In 1920 he left for Eretz Israel to head the Mizrachi Schools, but returned again in 1923. He died in 1930 and was succeeded by Dr. E. Munk of Berlin. Rabbi Munk later became the Rabbi of the Golders Green Beth Hamedrash, which first met in the house of Reuben Lincoln, then in the Lincoln Institute (which now houses a Sephardi congregation).

Rabbi Solomon Schönfeld (Fig. 99)

The short biography in the *Encyclopaedia Judaica*[4] does not begin to give a picture of Rabbi Schönfeld, or feeling for the life and work of this remarkable man, of whom one can say, like Sir Christopher Wren, "if you want my monument, look around you."

He was Rabbi of the Adass Yisroel Synagogue for 25 years – from 1933 – and also Presiding Rabbi of the Union of Orthodox Hebrew Congregations as well as Principal of the Schools, which flourished under him. His English translation of the Siddur, no doubt for use in 'his' synagogues, unfortunately cannot be said to be inspiring. However, he also seems to have been a successful marriage broker.

To know his greatest achievement, the reader should beg or borrow (but not steal) a copy of *Solomon Schönfeld. His Place in History.*[89] This combines a short biography with the recollections of those saved by him as Head, together with his father-in-law, Chief Rabbi Joseph Hertz, of the Chief Rabbi's Emergency Council, which saved Rabbis, their families and countless children before, during and after the Second World War. The testimonies of those he saved make moving reading. The story of his school for evacuee children in Shefford, under Dr. Grunfeld, is the subject of another book, and a miracle in itself.[90]

Rabbi Schönfeld was a man *"willing and able to turn the world upside down. No individual was too young or too insignificant to be taken care of – rich or poor, child or adult, student or teacher, every individual counted."*[89]

Fig. 99 ***Rabbi Dr. Solomon Schönfeld*** as a young man. He succeeded his father in the Rabbinate. (Reproduced from *Solomon Schönfeld. His Place in History.*[89])

THE NEW DALSTON SYNAGOGUE

BIRKBECK ROAD, E8,

LATER,

THE STOKE NEWINGTON SYNAGOGUE

SHACKLEWELL LANE, E8

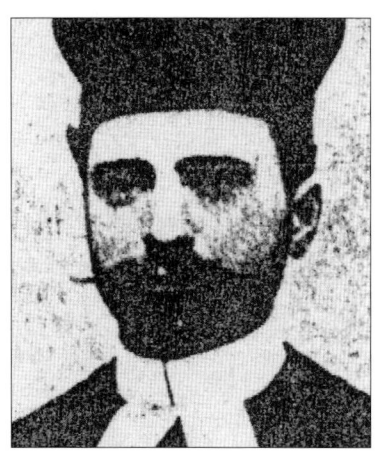

Fig. 100 ***The Revd. A. Feldman,*** first Rabbi of the New Dalston Synagogue. (Reproduced by kind permission of the *Jewish Chronicle*.)

זמירות ותהלות

לשיר במקהלות

ביום חנוכת בית הכנכת דאלסטא: החדשה

בלונדון הבירה יע"א

ביום א' י"ד מנחם אב

שנת תרח"ם לפ"ק

ORDER OF SERVICE

AT THE

CONSECRATION

OF THE

New Dalston Synagogue and Schools.

THE DEDICATION CEREMONY

WILL BE SOLEMNISED BY

The Rev. Dr. H. ADLER, Delegate Chief Rabbi

ON SUNDAY, JUNE 22ND, 5648

[illegible] the Rev. M. I. Cohen of the Borcugh Synagogue, with the Choir of the Bayswater Synagogue under the Direction of Mr. A. de Barraty.

LONDON:
PRINTED BY LEEP-BRIL AND SON,
82, BRICK LANE, SPITALFIELDS.

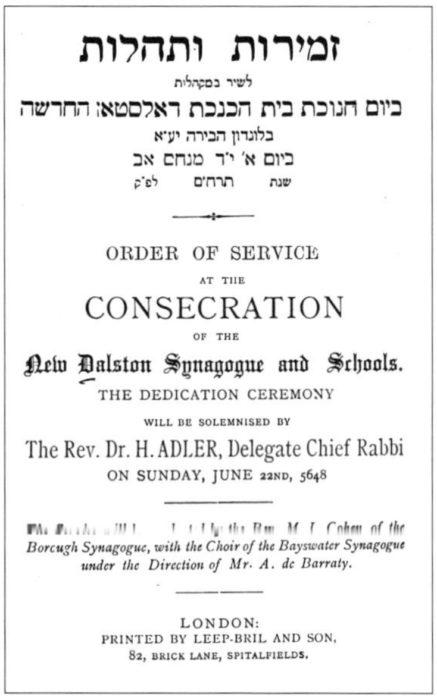

Fig. 101 Fronstipiece for the Order of Service at the consecration of the New Dalston Synagogue in 1888. (Courtesy of University College London.)

According to the history written by Dayan A. Feldman (Fig. 100; see also Appendix 5a),[91] the New Dalston Synagogue in Birkbeck Road was founded around 1888 (Fig. 101) in the face of much opposition from the congregation of the Dalston Synagogue at Poet's Road, just as that at the North London Synagogue in Lofting Road had objected to a new synagogue in Poet's Road and, later, as that at Shacklewell Lane would to the rebuilding of the New Synagogue in Egerton Road. At that time, however, there were so many Jews living around Dalston that they could, and did, fill many other synagogues locally. Its name – the New Dalston Synagogue – was used to distinguish this congregation from the older Dalston Synagogue in Poet's Road. The New Dalston Synagogue was the predecessor of the Stoke Newington Synagogue in Shacklewell Lane, which is actually in Dalston, while the Dalston Synagogue was situated in Islington, certainly not in what is understood as Dalston! Unfortunately, no photograph of the New Dalston Synagogue exists. When the building was sold and converted into a factory, the foundation stone was obliterated by the new owner.

The synagogue in Birkbeck Road was originally affiliated to the Federation of Synagogues; it had at first Hazzanim, but only visiting preachers. The first Hazzan at the New Dalston Synagogue, S. Manné (Fig. 102) subsequently went to Hampstead to be the first Hazzan there; he later emigrated to Johannesburg. The synagogue was on the first floor of the building, the prime site – the ground floor – being occupied by the religion school. The attached 'school' seems to have been more of a Talmud Torah than a proper day school, such as existed elsewhere, but proposals to set up a day school foundered. The Headmaster of the school was the renowned teacher Ish Kishor. The building proved unsatisfactory; the usual committee was set up and, in 1898, affiliation sought with the United Synagogue.

The Stoke Newington Synagogue, Shacklewell Lane

Initially, it had been planned to extend the building in Birkbeck Road, but the Committee favoured a new building. Houses were purchased in Shacklewell Lane and, as the congregation was affiliated to the United Synagogue, its architect Lewis Solomon was called upon to design the building, the cost of site and building being £13,000. This building, opened in 1903, still stands (see below) and has the distinction of being included in Rachel Wischnitzer's *The Architecture of the European Synagogue.*[24] She writes:

Fig. 102 *The Revd. S. Manné* (above), first Hazzan of the New Dalston Synagogue.

Fig. 103 *Stoke Newington Synagogue* (left), Shacklewell Lane, from a postcard around the time of the opening of the synagogue.

"Its couped round headed windows could fit either Renaissance or Romanesque design (Fig. 103). In the interior there is even a Moorish touch in the ring of decorative lozenges in the half dome of the apse (Fig. 104).

"The Synagogue is rather dull and uniform in appearance, but it is an 'efficient' building. The interior is spacious and well lighted. The upstairs meeting room at the back of the Western gallery … is connected to the Gallery by shiftable shutters which make it possible to extend the women's seating area … and there is a rolling skylight over the school area to convert it into a booth for the Feast of Tabernacles. The Synagogue is the first instance we find of planning for a 'dual function'. The Synagogue seats four hundred and thirty four men and two hundred and ninety five women (Fig. 105)."

Fig. 104 *Stoke Newington Synagogue* (below left). The interior at the time of the semi-Jubilee in 1928. (Reproduced from the semi-Jubilee history,[92] courtesy of Mrs. D. Lew.)

Fig. 105 *Stoke Newington Synagogue* (below right). An architect's drawing of the ground floor plan of the synagogue, school room and Succah. (Reproduced from the *Architect and Contract Reporter*, November 1903.)

The Hazzan at the New Dalston Synagogue from 1894 was the Revd. Coleman Davies (Fig. 106). He subsequently went on to serve the Stoke Newington Synagogue until his retirement in 1934. Of these early English Hazzanim, we know little – few recordings remain. I am informed that his

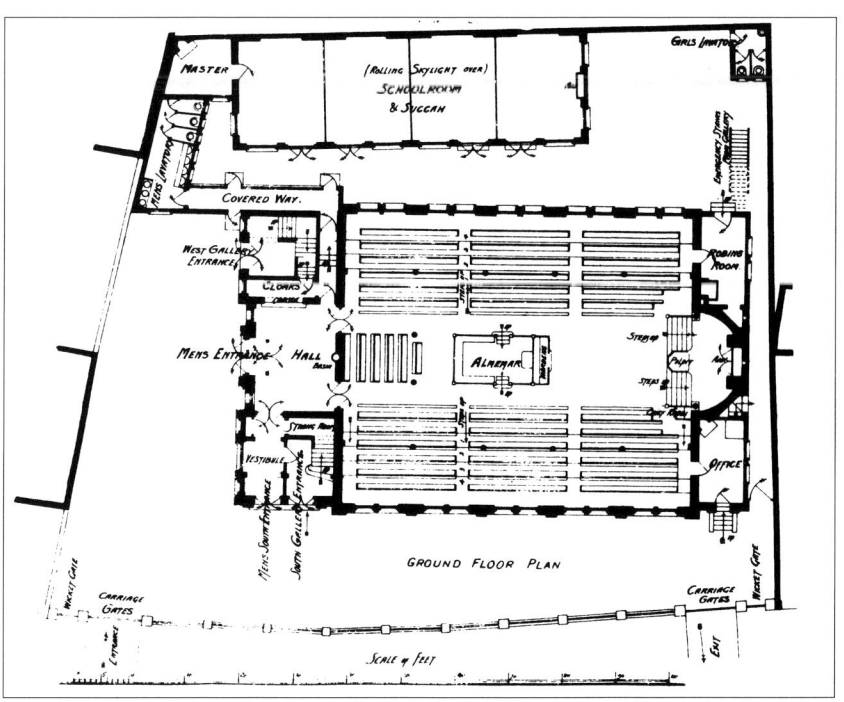

Fig. 106 *Rabbi Harris Cohen* (left) and the *Revd. Coleman Davies* (right). (Reproduced from the semi-Jubilee history,[92] courtesy of Mrs. D. Lew.)

voice was 'thin'.

The first preacher at the New Dalston Synagogue, Dr. Asher Feldman (see Fig. 100 and Appendix 5a), was appointed to Birkbeck Road in 1899 whilst still a student at Jews' College and remained there until he was appointed Dayan in 1902. He had been born in Russia. After arriving in England, he studied in Jews' College and at University College London, graduating in 1895; he was ordained Rabbi in 1899. He became a lecturer at Toynbee Hall and at Jews' College.

The first communal history of the Stoke Newington Synagogue, written by Rabbi Harris Cohen (Fig. 106), ends with the semi-Jubilee in 1928.[92] He had been chosen, even in those days (1903), not by public audition, but by a nominated Selection Committee. He preached first on the last day of the old building and at the opening service of the new, during which the Great Synagogue Choir performed under the direction of Mr. N. Peckar (see p. 30).

In 1925, a hall and cloakroom block was opened, bearing the name of the philanthropic Gustave Tuck in recognition of his services to the congregation, even though he had never resided locally. (Incidentally, Rabbi Cohen describes the Synagogue as a bulwark of conservative Judaism, showing how words can change their meaning over the years.)

The next history was written for the Golden Jubilee of the Synagogue in 1953.[93] In the photograph of the interior (Fig. 107), two huge lamps stand on the raised platform before the ark. Above the ark can be seen a large stone bearing the decalogue, which occupies much of the height of the heavily decorated, domed apse. Above the built-in ark itself, and over the domed apse, is written "Remember before Whom you stand". The marble pulpit had been donated by Gustave Tuck, who donated so much elsewhere.

Fig. 107 *Stoke Newington Synagogue*. The interior of the Synagogue at the Jubilee of the congregation in 1953. The large lamps on the Duchan were not present on the earlier photograph. (Reproduced from the Jubilee history,[93] courtesy of Mrs. D. Lew.)

Rabbi Cohen (see Fig. 106) was succeeded in 1934 by Dayan Lew (Fig. 108), who served until 1946 before going to Hampstead Garden Suburb. Rabbi Dr. A. Melinek served from 1947 until 1951 before going to Brondesbury. Rabbi Dr. I. Rapaport occupied the pulpit for one year, followed by the Revd. E. Morris in 1953.

The history notes a flourishing 'Welfare Centre', and 'Friendship Club' and a Youth Centre.[93]

When Hazzan Davies retired in 1934, the congregation obtained the services

Fig. 108 *Stoke Newington Synagogue*. The officers at the time of the induction into office of the Revd. S. Kusevitsky as Hazzan. He is shown in the front row with the Revd. (later Dayan Dr.) M. Lew on his right and the Revd. Coleman Davies on his left. (Photograph courtesy of the *Jewish Chronicle* and Mrs. D. Lew.)

of the great Hazzan, Simcha Kusevitsky (Figs. 18, 26 and 108). When Hazzan Kusevitsky went on to Duke's Place, he was replaced by the Revd. S. Einhorn.

Membership peaked at 568 males in 1950, but had declined to 343 by 1970, despite amalgamation with the Dalston Synagogue when that closed in 1967 (the number of male seatholders of both congregations in 1960 had been around 1,000). The numbers of the congregation continued to dwindle and, when the Stoke Newington Synagogue closed, its membership transferred to Hackney.

Today, in that part of north and north east London, the Hackney Synagogue is the only large United Synagogue still open, with a male membership of 300, including former members of the East London and Great Synagogues.

The building still stands today, in use as a mosque, in an area with a large Turkish population. A huge dome has been added to the roof (Fig. 109). I was allowed into the foyer, but could only glimpse the synagogue through the glass doors at the entrance to the synagogue proper. The exterior of the building is dilapidated, and the classrooms even more so. The foyer looks rather sad – just some stained wood panelling. Little seems to have been altered since the synagogue was closed. In the sanctuary the pews and the Almemar have been removed and the floor carpeted. The ark and surround remain, still in their faded 1960s pastel shades. The huge pulpit is still there, now draped with a green flag; the ark is now covered with a different sort of cloth.

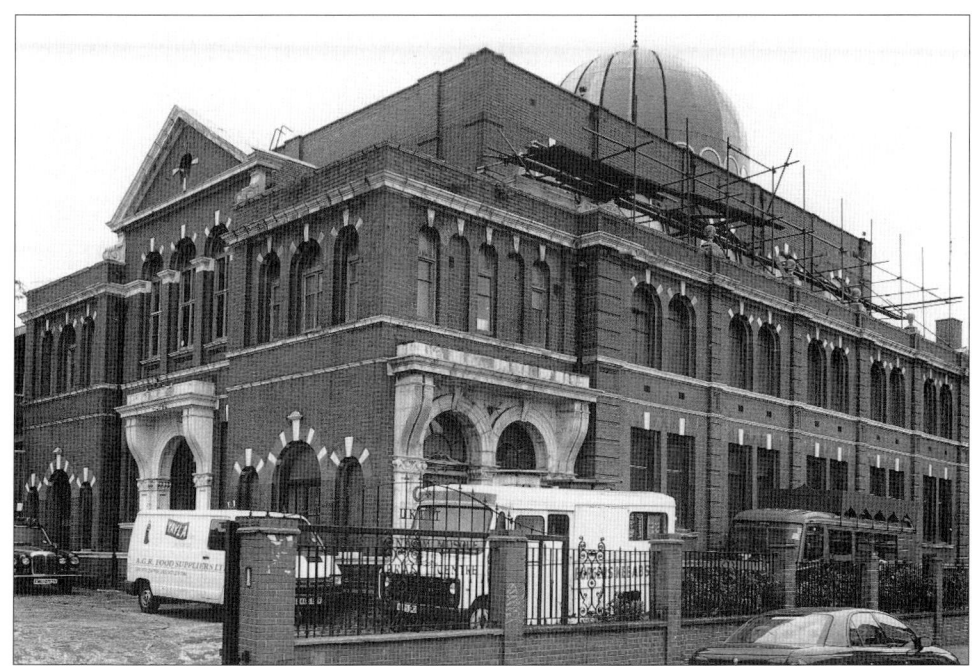

Fig. 109 *Stoke Newington Synagogue*. The Shacklewell Lane Synagogue is now a mosque. Note the dome.

THE SOUTH EAST LONDON SYNAGOGUE

NEW CROSS ROAD, SE14,

LATER, LAUSANNE ROAD, SE15,

LATER, NEW CROSS ROAD, SE14

A souvenir history was written in 1957 by Mr. Sam Wise.[94] The story of this community begins in 1888 when two local residents, Mr. and Mrs. Frank, could not get to the Borough Synagogue for the New Year services as Mrs. Frank was expecting a baby and could not walk very far. Mr. Frank placed an advert in the local paper asking local Jews to come to tea, with a view to setting up a quorum.

The first services were held in his house at 452, New Cross Road (there was even a kosher butcher on New Cross Road). Later, two rooms were obtained in Nettleton Road. These rooms eventually became too small for the membership and an old iron hut⋆ was erected in Lausanne Road, Peckham, in 1889. The ark and Almemar were placed at the eastern end; the hut also had a Gallery. The Order of Service is reproduced in Fig. 110.

Classes were rapidly established and a young minister, the Revd. Nehemiah Goldston, engaged (Fig. 111; see also Appendix 5a). He had the

Fig. 110 *South East London Synagogue* (above). Frontispiece for the Order of Service for the consecration of the Synagogue in Lausanne Road, Peckham, on Sunday, 7th April 1889. (Courtesy of University College London.)

Fig. 111 *South East London Synagogue* (opposite page). Frontispiece from the *Jewish World*, 17th March, 1905, showing the interior and exterior of the new Synagogue, together with its minister, the Revd. N. Goldston. (Courtesy of Dr. S. Cohen.)

Fig. 112 *South East London Synagogue* (right). An early photograph of the exterior. Those who worshipped there before the War tell me what a wonderful community it was. (Photograph courtesy of Dr. S. Cohen.)

⋆ The Portakabin of that time; many congregations started off in them.

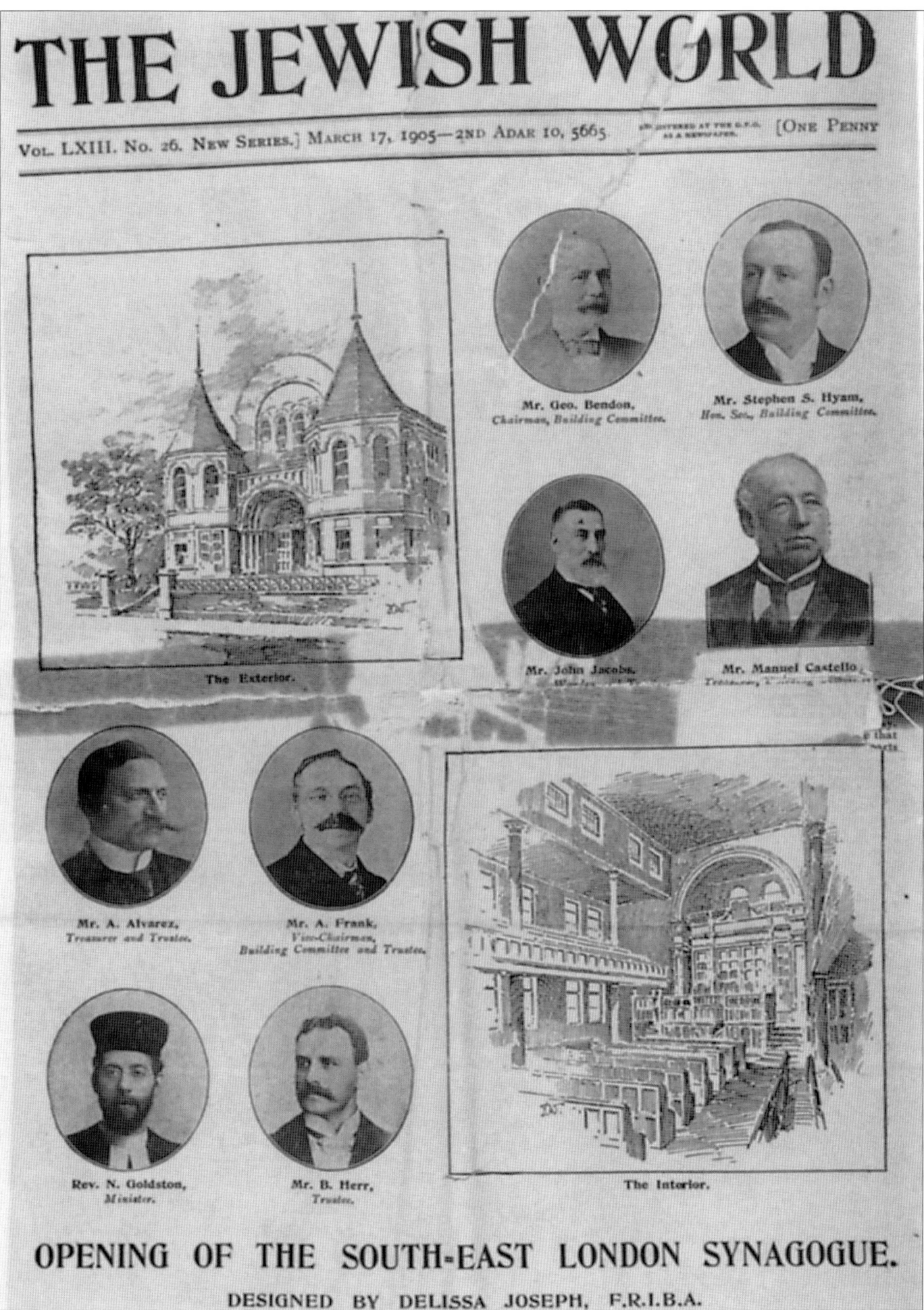

THE JEWISH WORLD

Vol. LXIII. No. 26. New Series.] March 17, 1905—2nd Adar 10, 5665   [One Penny

The Exterior.

Mr. Geo. Bendon,
Chairman, Building Committee.

Mr. Stephen S. Hyam,
Hon. Sec., Building Committee.

Mr. John Jacobs,

Mr. Manuel Castello,

Mr. A. Alvarez,
Treasurer and Trustee.

Mr. A. Frank,
Vice-Chairman,
Building Committee and Trustee.

Rev. N. Goldston,
Minister.

Mr. B. Herr,
Trustee.

The Interior.

OPENING OF THE SOUTH-EAST LONDON SYNAGOGUE.

DESIGNED BY DELISSA JOSEPH, F.R.I.B.A.

Fig. 113 *South East London Synagogue.* A later photograph of the interior - view towards the redesigned ark. (Photograph courtesy of Dr. S. Cohen.)

Fig. 114 *South East London Synagogue.* The rebuilt Synagogue, now a Kingdom Hall of Jehovah's Witnesses. The building is immaculately maintained.

reputation of being a flogger, wielding his cane mercilessly, but "*each one of his pupils, to this day, knows and understands the services*"!

Every Sabbath boys from a Jewish industrial school in Lewisham marched to the Synagogue, where they formed a choir.★ By 1896 there were 70 children taking part in the classes.

The hut was eventually condemned, and a new synagogue had to be built to serve the 130 Jewish families in the locality. The United Synagogue gave a loan to the young community and a parcel of land on the Hatcham Estate, belonging to the Haberdashers company, was acquired on an 81-year lease, at a ground rent of £25 per annum.

The New Cross Synagogue was consecrated in March, 1905. It was a rather strange-looking building (described as Romanesque), designed by Delissa Joseph. Its exterior was of red brick with stone dressings (Figs. 111 and 112). Initially, the interior was of panelled white wood and the rails of the Almemar similarly white (see Fig. 111).

By 1920 a Hazzan, the Revd. A. Lewis, had been appointed, a (mixed) choir was formed "*and the services took on a beauty and dignity which ... could never be forgotten.*"[94] The soprano in the choir was the BBC's 'Girl with the Golden Voice' Marjorie Savage.

The interior was remodelled in 1921, as shown in Fig. 113. Iron gates were added to the ark and the Wardens now faced the congregation. The Almemar and rails above were straightened. As at the Central and Borough Synagogues, a circular candelabrum was placed by the ark, one candle representing each soldier lost during the Great War. With its stained glass windows, gold chandeliers and the ark decorated with gold leaf , "*the effect was the most beautiful and dignified Synagogue one has ever seen.*"[94]

Mr. Goldston retired in 1934, after 45 years of service, and was replaced by the Revd. H. Bornstein, previously of the North West London Synagogue, Caversham Road (see Fig. 131). He in turn left in 1938 for Hampstead Garden Suburb and was replaced by the Revd. Simeon Isaacs, who later moved to the Central Synagogue (see p. 73).

In 1939 membership was at its highest, being 294 men and 128 women, with 93 children attending classes.

★According to the communal history,[94] but I can find no mention of such a totally Jewish school in the *Year Books*.

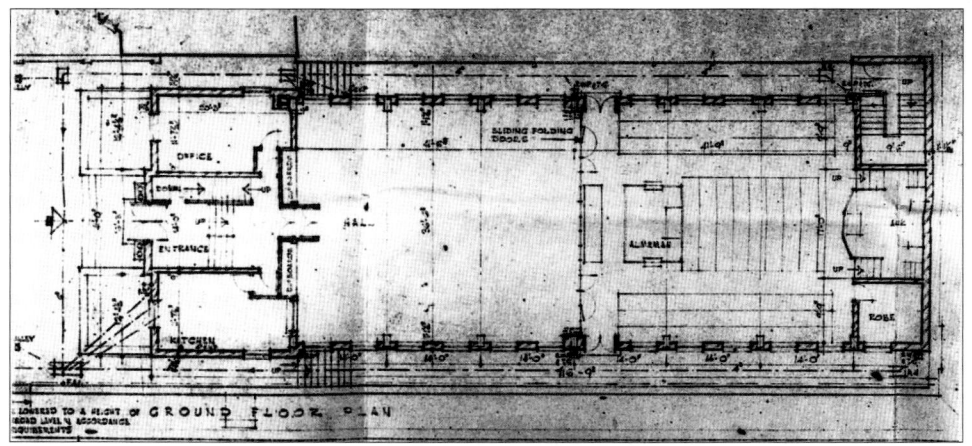

Fig. 115 *South East London Synagogue.* Plan of the interior of the last Synagogue of the congregation. The Almemar is towards the back of the Synagogue with fixed seating before it. Large folding doors lead into the hall behind, which seems of roughly equal size to the Synagogue, giving extra room during the High Holy days. (Photograph courtesy of Dr. S. Cohen.)

On Friday night, 27th December, 1940, the Synagogue was bombed and destroyed.

The Everlasting Light, however, continued to burn in the ruins and was to be used again, at 117 Lewisham Way. As Mr. Isaacs was now a Chaplain, the Revd. (later Lord) I. Jakobovits was appointed temporary minister.

A temporary hut was later erected on the old site and consecrated in 1946. A new building was erected in 1956 by the firm of C.P. Roberts, which had built the first Synagogue. The rather plain neo-Georgian exterior concealed a Synagogue, hall, classrooms and a kitchen (Figs. 114 and 115).

There were still 181 male members in 1970 but, by the 1980s, the congregation had declined and the Synagogue closed in 1985 when services could no longer be sustained, with only 56 male members.

The stained glass windows can be seen today in the Woodside Park Synagogue.

THE LIBERAL JEWISH SYNAGOGUE

HILL STREET, NW1,

LATER ST. JOHN'S WOOD ROAD, NW8

One of the earliest descriptions of the origins of the Liberal Jewish Synagogue is to be found in *The Reform Movement in Judaism* by D. Philipson.[61] This work, by an avowed Liberal and 'anti-orientalist', is of interest because it was written at the time of the foundation of the movement. Another useful article is by S. Bayme, entitled *Claude Montefiore, Lily Montagu and the origins of the Jewish Religious Union*.[95] For a description of its prayer books, see *Prayer Book Reform in Europe* by Professor J.J. Petuchowski.[64] In addition, the archivist of the Liberal Jewish Synagogue, Mr. B. Diamond, kindly made archival material available to me.

By the end of the 19th century, the West London Synagogue was no longer a force for change. Its minister, the Revd. Morris Joseph, had been vetoed by Dr. Adler for the post of minister at Hampstead because he would not pray for the restoration of sacrifices. He was a traditionalist and worked for communal harmony. He pressed for the retention of *Kashrut*, and said prayers for the restoration of Jewish statehood in Palestine. He took part in communal appeals together with his orthodox colleagues.

The foundation of the Jewish Religious Union was motivated by many factors. One was the drift away from religious observance, which it hoped to stem. Another was the arrival from Germany of 'higher Biblical criticism', the teachings of which were unacceptable to the relatively moderate Chief Rabbinate, while even Morris Joseph was against teaching Biblical criticism from the pulpit or to school children. Thirdly, according to Bayme,[95] social conflict, such as the position of women in Judaism and in the country generally, the Suffragette movement, and the need to suppress the white slave trade, united Jews of all theological positions, especially those of a modernising tendency from the United Synagogue and the Reform movement.

In order to attract Jews for whom the Sabbath had become a workday, Sabbath afternoon services began on 22nd February, 1890, at the Town Hall in Hampstead, conducted by Morris Joseph (then returned from Liverpool) with an order of service arranged by him.

The usual afternoon service was said but in the benediction "Retsei" the word 'songs' was substituted for 'burnt offerings'. The Hebrew portion of the services was followed by prayers, psalms and hymns in English (also used in Sabbath afternoon services at the orthodox New West End Synagogue). Men and women sat on the same level, but separately. Instrumental music and a mixed choir were used.

Philipson notes that these services were more 'reformed' than those at the Reform Synagogue.[61]

The preachers, besides Joseph, were the ministers of the West London Synagogue, as well as Claude Montefiore and Israel Abrahams (Simeon

Singer's son-in-law). These services lasted three years until Joseph was elected to the West London Synagogue.

After this, attempts were made to hold services on Sunday, as was already the practice in Berlin and in some cities in America, "*to form a bridge of religious fellowship and common worship across the gulf which has so far separated monotheists who are Jews, and monotheists who are not Jews.*"[96] These also failed and were discontinued, but the next attempt was more successful.

The Jewish Religious Union was organised in 1902 with Claude Montefiore as President. Simeon Singer and Lily Montagu were Vice-Presidents and A.A. Green, J.F. Stern and Morris Joseph were on the committee. The object of the Union was "*to provide means of deepening the religious spirit amongst those members of the Jewish community who are not at present in sympathy with the synagogue services or who are unable to attend them.*"[61]

For this latter reason services were again held on Saturday afternoons in rented rooms, usually at the Great Central (now Landmark) Hotel at Marylebone Station.[62] Prayers were in the vernacular, accompanied by musical instruments, and seating was mixed. Needless to say, the Chief Rabbi refused to allow these services to be held in a United Synagogue. Simeon Singer preached at the first service.

Eventually all the United Synagogue ministers withdrew from the movement. Morris Joseph however remained. An offer of hospitality from the West London Synagogue was obtained, but with certain provisos – amongst which were separate seating for men and women and what looks likes a fairly traditional Sabbath afternoon service – a reading from the scroll, Amidah, Olenu and Kaddish. These terms were unacceptable to the Jewish Religious Union, despite the pleadings of Mr. Joseph.

Fig. 116 *Liberal Jewish Synagogue*. The exterior of the original Synagogue in Hill Street, off Dorset Square, NW1, formerly a chapel. I am not sure when this photograph was taken - the building certainly looks very disused. (Photograph courtesy of Mr. Brian Diamond, archivist, The Liberal Jewish Synagogue.)

113

Fig. 117 *Liberal Jewish Synagogue*. The photograph of the interior shows the building in use as a synagogue. The Galleries were presumably for mixed seating when the ground floor was full. A prayer, in Hebrew and English, can be seen above the curtained ark – I presume the Prayer for the Royal Family. The Reading desk faced the congregation and probably doubled as a pulpit. (Photograph courtesy of Mr. Brian Diamond, archivist, The Liberal Jewish Synagogue.)

Branch services also commenced in the East End in 1903. In 1909 the committee, now without orthodox members, called itself 'The Jewish Religious Union for the Advancement of Liberal Judaism'. In 1911 services began in a disused chapel in Hill Street, NW1 (Figs. 116 and 117). In the same year, Rabbi Mattuck arrived from the Hebrew Union College.

By 1925 the membership outnumbered that of the West London Synagogue and a new Synagogue was opened in St. John's Wood (Fig. 118). The building had a handsome facade on the St. John's Wood Road, with a large Ionic portico of white stone extending up the entire facade of the building. The main walls were of red brick with bands of white stone. The architect M. Joseph described this as a fine and satisfying structure, the interior (Fig. 119) having "*a dignified beauty unknown to those of greater architectural pretension and elaboration.*"[44] I found it rather plain and too 'auditorium-like', though the ark was more ornate, of classical design, and reminiscent of that at the Golders Green United Synagogue.

The main auditorium had four recesses with angled corner walls (Fig. 120). The ceiling had a large dome. The walls were of a textured plaster surface and originally painted off-white. The building suffered damage in the War and, though rebuilt, was later replaced by a large modern synagogue

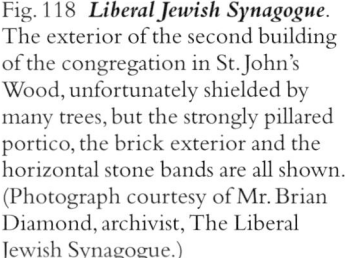

Fig. 118 *Liberal Jewish Synagogue*. The exterior of the second building of the congregation in St. John's Wood, unfortunately shielded by many trees, but the strongly pillared portico, the brick exterior and the horizontal stone bands are all shown. (Photograph courtesy of Mr. Brian Diamond, archivist, The Liberal Jewish Synagogue.)

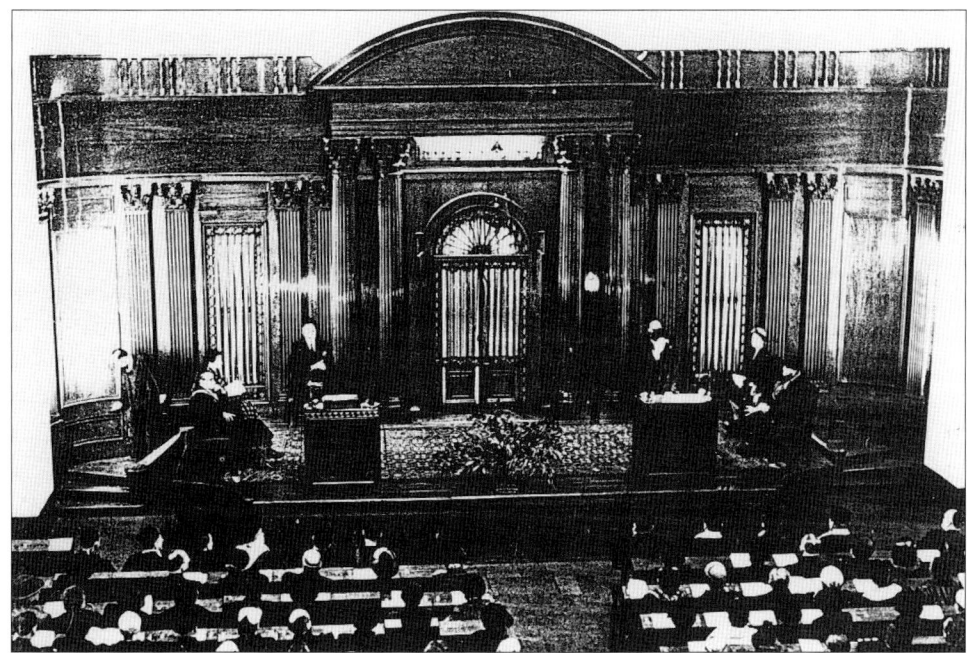

Fig. 119 *Liberal Jewish Synagogue*. The view towards the ark. With its polished wood and metal gate, the interior is reminiscent of that at the Golders Green United Synagogue. (Photograph courtesy of Mr. Brian Diamond, archivist, The Liberal Jewish Synagogue.)

and housing complex on the same site. There is still the massive and imposing portico of the previous building, but the interior is light and colourful and one of the most delightful of the modern synagogues in London.

For the early leaders of Liberal Judaism in England, see *Montefiore, Montagu and Mattuck, Pioneers of Liberal Judaism* by Rabbi Rayner[62] and *Some Recollections of Claude Goldsmid Montefiore* by Lucy Cohen.[97]

Claude Goldsmid Montefiore

Claude Montefiore (1858-1938) was one of the first Jews to graduate from Oxford University. There, he was encouraged to study Jewish texts from a critical perspective. Later studying in Berlin, he met Solomon Schechter, whom he subsequently brought to England. According to Bayme,[95] Montefiore's concept of Judaism, first described in the 1892 Hibbert Lectures, was a mixture of Biblical criticism which he wholeheartedly accepted, mysticism rather than rationalism, and a desire to study and learn from Christianity. Montefiore admired the mysticism and faith of Christianity and felt that Judaism should incorporate parts of it, including the New Testament, to attain the complete truth. These views were of

Fig. 120 *Liberal Jewish Synagogue*. The view towards the back of the Synagogue, showing the pews arranged in the Reform fashion, facing the eastern wall. (Photograph courtesy of Mr. Brian Diamond, archivist, The Liberal Jewish Synagogue.)

Fig. 121 *Rabbi Dr. Israel Mattuck*, the first ordained minister of the congregation. (Photograph courtesy of Mr. Brian Diamond, archivist, The Liberal Jewish Synagogue.)

course totally contrary to orthodox belief.

Rabbi Gollancz, in his New Year sermon for 1910 at the Bayswater Synagogue, was heavily critical of supplementary religious services, held on Saturday afternoons. He felt that the ordinary services should be sufficient and, if not, should be made to suffice the spiritual needs of the worshipper. He felt, as did Morris Joseph, that these were a signal *"for sects and schisms"* and that *"the Union was directed against the very principles and foundation of our Creed."*[76] Dr. Adler detected a hint of Unitarianism in the Jewish Religious Union.

It is to be noted that, while C.G. Montefiore was thanked for his help by Rabbi Singer in the Preface to early editions of his *Authorised Prayer Book*, Montefiore's name was deleted from later editions in an act of historical revisionism and replaced by 'an accomplished scholar'. Perhaps his second marriage – to a Gentile – was the final straw in his relationship with the orthodox community, who saw him *"not only as an innovator but as one who undermined the authority of their religion and weakened its moving spirit, which was to keep the Jewish community united."*[97]

Montefiore was an avowed anti-Zionist and felt himself to be English – calling them "my own people" – and was also heavily criticised by Zionists, both orthodox or not. Even the troubles in Germany did not alter his anti-Zionist stance.[95] Mr H.A.L. Fisher, who wrote the Foreword to his biography, called him *"a saint. Religion was his life, profound, exalted and all-pervading".*[97]

Lily Montagu (see Fig. 177)

Lily Montagu, the daughter of the first Lord Swaythling, though deeply religious,[62] was an early rebel against what she perceived as the subservient role of the woman in Judaism and was a strong supporter of Montefiore. According to Bayme, she *"quarrelled bitterly with her father over the ability of orthodoxy to stem the drift towards religious indifference. As early as 1905 she urged granting women the right to lead services and preach from the pulpit. She never suffered the invective that opponents of the Jewish Religious Union hurled against Montefiore."*[95] They both regarded social issues as having a moral and a religious dimension, including the campaign against the white slave trade and the Suffragette movement.

Rabbi Israel Isadore Mattuck (Fig. 121)

Israel Isadore Mattuck was born in Lithuania in 1883 and was taken to America as a child, educated first at Harvard, then at the Hebrew Union College, graduating in 1910. In 1911 he came to England to become minister at the Liberal Jewish Synagogue in Hill Street. He introduced confirmation at 16 years of age. Under Dr. Mattuck the congregation became the largest in Britain, with 1,300 members in 1927. He was a great propagandist for Liberal Judaism, both nationally and internationally, a prolific author and broadcaster, as well as editor of the Liberal Jewish prayer book. Later editions contained 26 different services to avoid repetition. A description of his life is to be found in the *Liberal Jewish Monthly* (memorial number) for June 1954.

THE NORTH WEST LONDON SYNAGOGUE

YORK ROAD, NW5,

LATER CAVERSHAM ROAD, NW5

Recent histories of Kentish Town devote no more than a few lines to the now defunct Jewish community. I have been working locally at what was a former workhouse for the last twenty-eight years and have driven past the two former synagogues of the congregation many times before realising their origin.

The arrival of the Jews in Kentish Town probably coincided with migration of Jews from the East End in search of economic opportunity and better housing, the Kentish Town Road being a prime example of housing 'over the shop'.

The North London Railway from Blackwall reached Camden Town in 1850 and the line from Kingsland to Broad Street opened late in 1865.[98] An extension from Camden Town to Hampstead Heath and beyond passed into Kentish Town West, the station there opening in 1867. The Northern line from Camden Town to Archway came later, opening in 1907, with two stations in Kentish Town connecting with trains to Moorgate and Old Street.[99]

Camden Town and Kentish Town never seem to have attracted Jews in the same number as Canonbury, Highbury and Dalston, but at least fifty families with seventy children resided locally, who would have had to worship at the North London Synagogue, Barnsbury.

The first synagogue at York Road, Kentish Town

The first organised Jewish congregation in Kentish Town – the North West London Synagogue at Clifton Hall – opened for public worship on Sunday, 18th May, 1890 (by the reckoning of the Hebrew Calendar Anno Mundi 5650). The site of the Synagogue is given as York Road (now York Way), Camden Road. The Post Office Directory for 1890 shows 143-147 York Road as the site of William Gittens' goods depository, just before Clifton Road (now called Cliff Road). The Directory for 1892 shows the North West London Synagogue lying between 143 and 147, with Mr. Gittens now described as an upholsterer. Clifton Road is where 153 would be. Clifton Hall is not listed in the Post Office Directory, either in York Road or Clifton Road; I can only conclude that it was part of Mr. Gittens' warehouse at 143-147 York Road. In the Ordnance Survey Map of 1894, Clifton Road is short, much of the south side being occupied by a reservoir. There does not seem to be a building recognisable as a separate hall.

Today, the site is still occupied by a large good depository lying on the Camden side of York Way, south of the Jews' Free School (Fig. 122).

The frontispiece of the Order of Service at the opening of the Synagogue is shown in Fig. 123. The name of the congregation in Hebrew is the direct equivalent of the English, that is, *Beis Haknesses* (House of Assembly) *Tsefonis*

Fig. 122 *North West London Synagogue.* Mr. Gittins' warehouse, the site of the first North West London Synagogue, York Road (now York Way).

Fig. 123 *North West London Synagogue.* Frontispiece for the Order of Service at the consecration of the first North West London Synagogue, Camden Road, 1890. (Courtesy of University College London.)

Fig. 124 *The Revd. Wolf Esterson,* minister at the North West London Synagogue from 1894 until 1899, and subsequently at the Hambro Synagogue. (Photograph courtesy of Dr. A. Goldberg, grandson of the Revd. Esterson.)

Maaravis (North West) *B'Kahal Kodesh* (in the Holy Congregation) *London Habiroh* (London the Capital). The Synagogue is described as *Mikdosh Me'at* – a small sanctuary. The Reverend Marcus Haines was not the minister of the congregation, but the Reader of the prestigious New West End Synagogue in Kensington. Mr. Davis was his choirmaster, hired for the day to beautify the service.

The Delegate Chief Rabbi, the Revd. Dr. Hermann Adler, preached the sermon and clergymen came from the Western, Hambro, Bayswater and Central Orthodox Synagogues; the Revd. Dr. Löwy of the Reform Synagogue also attended. The opening ceremony at Clifton Hall was fully described in the *Jewish World* and the *Jewish Chronicle,* of 23rd May 1890. The former is reproduced here:

"The consecration of this Synagogue – the latest addition to our metropolitan houses of prayer – in the Camden Road, took place on Sunday last, in the presence of numerous members and friends of the congregation, including many ladies. The hall which has been fitted up as a synagogue was profusely and beautifully decorated with various kinds of flowers, palms, ferns, &c., and presented quite a gala aspect. Among those present were the Revs. Dr. Adler, A. Löwy, D. Fay, and H. Gollancz. The service was impressively intoned by the Revd. M. Haines, and the choral portions were rendered by the choir of the New West End Synagogue in a manner which has rarely been equalled, and certainly never excelled. The choir was in the western gallery, whilst the organ was on the Almemar, and although no means of communication existed between the choir and their director, the numerous psalms and hymns, with fully choral afternoon service, were sung throughout with beauty of tone and delicacy of expression which, in some of the pieces, reached perfection. Mr. D.M. Davis (the choirmaster) directed the choir, and presided at the organ with his usual efficiency. The music was selected from the works of Mombach, Salaman, D.M. Davis, and other composers. The Psalms used were xxx., c., and xxiv.

"Mincha having been read, the Revd. Dr. Hermann Adler, who dedicated the synagogue to its holy purpose, preached a sermon from the text, "And they shall make Me a sanctuary and I will dwell in the midst of them" (Ex. xxv. 8).

"After the prayer for the Queen and Royal Family, and one for the wardens and founders of the synagogue, the ceremony was concluded with the singing of Adon Olam."

After the service, light refreshments were served in the Committee Room. Dr. Adler spoke and Dr. Löwy of the West London Synagogue responded for 'the clergy'. The Revd. J. Friedlander proposed the toast to "the Committee". Evidence suggests that he was the first minister and he certainly taught the children. The next minister on record to this small congregation was the Revd. Woolf Esterson (Fig. 124). Born in Edinburgh in 1872, he was educated in London at the Jews' Free School (then in the East End) and at Jews' College. He served the congregation from 1894 to 1899, when he became minister to the better known Hambro Synagogue. He died in 1958.[100] The late Dayan, Dr. Myer Lew, was his son-in-law.

The second Synagogue at Caversham Road, Kentish Town

Perhaps the lease on Clifton Hall had expired and could not be renewed. A site for a new building was secured in Caversham Road on land adjoining, and belonging to, the Midland Railway. The building was designed by A. Schonfield of Great Tower Street and seated 250 worshippers; it cost £1300 to build. Although it contained no Gallery, in accordance with orthodox practice men sat on one side of the Synagogue and women on the other.

The frontispiece for the Order of Service is shown in Fig. 125a. The opening ceremony had been delayed by over a month as the synagogue was still in an unfinished state. Sir Marcus Samuel, Bart, who opened the Synagogue, was the Chairman of the Shell Oil Company. The Order of Service contains an Appeal (Fig. 125b).

The service of consecration was again enthusiastically described in the *Jewish Chronicle* of 26th October, 1900. On this occasion we have the good fortune of having drawings of the exterior (Fig. 126) and the interior (Fig. 127).

Despite the small dimensions of the Synagogue, it was, to my eye, a building with a most beautiful and ornate interior, while the exterior clearly shows that it was a Jewish house of prayer.

A census of religious attendance on the first day of Passover 1903, coinciding with Easter Sunday, showed a total of 152 people attending the North West London Synagogue, as against 275 at the North London Synagogue in Lofting Road, N1; 1042 at the Central Synagogue in Great Portland Street; 376 men, women and children at the Western Synagogue, off the Haymarket; and the smaller Synagogue at Maiden Lane near Covent Garden managed 69 worshippers.

Of this small community, many must have been local shopkeepers.

Jewish traders in the Kentish Town Road
(taken from the Post Office Directory of 1900)

1c Isaac Disch – watchmaker
3 H. Weingold – hairdresser
55 L. Levien – confectioner
93 Barney Barnett – tailor
145 Milly Levy – fruiterer
157 Salmon Josephs & Son – oilmen
193 Barnett Isaacs – tailor
197 Salmon & Gluckstein – tobacconist
199 David Levy – fruiterer
284 Reuben Goldring – confectioner
314 Salmon Josephs & Son – oilmen
315 Ephraim Hart – china dealer
343 Robert Katz – hairdresser
351 Sally Freedman – tobacconist
389 Joseph Lipman – tailor

Incidentally, after the opening of the Synagogue, the congregation held a reception at which light refreshments were served, supplied by Messrs L. Levien of 55 Kentish Town Road, so there was a kosher confectioner or grocer there even at that time.

The Ministers

Revd. Esterson was succeeded as minister by the Revd. Walter Levin (Fig. 128) who was in post at the time of the consecration of the second, and final, home of the congregation in Caversham Road.

Walter Levin left in 1903 for the North London Synagogue in Lofting

Fig. 125 *North West London Synagogue.* (a) Frontispiece for the Order of Service at the opening of the second synagogue, Caversham Road, in 1900 and (b) an Appeal. (Courtesy of University College London.)

Fig. 126 *North West London Synagogue.* The exterior. (Drawn by Mr. Keith Ruggles from an original photograph in the *Jewish Chronicle.*)

Fig. 127 *North West London Synagogue.* The interior. (Drawn by Mr. Keith Ruggles from an original photograph in the *Jewish Chronicle.*)

Fig. 128   Fig. 129

Fig. 130   Fig. 131   Fig. 132

Fig. 128 *The Revd. Walter Levin*, minister of the North West London Synagogue, Caversham Road, from 1900 until 1903. (Reproduced by kind permission of the *Jewish Chronicle*.)

Fig. 129 *The Revds. S. Lipson* (left) and *Mendel Brown* (right), both of the North West London Synagogue, Caversham Road.

Fig. 130 *The Revd. E. Drukker*, minister at the North West London Synagogue from 1911 until 1915. (Reproduced from *The Jewish Communities of North East England* by Lewis Olsover (1980), published by Ashley Mark Publishing Co., Gateshead.)

Fig. 131 *The Revd. H. Bornstein*, the minister at the North West London Synagogue from 1932 until 1934. (Reproduced from *The History of the Hampstead Garden Suburb Synagogue* by I. Grose, published by the congregation.)

Fig. 132 *Rabbi B.D. Klein*, the minister of the North West London Synagogue from 1935 to 1965. (Photograph courtesy of his daughter, Mrs. Suffrin.)

Road (later becoming minister at the Bayswater Synagogue). He was succeeded by the Revd. S. Lipson (Fig. 129; see also Appendix 5a) who left in 1910 for the Hammersmith Synagogue. In the same year the Revd. B. Michelson of Newcastle was appointed at Caversham Road. Mr. Michelson was born in Middlesborough and was educated at Jews' College and University College London. He had previously served at Newport, Brisbane and Newcastle. From 1911 until 1947 he was the Welfare Minister to the United Synagogue, a member of Stepney Borough Council, and chaplain to Wormwood Scrubs Prison, devoting his life to prisoners' welfare and to the poor in Stepney.[101]

In 1911 the Revd. E. Drukker, who had been educated at Owen's School (then in Islington) and subsequently at Jews' College and University College London, was appointed. After four years he departed for Newcastle-Upon-Tyne (Fig. 130), where he spent the rest of his ministerial career.[102]

During the remainder of the First World War the post remained unfilled until, in 1918, the Revd. Mendel Brown was appointed (see Fig. 129; see also Appendix 5a). Mr. Brown had been educated at Portsmouth Grammar School, then at Aria College, Portsmouth (for the training of Jewish clergy) and finally at Jews' College and University College London, subsequently becoming an assistant minister at the East London Synagogue. He stayed at Caversham Road until 1932, when he made what proved to be an unfortunate career move – going to Shanghai, where he served as minister to the Ohel Rachel Synagogue. At the time, the Jewish community there was prosperous, with Sassoons and Kadouries in their midst. In 1942 he and his wife were interned by the Japanese, his wife dying due to the hardships endured in the camp. Mr. Brown died four years after the end of the Second World War, at the age of 64 years.[103]

Fig. 133 *The North West London Synagogue* after conversion into an architect's studio.

The next minister was the Revd. H. Bornstein (Fig. 131), serving from 1932 until 1934. He was later minister at the South East London Synagogue in New Cross and at the Hampstead Garden Suburb Synagogue. He died on active service during the Second World War in the Middle East.

He was succeeded in 1935 by Rabbi B.D. Klien (or Klein), MA (Fig. 132), who served till at least 1965. He lived in Tufnell Park Road* as the house next door to the synagogue was used for community purposes and also housed the caretaker. Rabbi Klien was renowned as a scholar and a gentleman of humble disposition who deserved a larger audience than that available at Caversham Road. He retired to Israel, and died there.

Rabbi Klien's daughter, Mrs. Suffrin, and other congregants have told me a little about the life of the congregation. There was a kosher butcher's shop in Drummond Street, Euston, and a kosher delicatessen in Camden Town just north of the underground station, behind where Sainsbury's is today. There were a few observant families locally with whom Rabbi Klien could study, but the congregation consisted mainly of shopkeepers who came early to Sabbath prayers, then returned to their businesses, occasionally having to be dragged back to keep the quorum going. Eventually, though, services could no longer be held on Friday nights and the few remaining members walked the short distance to the Highgate Synagogue on the Archway Road, itself now transferred to Highgate Village.

The last minister at Caversham Road was the Revd. L. Rosenberg. By 1975 the congregation had vanished and the building was abandoned, then vandalised. It was eventually purchased by an architect who put a new, larger skylight on the roof. The building still stands today (Fig. 133).

* In a recently published local history of Kentish Town it was stated that he lived next door to the Synagogue, but this is incorrect.

THE WOOLWICH AND PLUMSTEAD SYNAGOGUE

ANGLESEA ROAD, SE18

The Woolwich and Plumstead Synagogue closed in 1998, after over 100 years of Jewish communal life. The early editions of the *Jewish Year Book* list two congregations, one in Woolwich and another in Plumstead, the latter having more members. The addresses for the many congregations of the Federation of Synagogues were not given in early editions of the *Year Book*. I am indebted to Mr. E. Freedman, of Blackheath, for this history of the congregation.*

In the census taken in 1841 only five or six Jewish families are listed in the area. Late in the last century a Polish immigrant, Mr. Gluck, was a teacher of Hebrew in Prospect Place, implying a large enough Jewish community to warrant this.

Woolwich is a chartered market town with large open-air public markets, very suitable for peddlers. The area is easily accessible to East London via the ferry and the foot tunnel under the Thames. There was much employment to be had there, especially before the First World War, with the largest motorcycle factory in Europe, the firm of Siemens and, of course, the Arsenal, which churned out munitions for the Empire twenty-four hours a day and employed a vast number of people on a three-shift system. The Royal Artillery had a large garrison there. All these provided commercial opportunity for tailors and stall-holders. Surrounded by parks and woodland, the town was a welcome escape from the lack of open space in the East End.

The Woolwich congregation began in 1892, holding services in the Drill

Fig. 134 *Woolwich Synagogue.* The former St. Andrew's Church in Anglesea Road was the home of the congregation from 1925 until 1964. A Hebrew inscription is above the doors. (Courtesy of Mr. Albert Rosenberg; drawn by Keith Ruggles.)

Fig. 135 *Woolwich Synagogue.* The original ark from the first Synagogue on the Anglesea Road site. (Photograph courtesy of Susan Goldstein.)

* Personal communication.

Fig. 136 *Woolwich Synagogue*. The exterior of the new Synagogue. (Photograph courtesy of Mr. E. Freedman.)

Fig. 137 *Woolwich Synagogue*. The interior showing the Reader's desk and the Almemar at the eastern end of the Synagogue. Although this orthodox Synagogue was consecrated in 1961, this arrangement was used to increase the number of seats available. The women's section was behind a low, wooden barrier, but there also seems to have been some discrimination in the type of seats available for them. (Photograph courtesy of Susan Goldstein.)

Hall, Beresford Street and, later, in the Assembly Hall, Woolwich New Road, as well as in a house in Plumstead Road. By 1899 the congregation had moved to Brewer Street and, by 1906, to a former Welsh chapel in Parsons Hill.*

In the London Metropolitan Archives there are plans, dated 1906, drawn by Lewis Solomon for a purpose-built synagogue in Peakes Road. A single-storey building, 50' long by 25' wide, was proposed, with the Almemar at the front and the Ladies' section behind a grill at the rear. It was never built and planning consent was withdrawn in 1909.

By 1913 the two congregations had amalgamated, a converted house at 28, Beresford Street becoming the Woolwich and Plumstead Synagogue. In 1925 the former St. Andrew's Presbyterian Church in Anglesea Road became the penultimate home of the congregation (Figs. 134 and 135). In 1964 a new purpose-built Synagogue was completed and opened on this same site (Figs. 136 and 137); it was a fully equipped community centre with classrooms. Many of the members were shopkeepers, often of large stores,

* Information provided courtesy of Greenwich Public Libraries

Fig. 138 *The Revd. Gottlieb Rosenberg* pictured at the consecration of the last synagogue in Woolwich. (Photograph from the *Kentish Times*, dated 1964, courtesy of Greenwich Public Libraries and Mr. Albert Rosenberg)

but their children grew up and left the area. At its peak the congregation numbered 280 members, with fifty children attending classes, but at the closure of the Synagogue in 1998, only fifty people were left, mainly elderly; the classrooms were disused.

Reverend Gottlieb Rosenberg (Fig. 138)

Revd. Rosenberg, who already possessed Rabbinical ordination, arrived in Woolwich from Stabin, Poland, in 1910 to be the Hazzan of the community. Soon after arriving, he amalgamated the two congregations that he was to serve for the next 55 years, through two world wars and the move to a new, purpose-built synagogue. He remained so long in this post that he taught three generations of congregants!

The community – tradesmen, lawyers and doctors – offered hospitality to local Jewish soldiers stationed at the garrison, who were also always welcome in Revd. Rosenberg's home. His wife, Sarah, ran the local delicatessen, which was next door to the kosher butcher's shop of Mr. Woolmark. One of his sons, Louis Rosenberg, became minister at Staines, serving there also for 55 years, and his son-in-law, the Revd. S. Venitt, was a minister at Finsbury Park and Hammersmith Synagogue, but for only 50 years.

Mr. Rosenberg retired in 1965, having seen the new Synagogue open in 1964. The Revd. M. Gingold was the last minister and also served for many years.

THE WEST HAM (ASSOCIATE) SYNAGOGUE

EARLHAM GROVE, E7

Many communal histories are no more than a simple dry recitation of facts and dates. Some contain photographs, but very few give the 'feel' of the communities they describe. The recent history of the West Ham community by the local historian Howard Bloch is, however, a much larger book than most, and profusely illustrated.[104] It gives a lively account of events, is full of personal anecdotes, and brings the community to life; it is a model of what such histories should be like. The love of the members for the congregation and for their religion stands out.

West Ham was transformed from a collection of small villages into a major town with a large industrial area around docks and factories, whereas East Ham remained a largely residential suburb. Prosperous Jews moved into the larger houses of Stratford, Forest Gate, Manor Park and East Ham, while poorer Jews moved to the area of the street markets and small shops in Canning Town. Forest Gate in particular was a very desirable residential district.

The Order of Service for the consecration of the West Ham (Associate) Synagogue in Forest Gate, dated 9th April, 1911, contains the history of the congregation from 1897. At that time Jews were already residing in Stratford, but the nearest synagogue in the East End was four miles away. For the years 1897, 1898 and 1899 adverts were placed in the Jewish press announcing that services for the High Holy days were being held in a local hall, the Scrolls being borrowed from the New Synagogue. A *Cheder*, with

Fig. 139 *West Ham Synagogue.* The exterior, from a pamphlet produced at the opening in 1911.

Fig. 140 *West Ham Synagogue.*
The original interior before
reconstruction and enlargement,
at the time of the opening of the
Synagogue.

twenty five pupils, was started in 1897 in a house purchased in Forest Gate.
Services commenced in 1900, Mr. G. Rosenthal being the Reader. As the
congregation increased in number, the house became too small and 95,
Earlham Grove was purchased for £1,200.★ The adjacent house, No. 97, was
purchased a few years later, in 1904.

By 1908 the Appeals Committee included not only Rabbi Mendelsohn
(see below), but also the Revd. Morris Joseph, by then senior minister at the
West London Synagogue (things were different in those days).

The building works commenced in August, 1910, and the foundation
stone laid on 27th October. The Chief Rabbi conducted the opening
service, together with the Revd. Solomon Levy and the Choir of the New
Synagogue. Among those present were the Reverends Joseph, Stern and D.
Wasserzug.

The exterior of the building, shown in a contemporary photograph, can
be seen in Fig. 139. The arch over the main door has, in metallic letters, the
words "How goodly are thy tents, O Jacob". The front is recessed and, at the
sides, are further doors, presumably leading to the Galleries. On examination
of the photograph, it would appear that there was a dome over the roof.

The *Jewish World,* quoted by Bloch, noted that "*the Synagogue is designed in
the Romanesque style and will accommodate 426 ladies and gentlemen. The interior
presents a handsome appearance. The ark and Almemar (all in one at the eastern end)
are of solid English oak.*" (The ark is actually a large 'chest' built into an apse with
no gallery, but two large tablets above.) "*The exterior is of yellow facing bricks with
red handmade brick bands and semicircular arches over the door and windows.*"[104]

The *Jewish Chronicle* further noted that "*the windows are of stained glass, the
portion above the ark a work of rare beauty.*" Prayers, presumably for the Royal
family, can be seen on either side of the ark.

The interior is not ornate and was built in a simpler (and cheaper)
manner than many of the other late Victorian synagogues, but the ark and
Almemar had a dignified appearance (Fig. 140).

In 1927 a communal hall and classrooms were built, again to a design by

★ A matinée at the Borough Theatre
in Stratford had raised £250 towards
the cost. This theatre was owned by a
relative of the Synagogue Treasurer's
wife and two concerts were given
there, gratis. The architect of the
West Ham Synagogue, B. Crewe
(who also designed the Golders
Green Hippodrome) had trained
in the office of Frank Matcham, the
renowned theatre architect, who had
designed the Borough Theatre.

Crewe, the classrooms arranged around a large hall. A kitchen was installed in the basement, with a lift to serve the floors above.

In 1933 the Synagogue was enlarged to the design of C.J. Eprile (who also designed the new Cricklewood and Hendon Synagogues). Nearly 200 extra seats were provided, and also a choir gallery (the mixed choir had originally sung at the back of the Ladies' Gallery).

This wonderful history tells how, during the Second World War, the community established a home for refugee children and maintained close links with its evacuee children in Cornwall. Several members were killed when a V2 rocket bomb fell opposite the Synagogue; it also partially demolished the minister's residence.

Bloch notes that, by the 1960s and 1970s, the Jewish population was very much in decline; the Jewish shopkeepers had retired, streets were being redeveloped, and members of the congregation were moving further east. The Hebrew classes ceased in 1975 – by then, only 12 children attended. In August 1984 the Synagogue and its Scrolls were destroyed by fire.

The number of male seat holders peaked at 561 in 1950, but had declined to 296 in 1970. Today, the congregation worships in the former youth synagogue on the same site, which had been opened in 1959 by Dayan M. Swift, the minister, Revd. G. Schneider, and the Hazzan M. Woolf, and whose ark and seats had been made by one of the members.

The Reverend, later Rabbi, later Dayan Louis Mendelsohn

In 1903 the Revd. L. Mendelsohn, MA, was appointed as minister to the congregation. He passed the examination for the Rabbinical Diploma in 1913 and gave an interview for the *Jewish Chronicle*. "*His kindly twinkling eyes speak of hopefulness buoyed up by a strong sense of humour,*" wrote the correspondent. His sermons were said to be "*literary models of neat phraseology and delicately balanced periods.*"[105]

After leaving Jews' College (which was then in Tavistock House, the previous home of Charles Dickens), he travelled to Melbourne in Australia to take up his first ministerial post. "*On board ship was a Jewish girl, very 'frum' and very proper, who was to meet her fiancé at Melbourne, but when the boat arrived she absconded with the Second Officer.*"[105]

His next post was at Newcastle-Upon-Tyne, where he succeeded the Revd. S. Friedeberg (who later changed his name to Frampton because of anti-German agitation during the First World War). From there he moved to Bristol and, subsequently, to Dublin. Here, he notes, many Jews were 'packmen' (itinerant peddlers) and "*a feeling of irritation was worked up against them.*" (Jew-baiting was common in Limerick and Cork, but not in Dublin.)

He eventually returned to London to become Rabbi of the Burial Society (there is a large cemetery at Plashet, which has now closed). He was also Visitor to the Parochial Schools in Essex where, he noted, abandoned Jewish children were left "*to the Parish*".

His photograph, together with that of Hazzan Rosenthal, can be seen in Fig. 141 (see also Appendix 5a). These delightful montages, found in synagogal histories of the early twentieth century, show worthies with fierce moustaches, or more prosperous statesmen with beards, posed looking in different directions – men of substance all. Revd. Mendelsohn (later to become Dayan) is shown to be beardless and wearing a Roman collar, while Hazzan Rosenthal is probably wearing a blouse and a simple shawl-like *Tallit*, in the manner of the Continental Reformers, although he is bearded.

Fig. 141 *West Ham Synagogue.*
Past and present officers of the
Synagogue, including the Revd. L.
Mendelsohn and Hazzan Rosenthal.

THE EAST HAM AND MANOR PARK SYNAGOGUE

CARLYLE ROAD, E12

Fig. 142 *East Ham and Manor Park Synagogue*, Carlyle Road, E12. Now a Hindu temple, there is nothing to show that it was a Jewish house of worship. Replacement windows can be seen at the front. Were there stained glass windows here previously?

The East Ham and Manor Park Synagogue had been founded in 1900 (Fig. 142). There were 315 male seat holders in 1950 but, by 1970, only 184; by 1985 a mere eighty four remained.

The Synagogue closed in 1986; only fifty male and female members transferred to West Ham. Joint membership of the three local amalgamated congregations (West Ham, East Ham and Upton Park) currently is 131 men and 154 women.

THE BRONDESBURY SYNAGOGUE

CHEVENING ROAD, NW6

Two histories are available – a Silver Jubilee record written by Dayan Harris Lazarus in 1930[106] and a second, for the Golden Jubilee in 1955, by Rabbi Dr. A. Melinek.[107]

By the late nineteenth century, Jews had begun to settle in the new suburbs of Brondesbury and Willesden, encouraged by the opening of the Metropolitan railway. The nearest Synagogue in Hampstead was too far away to walk to and so, in 1900, meetings were held to discuss the building of a local Synagogue with the support of the United Synagogue and Dr. Löwy, the Emeritus minister of the West London Synagogue.

A site was found and the freeholder, Solomon Barnett, accepted a price far below its real value. Hebrew classes started at the Kilburn Grammar School. The Headmaster was the Revd. D. Wasserzug, later of the Dalston Synagogue. Mr. Barnett erected the usual corrugated iron hut on the land. A subsequent fund-raising Bazaar was opened by Lady Samuel and Mrs. Montefiore.

The Brondesbury Synagogue, designed by F.W. Marks, opened in 1905. At the ceremony were the Chief Rabbi and the Revd. Morris Joseph of the West London Synagogue, as well as the *Haham,* Dr. Gaster, the previous minister S. Rappaport, and the new, H. Lazarus, all of whom carried scrolls

Fig. 143 *Brondesbury Synagogue.* The facade. (Photograph produced from the semi-Jubilee history.[106])

Fig. 144 *Brondesbury Synagogue*. The interior, looking towards the ark, as built. The Moorish arch over the ark had space for a choir. The Reader's desk was at the eastern end of the Synagogue and the Wardens' benches faced the congregation. There were further arches over the Ladies Gallery. (Photograph produced from the semi-Jubilee history.[106])

into the new synagogue. The Secretary was Philip Ornstien.

The exterior was of red brick. Vaguely Moorish windows over the entrance doors and two large, copper-covered onion-domes, which terminated in long spikes rising out of a coronet, gave the building an oriental or Moorish character. There was a large circular window in the tableau with a central Star of David (Fig. 143). Because the synagogue lay on the crest of a hill, it was possible to provide a hall beneath the main building.

From the photograph of the interior, taken in 1930 (Fig. 144), it can be seen that the Reader's desk on the Almemar is at the eastern wall, with transverse seating up to the ark; the Wardens' seats face the congregation. The location of the Almemar was a matter of controversy, only settled when the architect informed the Committee that a central location would entail the loss of 40 seats.

At the opening of the Synagogue, the Almemar had two levels, the lower several steps below the upper, at the ark. Because the Galleries were so high, however, it was impossible to see the Reader's desk and pulpit from them.

At reconstruction, in 1924, the lower platform of the Almemar was elevated, improving vision, but stunting the appearance of the ark. At the same time the railings and tablets in the Choir Gallery above the ark were added.

The whole apse was surmounted by a Moorish-looking arch and the ceiling over the nave was vaulted above further Moorish arches. At the time of the semi-Jubilee, the Synagogue is recorded as being decorated in red, green, blue and gold. The Synagogue was destroyed by arson in 1965, but was subsequently completely rebuilt and reconsecrated. Membership had been stable between 1930 and 1950 at around 500 male seat-holders, but by 1970 had declined to half that number. Despite the good quality of housing locally, a general migration of Jews away from Brondesbury, Willesden,

Fig. 145 *Brondesbury Synagogue*. The Synagogue is now an Islamic school. The facade is unaltered but the Star of David in the large window over the entrance has been replaced by Islamic symbols. The building was rebuilt after a fire, but the Hebrew congregation closed shortly after.

Photo by Vaughan & Freeman
DAYAN H. M. LAZARUS, M.A.

Photo by Vaughan & Freeman
THE REV. N. PECKAR.

Fig. 146 *Dayan Harris Lazarus* and the Reader, the *Revd. N. Peckar* at the time of the semi-Jubilee of the Brondesbury Synagogue. (Photograph produced from the semi-Jubilee history.[106])

Cricklewood and Dollis Hill resulted in the closure of the Synagogue in 1974. The congregation merged with that at Willesden. Currently, the two synagogues have a joint male membership of 141. In 1970 there had been 800 male members jointly.

The building was originally sold to the Kilburn and Brondesbury School, who later sold it. The use of Moorish motifs – a feature of nineteenth century synagogal architecture which was felt to be in keeping with a religion originating in the east (but actually derived from Moorish architecture in Spain) – is ironic, in view of the later use of the building, now an Islamic mosque (Fig. 145). Rosenberg[108] notes that the interior has been cleared of seats and has been painted white (as at Stoke Newington Synagogue); where the ark stood there is now a niche facing Mecca.

The ministers

The first choirmaster, N. Peckar (Fig. 146), became the first Reader. Mr. Peckar was also a tutor in Hazzanut at Jews' College. He retired in 1933 and was replaced by Hazzan Elfand from Warsaw.

Dayan Lazarus (Fig. 146; see also Appendix 5a) resigned in 1938 on his appointment as Senior Dayan of the Beth Din.

Further ministers who served there were Revd. I. Jakobovits (see under South East London Synagogue, p.108.), who later became Chief Rabbi, and Dr. A. Melinek.

THE BRIXTON SYNAGOGUE

EFFRA ROAD, SW2

The history of the Brixton Synagogue was written for the Golden Jubilee of the congregation by Mr. Leonard Cohen.[109]

Whilst there were large houses locally for the better-off, the Jewish newcomers were "*mostly of the working and business type*". The opening of the tramlines and the Northern line also made this area more accessible to the City.

The first services, in September 1905, were held in the Carlton Hall, Turnstall Road; this contained a small hall, which was used for services, and a large hall, used for social events. Leonard Cohen was the first *Barmitzvah* in October of that year and his father was the first Warden. Later that year, the Revd. A. Mishcon of Derby was appointed to the congregation, which was independent at that time. The United Synagogue had been initially approached for burial rights and had suggested an amalgamation with the Borough Synagogue (which did eventually happen but only many years later, after the Borough Synagogue had closed). Initially, the members had to belong to the Western Synagogue Burial Society, as did so many other new communities.

In 1909 the lease of the Carlton Hall expired and the congregation then held Sabbath services at 44 Brixton Hill; New Year services had be held in various halls.

Fig. 147 *Brixton Synagogue*. Rabbi Mishcon, Chief Rabbi Hertz and civic dignitaries at its opening service. (Photograph reproduced from the communal history.[109])

Fig. 148 *Brixton Synagogue*. The
interior of the Synagogue, as
illustrated on a certificate given at the
Festival of the Rejoicing of the Law.

Eventually a building, Rutland Lodge at 49 Effra Road, was purchased. This was a large house with a large garden, in which a single-storey synagogue was erected. The Synagogue opened in 1913, the congregation having been admitted to the United Synagogue in 1912. Inside, the men were seated on the right and the women on the left, with a partition between them. The ark and the Almemar were at the eastern wall.

The congregation itself also opened a local kosher shop.

Because of a large influx of Jews to the area, a larger building became necessary and was opened in 1921 on the same site in Effra Road, with seating for 429 men and 191 women; the old Synagogue still remained in use for classes and overflow services. During the late 1930s a hostel was opened for Jewish refugee children and, by the beginning of the Second World War, 260 children were attending the Hebrew classes.

The photograph of the exterior of the new building (Fig. 147) shows a

Fig. 149 *Brixton Synagogue*. The Hebrew classes circa 1958. Some of my neighbours recognise themselves in this photograph. There are a large number of people present, yet the congregation vanished in a few years. (Photograph produced from the communal history.[109])

Fig. 150 *Brixton Synagogue*.
The present day exterior.

Fig. 151 *Rabbi A. Mishcon.*
(Photograph produced from
the communal history.[109])

Fig. 152 *Rabbi, later Dayan Morris
Swift.*

columned portico with laterally situated, projecting blocks containing staircases and cloakrooms. Semi-circular domes over these blocks gave a vaguely 'oriental' appearance to the classical facade, which was built entirely of stone.

The plan of the interior was of the conventional orthodox type, the Almemar being towards the back of the sanctuary, with three banks of seats behind, facing the ark, and four blocks of seats aligned along the sides (Fig. 148). A central pulpit stood before the ark, which was redesigned in 1929 with new canopy.

The Galleries were supported on large, square pillars, with smaller round pillars reaching the roof. The choir, when I attended the Synagogue, had sung on the Almemar.

When the newly refurbished Synagogue Hall was damaged by fire in 1956, the neighbouring Unitarian Church offered their premises for the kindergarten (a reciprocal kindness, as when the Unitarian Church had been bombed during the War, the hall had been lent to that congregation for its Sunday services).

At its peak, in 1960, there were 614 male members, but the numbers subsequently declined. The Borough Synagogue amalgamated with the Brixton Synagogue in 1961, bringing some of the 130 or so of its remaining members, so that in 1970 there were 526 male members of the joint congregation, while at the Streatham Synagogue in the same year there were some 250 members.*

The photograph of the classes in 1958 (Fig. 149) shows very many youngsters. When I worshipped at the Synagogue in the 1960s, it was always reasonably full. Yet the congregation melted away over a relatively short time and the building finally closed. Social conditions had changed considerably locally since the turn of the century; the area had become run-down, and there had even been civil unrest and street riots. The Synagogue amalgamated with Streatham Synagogue on a new site in Leighham Court

* The congregation in Streatham had separated from that in Brixton in 1947.

Road (see the *Year Book* for 1986). There are now 191 male members in the joint community, down from 390 in 1984 and 277 in 1989.

The facade of the Synagogue building remains as a landmark in Brixton, a relic of a vanished local way of life (Fig. 150).

The ministers

Rabbi Mishcon (Fig. 151) died in 1935, at the age of 55 (Lord Mishcon is his son). He was succeeded by Rabbi (later Dayan) Morris Swift.

Rabbi, later Dayan Morris Swift (Fig. 152)

Rabbi Swift was born in Liverpool in 1907. Although his father had been a layman, he and his two brothers became Rabbis, all different in appearance and all with a different style of preaching. Morris was the greatest in the pulpit, speaking without notes, keeping the congregation spellbound with his fiery oratory.

After Manchester Yeshiva, Morris Swift had gone to Ponevez and Mir; he returned to England to become Rabbi at the Shepherd's Bush Synagogue before succeeding Rabbi Mishcon at Brixton. During the War, he also administered to the congregation at High Wycombe. In addition, members were moving to nearby Streatham and local services were set up there. Mr. (later Rabbi) A. Super was appointed Assistant Minister to the Brixton Synagogue.

In 1946 Rabbi Swift resigned and emigrated to Johannesburg. From there he moved to Los Angeles, before returning once more to England as Senior Dayan at the London Beth Din. He was a man of compassion, but uncompromising in his beliefs; it was a privilege to know him and a delight to hear him.

Rabbi, later Dayan Meyer Steinberg (Fig. 153)

In 1950 the Revd. R. Turner was appointed Reader and, in 1952, Rabbi (later Dayan) Meyer Steinberg became minister in place of Rabbi Swift.

Dayan Meyer Steinberg came from Poland and was a chaplain to the Polish Forces in exile during the Second World War. His wife and daughter, meanwhile, were sent to Belsen. They were reunited after the war, in Paris. Coming to England, Rabbi Steinberg was at the Notting Hill Federation Synagogue before being appointed to the Brixton Synagogue. A most kindly and gentle man, he was involved in matters of adoption and personal status at the Beth Din. He died in 1971.

Fig. 153 *Rabbi, later Dayan Meyer Steinberg.* (Photograph produced from the communal history.[109])

THE BERMONDSEY AND ROTHERHITHE SYNAGOGUE

JAMAICA ROAD, SE16,

LATER ROUEL ROAD, SE16

Fig. 154 *Bermondsey and Rotherhithe Synagogue.* The Synagogue in Rouel Road was formerly a congregational church and is seen here in a Victorian engraving. (Courtesy of Southwark Public Libraries.)

The congregation was said to have been founded in 1911, but first appears in the Jewish Year Book for 1915 at 4, Union Road (now known as Jamaica Road), SE16.★ Rotherhithe is east of Bermondsey, directly south of Whitechapel and Stepney via the Rotherhithe tunnel, but still quite a walk away.

In the 1916 edition of the Year Book, the Synagogue is listed as being at 31, Old Kent Road (in the back of a hairdresser's shop), but this low street number is much nearer Walworth than Rotherhithe. At this time the Revd. S. Anekstein was the minister. Classes were held every weekday evening, with 50 children attending. By 1917, however, the congregation is shown as having moved back to Union Road, where it remained for the next 19 years. Perhaps the synagogue in Union Road was being rebuilt in 1916.

In 1936 the congregation found a home in the former Congregational Church in Rouel Road, SE16 (Fig. 154), the minister at that time being Rabbi M. Davidson, who later went to the South West London Synagogue (see Fig. 158). Rouel Road is actually near nowhere in particular, but runs into Southwark Park Road, where most of the local shops were closed on the Jewish High Holy days. The Synagogue in this large former church had a youth club – the Southbank Jewish Club.

Many Jews left the district during the Blitz. The Synagogue no longer appears in the Year Books after 1970. (See also the chapter on the Federation of Synagogues on p. 169).

★ A recently published local history of Bermondsey, Rotherhithe and Southwark made no reference to the local Jewish communities. When I wrote to the author pointing out his omission, he could not believe that there had been Jews locally, especially in Rotherhithe, although he realised there may have been a few Germans active in the leather trade in the area. This correspondence was one of the inspirations behind this current monograph.

HORNSEY AND WOOD GREEN SYNAGOGUE

Green Lanes, N8,

later Wightman Road, N8

The *Jewish Year Books* for 1911, 1912 and 1913 list the Wood Green Synagogue at Queen's Parade, Green Lanes, with a minister, the Revd. S. Michelson. The congregation was an independent one.

By 1914 services were being held in Clarence House, Tottenham Lane. The congregation remained there, being admitted to the United Synagogue in 1920. Shortly after, the synagogue moved to Wightman Road, N8, where it stayed until closure in 1987.

In 1950 there had been 106 male seat holders, declining to 87 by 1970 and to 60 by 1984. On closure, the few remaining members transferred to the congregation at Muswell Hill.

I was unable to obtain a photograph of the interior. It seems that the Almemar had been against the ark; as there had been no Ladies' Gallery, the women sat to the left of the central aisle.

Wightman Road is a long road running from Turnpike Lane to Finsbury Park, becoming progressively more dilapidated. The Synagogue was in a side turning, near Turnpike Lane itself; it is now a mosque (Fig. 155). The building in the illustration is clearly post-war and prefabricated; it cannot be the original Synagogue in Wightman Road. Apparently the building shown in Fig. 155 had been extensively refurbished in the early 1980s, but closed around seven years later (the last entry in the *Year Book* is 1987).

The long-serving minister at the Synagogue between the Wars was the Revd. H. Goodman (see Appendix 5b).

Fig. 155 *Hornsey and Wood Green Synagogue*. Now a mosque, the building is of brick externally but has a rather prefabricated appearance. It presents a rather sorry sight.

THE MUSWELL HILL SYNAGOGUE

FORTIS GREEN ROAD, N10

Fig. 156 *Muswell Hill Synagogue.* An old postcard showing the Athenaeum, Fortis Green Road. The building, initially a concert hall, subsequently a cinema and a dance hall, was then bought by the congregation. It was demolished in 1966.

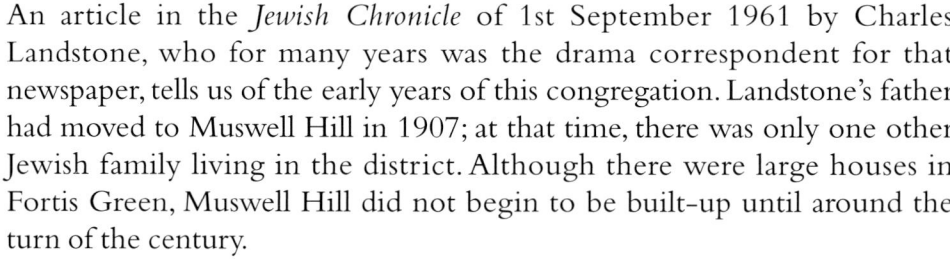

Fig. 157 *Muswell Hill Synagogue.* The Art Deco facade of the ark in the small hall of the Athenaeum. (Drawn by Mr. Keith Ruggles from a photograph in the *Jewish Chronicle.*)

An article in the *Jewish Chronicle* of 1st September 1961 by Charles Landstone, who for many years was the drama correspondent for that newspaper, tells us of the early years of this congregation. Landstone's father had moved to Muswell Hill in 1907; at that time, there was only one other Jewish family living in the district. Although there were large houses in Fortis Green, Muswell Hill did not begin to be built-up until around the turn of the century.

In 1911 a Mr. Milstone opened a tailor's shop and, as he had many children, a *Minyan* was assured.

Initially the congregation of only twenty hired the small hall in the Athenaeum; by 1930 the membership had increased to fifty. Services for the High Holy days were held in the large hall. The Athenaeum (Fig. 156) had been built as a dance hall but was also used for amateur theatricals and public meetings. It was also a cinema during the era of silent films.

In 1937 the Revd. M. Shechtman of the Redmans Road Talmud Torah was invited to reside in the district. Sabbath services and Hebrew classes for children were then held in his house at No. 6, Methuen Park. By 1942 there were 142 attendees at High Holy days, in part due to the influx of refugees from Europe. In 1945 membership had swollen to 250 people.

Soon after this the members formed a limited company which bought the Athenaeum. Shares at £75 each were issued to members. The small hall dedicated as a Synagogue in 1950, was in the Deco style (Fig. 157), but the large hall continued to be used during the Festivals. In 1960, 700 people attended services.

As the large hall of the Athenaeum had been a dance hall, it contained a bar – closed, of course on Yom Kippur – and turnstiles into the toilets.

The building was later sold to Sainsbury's, who demolished it, and a supermarket, with flats above, now occupies the site. The ark from the Athenaeum was moved to the Beth Hamedrash of the new Synagogue.

The new Synagogue of the congregation, designed by Mr. J. Mendleson, with a window by Abraham Games, was built in 1963 on the grounds of a large house in nearby Tetherdown, the plot having been sold to the congregation on favourable terms by the Maurice family. Membership of the congregation had risen progressively from 203 males in 1950 to 354 in 1970, but in 1997 the numbers had declined somewhat to 230.

THE SOUTH WEST LONDON SYNAGOGUE

104, BOLINGBROKE GROVE, SW11

Fig. 158 **Balham Synagogue**, 47 Boundaries Road. The original site of the congregation in Balham.

Fig. 159 **South West London Synagogue.** The exterior after closure. The Synagogue was situated in a house at 104, Bolingbroke Grove and was extended into the back garden of the house, which belonged to the Revd. Ostroff. Building work was completed in 1927.

The *Jewish Year Books* for 1911-1913 list a Balham & Tooting congregation at 47, Boundaries Road in Balham (Fig. 158), and a Wandsworth & Battersea congregation at 563, York Road in Wandsworth. In 1914 there is a new congregation – the Wandsworth & Balham – at 77, Bolingbroke Grove, Wandsworth, an amalgamation of the two mentioned above. By the following year, in 1915, this congregation had moved to 104, Bolingbroke Grove, in the 'Synagogue House', with a Reader, the Revd. I. Ostroff. The Synagogue was apparently in Mr. Ostroff's house, but subsequently was extended into the garden as a proper, large synagogue – the South West

Fig. 160 *South West London Synagogue.* The interior of the Synagogue photographed during a wedding service conducted by Rabbi Davidson. This is the only photograph of the interior I was able to obtain and shows how spacious the Synagogue was, and how beautifully furnished, with a large central Almemar, a wooden ark and wooden facings to the Ladies Gallery. The interior furnishings coming from the original Borough New Synagogue. Rabbi M. Davidson served from 1944 until 1975. (Photograph courtesy of Mr. Cyril Davidson.)

Fig. 161 *New South London Synagogue.* This Synagogue in Balham High Road incorporated the former Balham & Tooting and Wimbledon Hebrew congregations. (See the *Jewish Year Book* for 1939.) (Photograph courtesy of Dr. Nick Hollings.)

London Synagogue (Fig. 159).

According to the Revd. A. Greenbat,* the fixtures of the original Borough Synagogue were installed here when that congregation moved to the Surrey Tabernacle (Fig. 160).

Just around the corner, at 105 Nightingale Lane, was (and still is) the Home for Aged Jews, a union of the 'Hand in Hand Asylum', the 'Widows' Home' and the 'Jewish Home', as well as the 'Jewish Home of Rest' (*Bayis Shalom*) "*for those of our faith who are suffering from diseases that have ceased to respond to hospital treatment – £500 will name a bed, £1,000 a ward*"** Also in Nightingale Lane, at No. 101, was the Jews' Deaf and Dumb Home for Children, founded in 1863 for those aged between 8 and 16 years. Here they were taught "*carpentry, boot repairing, tailoring, dressmaking and housewifery.*"

In its early days the community must have been active; they ran two sets of Hebrew classes – one in the Synagogue and one in an London County Council School in Tooting.

The long-serving, and last, minister of the South West London Synagogue was Rabbi M. Davidson, previously at the Rotherhithe Synagogue in Rouel Road.

The Synagogue closed in 1997. Membership had peaked at around 230 males between the years 1950 and 1960, but at closure there were only fifty two. The newly built and renamed South London Synagogue situated in Streatham Road, incorporating the Brixton and the Borough Synagogues and presumably these fifty two men, has a current male membership of 191.

Between 1934 and 1935 another new congregation had arisen locally – the Balham & Tooting congregation – whose Secretary, Mr. M. Schwartz, lived in Balham Hill. Its address is given as being at 277, Balham High Road (Fig. 161). In 1940, it moved to 239, Balham High Road, changing its name to the New South London Synagogue and incorporating the Wimbledon Synagogue; its minister was the Revd. M. Schwartz (presumably the same person as the Secretary above). While it was listed in the Year Books as an 'affiliated' synagogue, it does not appear in the centenary history of the United Synagogue. It ceases to appear in the Year Books after 1945.

UPTON PARK SYNAGOGUE

TUDOR ROAD, E6

Fig. 162 *Upton Park Synagogue* (above). A drawing of the exterior. (Courtesy of Mrs. Benjamin, Secretary of the West Ham Synagogue.)

Fig. 163 *Upton Park Synagogue* (below right). The Synagogue in its current state, now used as a church.

The history of this Synagogue, written by Cyril Wiseman, is included in the West Ham history.[104]

The congregation first met in 1911 in the house of a Queens Road market trader. Later, a shop and house at 38, Plashet Grove, East Ham, was converted into a synagogue and, in 1918, a larger house in Katherine Road purchased. Subsequently, a new synagogue was erected on a site in Tudor Road (Fig. 162), with seating for 310 men and women, as well as classrooms.

Many of the congregants were market traders, which seems to have affected Sabbath attendance (although not at New Year). On the Days of Awe, the market was closed.

Bombing during the Second World War altered the district and the Jews moved out. A large communal hall was opened in 1960, but was no longer viable. In 1970 there were 169 male seat holders, down from a peak of 237 in 1950. The Synagogue amalgamated with West Ham in 1972.

The building is now a sectarian church (Fig. 163).

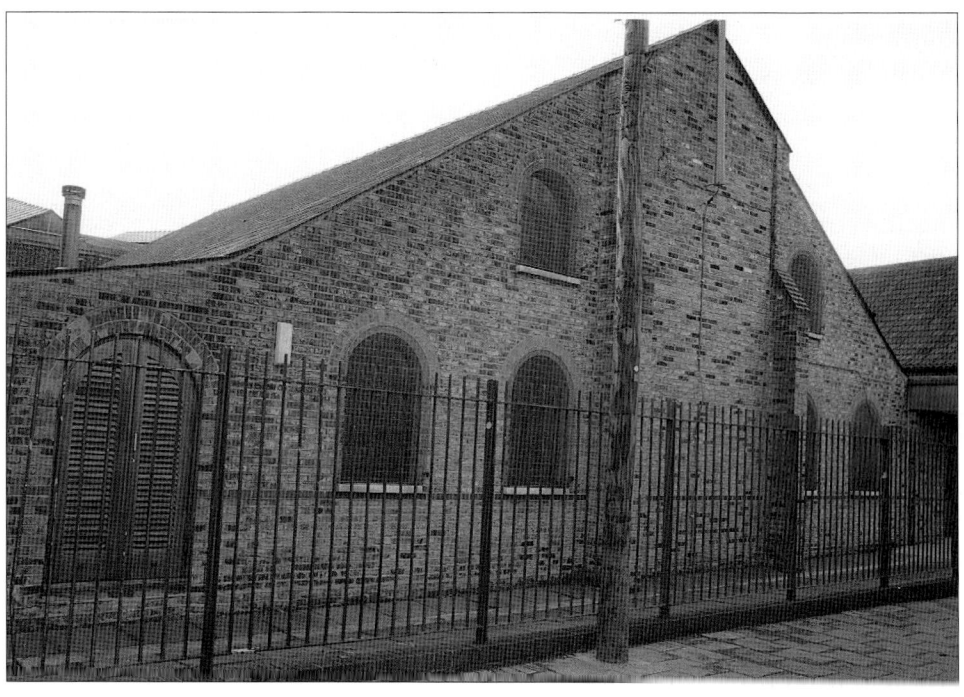

THE RICHMOND SYNAGOGUE

PARKSHOT,

LATER SHEEN ROAD, RICHMOND

There is a long history of Jewish settlement in Richmond which first took place in the late seventeenth and early eighteenth centuries, as described by Rachel Daiches-Dubens.[110] She notes that Richmond had (and still has) an exquisite situation and beautifully laid-out estates. It was also not too far away from the City.

Needless to say, the Jews who settled there in those days were extremely rich, the first being Solomon de Medina, a banker, the first professing Jew to be knighted. He was also a generous benefactor to Bevis Marks. Another immigrant who made it was Moses Hart of Breslau, a government agent under Queen Anne. A benefactor of the Great Synagogue, he brought his brother, Aaron, over to be its Rabbi. Isaac Nunes, the Warden at Bevis Marks was also a resident of Richmond.

As these were orthodox Jews, Daiches-Dubens believes that there must have been more, if only to make up a quorum for prayer. It seems there was also considerable settlement over the river at Isleworth and Mortlake. Here lived the very wealthy and inter-related Franks families.*

Judith Levy, the daughter of Moses Hart, was born in 1706 and died in 1803. She was said to be "*the richest women of the tribe of Judah*".[111] She donated £4,000 to the rebuilding of the Great Synagogue in 1790 and lived in Maids of Honour Row. During her life she was known as the "Queen of Richmond Green". Her sister, Rachel, lived nearby in Old Palace Court.

Benjamin Goldsmid, of a Dutch family, married Jessie Solomons of Clapton, who came with a dowry of £100,000 *then*. In addition to a town

Fig. 164 *Richmond Synagogue* (above left). The building in Sheen Road was a former chapel. The entrance door was directly off on the main road. (Drawing by Mr. Keith Ruggles from a plan kindly supplied by Ms Jackie Lang of the synagogue administration.)

Fig. 165 *Richmond Synagogue* (above right). Plan of the interior. (Drawing by Mr. Keith Ruggles from a plan kindly supplied by Ms Jackie Lang of the synagogue administration.)

* This well-researched article by Daiches-Dubens notes that the Franks family rapidly out-married and assimilated into the Christian majority.

145

house, he purchased an estate in Roehampton, building a mansion that *"excited the admiration of all who beheld it".*[110,111]

Daiches-Dubens' enthralling article carries on listing Jews, all recently arrived, who amassed enough money to become assimilated into English Society at a time when many of their co-religionists were mere peddlers.

The history of the present community is less romantic.[112] The Diamond Jubilee of the modern congregation was celebrated in 1976. Mr. Arthur Howitt established the congregation, the first to be formed outside London by the United Synagogue. Mr. Howitt, later first Jewish Mayor of Richmond, was a benefactor of the Jewish Museum and later associated with the Western Synagogue. He also wrote a book on the Jews of Richmond.[111]

According to the short history published by the congregation, which gives no author, initial services were held at the Central Hall, Parkshot, consecrated in 1916.[112] The Synagogue transferred to a converted chapel in Sheen Road in 1938 (Figs. 164 and 165), which was later demolished. A new synagogue was erected in Litchfield Gardens in 1986.

Rabbi Dr. M. Ginsberg, AKC, (see Appendix 5a) was the minister from 1922 until 1961.

THE CHELSEA SYNAGOGUE

(THE VICTORIA AND CHELSEA SYNAGOGUE)

SMITH TERRACE, SW3

The present Chelsea Synagogue, designed by the architect Cyril Adler and built in 1959, is a little gem.

The recent history,[113] written to celebrate the 80th Anniversary of the congregation, unfortunately does not illustrate the old Synagogue and, despite help from the descendants of the first two ministers, and from pre-War members, I have been unable to trace a photograph. Although it was situated in Smith Terrace – a well-trod street of former artisans' cottages – no photographic records exist in the various Local Government and municipal archives.

In 1913 two local residents, Woolf Adler (the father of the above architect) and Julius Nelken met by chance in Battersea Park and decided to organise a local congregation. A property was finally purchased in 1916 – a former artist's studio, the Red House, in Smith Terrace, the last house in the street. Its entrance was next to the gate of a scrap or builder's yard, which was also purchased for the new synagogue.

The downstairs part of the house was used for a *Cheder*, Literary Society meetings, and various social activities. A *Succah* was erected in the garden. The upstairs part was the synagogue proper, with ceiling 'lights'. The women sat on the right-hand side of the room, behind an ornamental grill without a curtain. In front of the grill sat the male choir and the Choirmaster (the Rabbi's wife, Mrs. Miller) conducted the choir from behind the grill – by all accounts it was a very good choir too. The wardens sat in front of the men's seats.

Many of the members were shopkeepers. Services finished early. Rabbi Miller's daughter told me that Jewish refugees from Germany were brought to the Cadogan Pier by boat (presumably from Tilbury) and were taken straight to the Synagogue.

The freehold for the Red House had been purchased in 1949 for £500 and the adjacent site for £3,500. In 1957 the old building was demolished and the new one erected on the same site.

The builders of the new Synagogue, Gilbert Ash, deferred their profit for a year in order to assist the congregation. The number of male seat holders peaked at 145 in 1960.

THE SETTLEMENT SYNAGOGUE

BETTS STREET,

LATER BERNERS (HENRIQUES) STREET, E1

Fig. 166 *The Oxford and St. George's Settlement.* The initial building in Betts Street. The Settlement was founded as a War Memorial by the West London and Liberal Jewish Synagogues. (Photograph courtesy of Rabbi L. Rigal.)

* The term 'settlement' refers to a group of social workers from a college, etc., who establish themselves in a poor or crowded district in order to provide education, recreation, etc., for the inhabitants.

Rabbi L. Rigal, the current minister to the congregation has written a brief account of the history of the Settlement Synagogue.[114] Its founder, Basil Henriques, came from a long-settled and well-to-do Spanish and Portuguese family devoted to good works. His grandfather, Jacob Henriques, was one of the founders of the Reform Synagogue, which his father – a Governor of the Jewish Orphanage – regularly attended. His mother – the 'Chairman' of a 'lodging house for respectable girls' – was a great-niece of Sir Moses Montefiore. She was deeply spiritual, but rarely attended the Reform Synagogue as she disliked, as a woman, sitting in the Gallery. Both his parents are buried in the Reform Cemetery in Hoop Lane, where there is also a memorial to Basil's brother, killed in the First World War, who lies in France.

Basil Henriques was educated at Harrow and University College, Oxford, where he was much moved by the atmosphere of the Church, but not its doctrines. Conversely, he loved Jewish doctrine, but could not tolerate the atmosphere of the Synagogue. He grew up in a large house in Sussex Square, attended by butlers and footmen, but after university and a term in the Army – he served in the First World War and took part in the first tank battle- spent his life in London's East End, shared with his charges.

Three turning points in his life were his meetings with Claude Montefiore (see p. 115) and his tutor, who was the Oxford representative of Toynbee Hall, and thirdly, reading a book about poverty in Bermondsey.

In March 1914 he opened a boys' club in Cannon Street Road in the area known as 'St. George's' and, as he had recently come down from Oxford, the club became known as the 'Oxford and St. George's'. A girls' club was opened in 1915 in two rooms in a house in Betts Street by Rose Loewe, who later became Henriques' wife. Together, after the First World War, they set up a club and settlement* in Betts Street within a building next to the girls' club which had previously been 'the Bridge of Hope' – a refuge for fallen girls (Fig. 166). The money for this was provided by Viscount Bearsted, in memory of his son killed in the War. The place, Henriques wrote in his autobiography *The Indiscretions of a Warden,* "*looked dreary. It was in a side street off Cable Street … where all the goods looked shoddy and all the goods displayed second-hand … Next door were stables which stank, and brothels.*"[115] Henriques sought assistance from the Reform and Liberal congregations, and the Settlement congregation has been associated with these movements ever since.

A room was set aside in the Club for use as a synagogue, with pews presented by a Methodist church. The girls of the Club formed a choir and Mrs Henriques played the organ.

Describing the interior of his Synagogue at High Holy day services in the

Whitechapel Art Gallery, Henriques wrote: "*We possessed no vestments or ornaments, and had to make shift in a manner which many may hold to be sacrilegious. For an Ark we had a wardrobe from our bedroom. Although we had a scroll of the Law, there were no silver bells which are usually placed over the handles. My wife concocted these with silver tea-spoons. The pulpit covering was a bedspread. Behind the apertures of the reading-desk were hung white hand-towels. There was a glorious array of flowers, and the whole effect was one of beauty and sanctity, incredible as it may sound from this description.*"[115]

Henriques was deeply religious but not orthodox. A Justice of the Peace, he was later knighted for his work. He devoted his time to the service of others in a way that is scarcely believable today (Fig. 167). Basil Henriques seems to have been of a type peculiar to his generation. Coming down from university, he devoted his life to helping others less fortunate – setting up clubs, ensuring moral and religious leadership, making sure boys put on *Tephilin*, taking them to camps (for many their only holiday). It seems perhaps rather like a full-time 'scouts' but Henriques succeeded in retaining the religious loyalty of many who would otherwise have opted out of the community. In fact, he was "*much concerned with the Jewishness of his camps.*"

"*The planning of the Sabbath in camp must be above all on the basis of its delectability. The family feast on a Friday evening in the dim light of the Sabbath candles on the white table; the quality and quantity of the food provided, the glow that comes through saying the Sanctification … the peace, the love, the sense of brotherliness …The Friday evening fails completely and utterly in camp unless those who attend it have had deeply imprinted on their hearts that it is something good in itself, something to be emulated and repeated in their daily lives at home.*"[116]

In 1929, the Settlement moved into a new building in Berners Street (now called Henriques Street) in the East End and became known as the

Fig. 167 *Sir Basil Henriques* in later years. (Reproduced by kind permission of Mrs. A. Loewe and Routledge, Kegan Paul, publishers.)

Fig. 168 *St. George's Settlement, Bernhard Baron House*, Berners Street (later Henriques Street). A drawing of the exterior. (Courtesy of Rabbi L. Rigal.)

Fig. 169 *St. George's Settlement, Bernhard Baron House*. Interior of the Synagogue. The ark is built directly into the wall. There is no fixed seating. (Photograph courtesy of Rabbi L. Rigal.)

Bernhard Baron St. George's Jewish Settlement – a large, purpose-built centre with a dedicated settlement (Figs. 168 and 169).

Henriques was himself a member of the Reform Synagogue and an admirer of C.G. Montefiore. Whilst the Synagogue was in the Reform style, the local boys and girls came from orthodox backgrounds, most of the member children being of recent immigrant stock from Russia and Poland. The prayer book was a mixture of traditional and Liberal, with Hebrew prayers mixed with English hymns written by Henriques and sung to music composed by his wife, who also played the harmonium during services.

With the movement of Jews away from the East End, the clubs moved to Whetstone, but are again to be closed. The Synagogue remained in the East End but recently it too closed, moving to Essex and amalgamating with the South West Essex Reform Synagogue.

CRICKLEWOOD SYNAGOGUE

WALM LANE, NW2

Fig. 170 *Cricklewood Synagogue.* The Synagogue in Walm Lane after its opening. It is a handsome and large building in the contemporary 1930s style. The tablets containing the Decalogue stand on the very top of the front entrance. (Photograph courtesy of Brent Public Libraries.)

The history of the Synagogue by B.B. Lieberman was written on the occasion of the Silver Jubilee of the congregation in 1956 but, unusually, it contains no illustrations.[117]

A public meeting to launch the congregation was held at the Crown Hotel, Cricklewood, on 30th December, 1923. It was originally called the Willesden Green and Cricklewood congregation, but in 1931 was renamed the Cricklewood Synagogue. Initially, it had been hoped to build a new synagogue serving both Cricklewood and Brondesbury with 1,200 seats, but the scheme fell through.

A site was found in Walm Lane and the usual hut, previously at Waterloo Station, was erected there. Festival services were held in the adjacent St. Gabriel's Hall. Whilst the synagogue was being built, services were held in the neighbouring Congregational Church Hall, lent freely by the unanimous vote of the church members. Mr Lieberman notes that the hut was then given to a new Congregational Church in Wembley – *"thus does one good deed produce another."*

The foundation stone of the new synagogue was laid on 14th September, 1930, the architect being Mr. C.J. Eprile. On the front of the building were two vertical pillars supporting the two tablets for the Ten Commandments, which have now been transferred to the front of the new Synagogue. The exterior of the brick-faced building is handsome (Fig. 170), (although I prefer Eprile's designs for the exterior and interior of Hendon Synagogue, which unfortunately has not been well maintained).

The finished building could accommodate 1,100 worshippers and the

Fig. 171 *Cricklewood Synagogue.* Interior view, looking towards the imposing ark. Note the barrel-vaulted roof. The choir sat above the ark. (Photograph courtesy of Mr. Stephen Rosenberg.)

Ladies' Gallery was built without supporting pillars. The Almemar was central and the choir was over a handsome wooden ark, the effect of which was slightly spoilt by having metal doors opening outwards, rather than sliding into the adjacent eastern wall (Fig. 171).

The stained glass windows were designed by David Hillman – 55 in all – symbolising the Festivals (see inside back cover). Other examples of his work can be found at Great Portland Street, St. John's Wood, Hampstead Garden Suburb, and the Hendon Reform Synagogue.

Rabbi Louis Rabinowitz (Fig. 172), then at South Hackney, was installed as Rabbi in 1932. Subsequently a chaplain during the Second World War and then the Chief Rabbi in Johannesburg, he retired to Israel, continuing to write for the *Jerusalem Post* and the *Encyclopaedia Judaica*.

While he was away on military service, his place had been taken by an emigré Rabbi, Dr. Isaac Lichtigfeld (Fig. 173). Born in 1894 in Galicia, he died in Frankfurt in 1967 and was buried in Israel. He was Rabbi in Frankfurt and the Land Rabbi of Hessen between 1954 and 1967.

Rabbi Rabinowitz did not return to Cricklewood after the War and Rabbi Lichtigfeld was succeeded in 1947 by Rabbi M. Landy, a powerful preacher and a pioneer of Jewish education locally.

Hazzan A. Shechter of Westcliff had been appointed as Reader in 1929. He died, on the Almemar, at the end of what he had intended to be his last service prior to retirement. He was succeeded by the Revd. P. Faigenblum, previously at Willesden, whose marvellous recordings with the London Jewish Male Voice choir are still available.

In the 1970s and 1980s the many local congregations were in decline. The main Cricklewood Synagogue had had 742 male seat holders in 1950, but the number declined slowly to 519 in 1970. The Synagogue closed in 1989, when only 153 male members remained, and the building was sold for conversion into flats (this conversion cost £1,000,000 in 1989) (Fig. 174).[108] The former Hall next door then became the Synagogue, albeit of much

Fig. 172 *Rabbi Dr. Louis Rabinowitz*, the first minister of the Cricklewood Synagogue.

Fig. 173 *Rabbi Emil Lichtigfeld*, minister at the Cricklewood Synagogue during the Second World War.

Fig. 174 *Cricklewood Synagogue* (left). The building today, after conversion of the Synagogue into flats. The Decalogue has been removed and is shown on the wall of the building on the left – the former communal hall, which now functions as the current Synagogue. The stained glass windows have also been removed from the stairs leading to the Gallery and replaced with ordinary glass, giving light to the flats. Time has passed since the first photograph (Fig. 170), as shown by the growth of the trees.

reduced size, with seating for seventy men and fifty women. Proceeds from the sale of the main Synagogue covered the conversion costs of the Hall – £150,000. Twenty eight of the stained glass windows were retained in the new Synagogue (some went to the Hendon and some to the Kenton Synagogue). The original ark, reduced in size, was also fitted into the new Synagogue, as well as much of the original furniture.

A small congregation of ninety eight male and 128 female members remains.

The stained glass windows at the **Cricklewood Synagogue**, designed by David Hillman.
(Photographs courtesy of S. Ussiskin and I. Donoff.)

WILLESDEN SYNAGOGUE

COLLEGE ROAD, NW10

LATER HEATHFIELD PARK NW2

The history of the congregation was written by Rabbi Dr. Bernard Susser on the occasion of the Diamond Jubilee of the congregation in 1994.[118]

Earlier congregations had begun in Brondesbury in 1905, and in Walm Lane, Cricklewood, in 1923. Some Jews living further west around the High Road, Willesden, and on the Stonebridge Estate established congregations in private houses. Two separate groups emerged – the West Willesden Synagogue, affiliated to the United Synagogue, and the Willesden Green Synagogue, which affiliated to the Federation.

The United Synagogue congregation started in Stonebridge Park in 1926. In 1928 they moved to a scout hut in the grounds of a convent in Crown Hill Road, NW10, in the centre of Harlesden, and became the Harlesden Hebrew congregation.

In 1933 the congregation became a District Synagogue and acquired a plot in College Road, slightly nearer Willesden than Harlesden.

A public meeting in 1934 raised £200 towards the £1,000 needed to commence building and, in May 1934, the foundation stone of the Willesden District Synagogue Communal Hall and classrooms was laid. The building opened in September of that year (Fig. 175).

The initial building was really a communal hall, seating 500, with a facility for services and classes. It rapidly proved too small and services were soon overflowing. Moreover, it proved to have been built in the wrong place – nearer Kensal Rise rather than the better class of housing in Willesden on the Dobree Estate; the members in the main no longer lived around Harlesden, but rather towards Willesden Green. Despite the recent opening of the

Fig. 175 *West Willesden (United) Synagogue, College Road.* The original building, erected by the United Synagogue, opened on 13th September, 1934. When it closed it was rented out as a warehouse. (Reproduced from *The History of the Willesden and Brondesbury Synagogue, 1934–1994* by Rabbi Dr. Bernard Susser, courtesy of David Selman.)

Fig. 176a

Fig. 176b

Fig. 176a **Willesden Federation Synagogue, Heathfield Park.** The interior, as sketched by the original architect, F. Landauer. (Courtesy of the Royal Institute of British Architects.)

Fig. 176b **Willesden Federation Synagogue, Heathfield Park.** The exterior, in the 1930's style. Of interest is the metal work in front of the upper floor lobby. The front has been boarded up and the building is for sale. The brick extension at the back can be made out. A similar extension on the other side of the building gives a cruciform plan to the interior.

Fig. 176c **Willesden Federation Synagogue, Heathfield Park.** The interior of the Synagogue, still in use in November, 1999. Built with a flat roof which now leaks, the interior has not been redecorated for many years.

Fig. 176d **Willesden Federation Synagogue, Heathfield Park.** The small prayer room lies off the main entrance hall to the Synagogue and will also be closed when the Synagogue is sold.

Fig. 176c

Fig. 176d

★ Mr. Landauer's drawings for the Willesden Synagogue have been deposited in the Royal Institute of British Architects' print collection, Portman Square. His sketch for the interior of the Willesden Synagogue is shown in Fig. 176a. The front facade of the building, facing Heathfield Park, is as he designed it (Fig. 176b).

Synagogue, therefore, a new site was sought, nearer the centre of the Jewish population in Willesden Green.

Meanwhile, the group affiliated to the Federation of Synagogues had begun to hold services in 1933, initially in a house in Park Avenue (near Gladstone Park) and then in a house at Heathfield Park, which was subsequently converted into a synagogue, opening in 1934. This Synagogue seems never to have attracted members in any great number and was always in debt. Even so, a large Synagogue was erected on the site to the plans of F. Landauer (Fig. 176a), who had earlier designed a remarkably beautiful synagogue in Plauen, Germany.★ A description of the new building in Heathfield Park was published in the *Architects' Journal* for 14th April, 1938. It seated only 500 worshippers – too few, it was thought at the time. A further extension was then built at the ark end, that is, at the Brondesbury Park end, enlarging the capacity to 1,000 seats. At the same time, the central Almemar of the Federation Synagogue was placed towards the ark (this was moved back again in 1950).

This building resulted in a massive debt of £11,000. The builders sued the Trustees of the Synagogue for the monies owing. The congregation then voted to close and to join the United Synagogue as a constituent synagogue amalgamated with the West Willesden United Synagogue on the Heathfield Park site. The College Road site reverted to the United Synagogue and was sold.

The synagogue in Heathfield Park is now up for sale (1999), its estimated worth £500,000. It presents a sorry sight – the front door is bolted, the austere interior has faded and the roof leaks (Figs. 176b and c) The congregation, now small, will worship in the communal hall at the rear. The Beth Hamedrash (Fig. 176d), situated near the front door of the main building, will also close.

MILE END AND BOW UNITED SYNAGOGUE

HARLEY GROVE, E3

The Mile End and Bow (District) Synagogue was admitted to the United Synagogue in 1927. The 1929 *Jewish Year Book* gives the address as Harley Grove (Bow).*

The Rabbi in the 1930s was J. Lew, then the only Hassidic Rabbi in the employment of the United Synagogue. One of his sons was Dayan M. Lew and another Rabbi Maurice Lew.

In 1940 there were 382 male seat holders, in 1960 still 292, but by the late 1970s only 208. The Synagogue closed in 1977.

The building is now a very well maintained Sikh temple (Fig. 177).

Fig. 177 *Mile End and Bow District (United) Synagogue*. The building, formerly a church, is now a Sikh temple. The exterior is well maintained.

* The same *Year Book* also mentions a Federation Synagogue (Mile End New Town) in Dunk Street, E1.

THE WEST CENTRAL LIBERAL SYNAGOGUE

ALFRED PLACE, WC1,

LATER WHITFIELD STREET, W1

The history of this congregation was written by Rabbi L. Rigal on its 50th Anniversary in 1978.[119] In the 1920s and 1930s there was a large Jewish working-class settlement in Soho and around Cleveland Street, east of Great Portland Street. There was then a sense of *noblesse oblige* amongst the better-off, which led to the Settlement movement in the East End. In the West End, the West Central Jewish Girls' Club was established in 1893 in Dean Street, by the sisters Lily and Marian Montagu, daughters of the first Lord Swaythling, a strictly orthodox Jew who was also instrumental in founding the Federation of Synagogues.

The Girls' Club moved to Alfred Place in 1914, adjacent to the Western Synagogue, which was being rebuilt at that time. The West Central branch of the Jewish Religious Union, formed in 1913, then held its services in the newly opened Club Hall.

In 1941 both the Western Synagogue and the adjacent Club were destroyed by bombing. No-one was hurt in the Western, but twenty-seven people sheltering in the Club were killed. Following this, the congregation worshipped in the Whitfield Tabernacle and at the Mary Ward Settlement off Woburn Place.

The congregation then built a Synagogue on the corner of Whitfield Street and Maple Street, in a district once Jewish but now essentially devoid of Jews. The complex was built in stages, so that the Synagogue was moved upstairs when the upper floor was added in 1960. This building, now

Fig. 178 *West Central Synagogue*. The interior. (Photograph courtesy of Rabbi L. Rigal.)

158

Fig. 179 *West Central Synagogue*. The interior during a service, with Rabbi Edgar in the centre and Lily Montagu on the far left. (Photograph courtesy of Rabbi L. Rigal and Mr. Lawrence Miller.)

demolished and replaced by a mixed development of housing, Synagogue and offices, was spartan on the exterior, of unadorned brick with an external stairway leading to the first floor. The sanctuary (Fig. 178) was quite large, with the Reader's desk in the front of the ark, facing the congregation. The walls were painted light green when I saw them. The overall effect was one of austere simplicity.

Services continue to be held on Saturday afternoons, continuing the traditions of the Jewish Religious Union. Many worked a five-and-a-half day week, and it was to these that the services were directed.

Lily Montagu officiated here and conducted marriage services, the first Jewish woman minister in Great Britain (Fig. 179). She was one of the first women to be a Justice of the Peace; she was also a founder of the National Organisations of Girls' Clubs and also one of the founders of the World Union for Progressive Judaism. She died in 1963, aged ninety years.

A fuller description of this congregation and of the Jewish clubs in the West End can be found in *Living Up West*.[1]

HARROW SYNAGOGUE

FORMERLY HARROW (KENTON AND DISTRICT) HEBREW CONGREGATION, Sheepcote Road, later, Vaughan Road, Harrow

Fig. 180 *Harrow Synagogue*. I arrived too late; the former prefabricated Synagogue had been taken over by the Hindu community, but they have recently built a large temple nearby and left Vaughan Road, demolishing their previous building. The prefabricated iron church next door, however, remains in excellent condition, and I wonder if the Synagogue was built to the same design.

An article by Randolf Sinclair, kindly provided by the Pinner Synagogue, entitled *Historical Wanderings of Harrow and Pinner*, describes the history of Jewish settlement there.[120] Mr. Sinclair arrived in Harrow in 1931, but he thinks that the first Jewish family arrived in 1923, followed by the daughter of the Reader of the Hackney Synagogue (Revd. Blachman) and her husband (Mr. and Mrs. Klein) in 1924.

In 1928 Mr. Phillips, a solicitor, gave a house in Sheepcote Road (No. 28) for use as a synagogue. In 1936 the first minister, Isaac Cohen, was appointed. High Holiday services were held in halls, or over a bakery in Station Road – the smell of fresh bread on Yom Kippur a torture!

Major Salmon, the local Conservative MP was a member, as well as a certain Mr. Mandelson of the *Jewish Chronicle*.

Revd. Cohen left in 1939 to be followed by a minister, Mr Hooker, who died on active service during the Second World War.

Because of bombing during the Second World War, many families left central London. Railway communication with central London is of course excellent and rapid and the area as a whole, "Metroland", was developed as result of the building of the Metropolitan line.

In 1950 there had been 275 male members of the Harrow Synagogue but, with the move from Sheepcote Road to Vaughan Road (another two and a half miles to walk), those who lived in Kenton started services there in

1949. Eventually, the 'daughter' congregation there eclipsed the 'mother', which eventually closed. The Kenton Synagogue was admitted to the United Synagogue in 1949 and, by 1960, had a male membership of 534, which had increased to 1007 ten years later .

I knew that the Harrow Synagogue in Vaughan Road, which opened in 1946, had closed in 1972 and that members whom I knew had transferred elsewhere. In 1950 there had been 275 male members but, by 1970, only eighty five remained. I was told that the building – a tin hut – had become a Hindu Temple. By the time I went to photograph it, only a wasteland remained (Fig. 180), even though the tin hut next door, a Pentecostal Church, was immaculate. There was a large, new Hindu Temple nearby.

I made numerous phone calls to old congregants, local papers and dignitaries, but was unable to find a photograph of the interior or exterior. All tangible evidence of it has literally vanished.

DOLLIS HILL SYNAGOGUE

PARKSIDE, NW2

Fig. 181 *Dollis Hill Synagogue*. A current photograph of the exterior of the Synagogue. The hexagonal windows originally contained Stars of David, while the inverted windows in the side buildings contained candelabra as their motif.

Fig. 182 *Dollis Hill Synagogue* (below right). The interior of the building, looking towards the ark. A very large Almemar is united with the ark on the eastern wall, while the Wardens face the congregation. The original interior has been panelled. The lights are entirely in keeping with the design of the interior. (Photograph courtesy of National Monuments Record.)

The story of this unique synagogue is to be found in Rachel Wischnitzer's *The Architecture of the European Synagogue*[24] and, at greater length, in *Synagogues of Europe* by Carole Herselle Krinsky.[121]

Dollis Hill lies to the north of Cricklewood and Willesden, and to the south of the North Circular Road, in an area of typical inter-War speculative development. Krinsky[120] notes that the congregation first met in a private house in 1929. Services were also held in the Neasden Mission Hall until 1933, when a small synagogue, later the community centre, was built at a cost of £1,400.

The foundation stone of the Dollis Hill Synagogue was laid in 1937. This building, according to Krinsky, looks like nothing else in Britain. It was uncompromisingly modern, both within and without (Fig. 181). The designer, Sir Owen Williams, was not an architect, but an engineer, whose other major works included the old Daily Express building in Fleet Street, the Boots (the Chemist) Factory in Nottingham, and the bridges spanning the M1 motorway.

Cantilevered Galleries, fixed onto corrugated walls, did away with the need for supporting pillars, thus giving unobstructed views. The roof was also corrugated, again dispensing with the need for supporting beams. Inside, the ceiling lights were totally in keeping with the modern style. Originally, the internal walls were of plain concrete, but these were later covered with wood panelling to give both warmth and a warmer look. The Almemar was at the eastern end with the decalogue above the plain curtained ark. The choir gallery projected out over the ark. The Synagogue had 524 seats for men and 392 for women (these seats were padded but look rather uncomfortable) (Fig. 182)

The hexagonal windows lent themselves to a central hexagram – a Star of David (later replaced by stained glass) – while in the adjacent Hall, the rectangular windows had a rounded lower edge into which fitted the outline of a *Menorah*.

Male membership peaked around 1960, when there were 640 members. In 1970 there were still 500, but membership gradually declined – to 255 by 1984 and 176 by 1989. In 1997 only 106 male members remained.

Recently the congregation has moved into the Hall, and the Synagogue building is now in use as an Orthodox Jewish School but, as there are few such children locally, they are bussed in from other areas.

HIGHGATE SYNAGOGUE,

ARCHWAY ROAD, N6

This Synagogue was admitted to the United Synagogue in 1935 but is listed in the latter's centenary history as having 59 male members in 1930. It is not listed in the 1929 *Jewish Year Book*.

In 1939 the minister was Maurice Lew, later of the Dean Street Synagogue, while the President of the congregation was Sir Robert Waley-Cohen, also President of the United Synagogue, who resided in splendour in Hampstead Lane.

The Synagogue was originally at 88 Archway Road but this apparently unattractive building has since been demolished as part of a road widening scheme; I could find no photograph of it. The congregation then moved up the road into a church. The steep gradient of the side road allowed access to the Waley-Cohen Hall below the Synagogue (Fig. 183). The interior of the building can be seen in Fig. 184, prior to the installation of fixed pews. Rabbi E. Nemeth was the long-serving minister.

In 1950 there were 308 male members and, by 1960, 361 (there is some very attractive housing locally, even if the Archway Road itself is rather seedy). Numbers then began to decline. After the Synagogue was gutted by fire in 1976, the congregation initially worshipped in a local church hall in Pond Square and then transferred to Highgate Village. It now has 128 male members.

The building in Archway Road is now a Hindu temple.

Fig. 183 **Highgate Synagogue** (right), Archway Road. Previously a church, now a Hindu temple. The congregation moved out after the Synagogue was gutted by fire. The steep gradient of the side road allowed access to the Waley-Cohen Hall below the Synagogue.

Fig. 184 **Rabbi E. Nemeth** conducting a wedding prior to the introduction of fixed pews (below). The congregation had recently moved from 88, Archway Road. (Photograph courtesy of Mrs. Nemeth.)

THE PINNER SYNAGOGUE

CECIL PARK, PINNER

Set in a historic village with much new building around the Metropolitan line, synagogue services were started in Pinner in 1941, again presumably by evacuees from central London. Initial services were held in a local school in Cannon Lane.

In 1950 a building was purchased in Cecil Park. Initially a chapel (Fig. 185), then a YMCA Hall, the single storey building (Fig. 186) had separate seating for women behind a low railing. The ark was a simple cupboard and the Almemar central. There were no permanent seats (Fig. 187). There were attractive stained glass windows depicting the Sabbaths and Festivals.

The congregation grew due to an influx of young married couples, but the local Council always objected to a rebuild on a new site. A new building was erected on the old site in 1981.

Rabbi Grunewald has been the minister there since 1976. Previous ministers had been Rabbis Warshaw, Cofnas and Katz.

Fig. 185 *Pinner Synagogue.* A view of Pinner in its rural days. Marsh Lane is a dirt track. The telegraph has arrived, but not motor transport. The rear of the chapel is shown on this charming photograph. The window was subsequently filled in (Photograph courtesy of Mr. Don Walters.)

Fig. 186 *Pinner Synagogue* (below left). The exterior of the first Synagogue in Cecil Park. Stained glass windows are shown in the side wall. The apse behind the building, seen on the previous photograph, is still present. It was a chapel before becoming a YMCA building. The current Synagogue stands on the same site. (Photograph courtesy of the congregation.)

Fig. 187 *Pinner Synagogue* (below right). Despite its small size, the Reader's desk was in the centre of the Synagogue. The women sat at the back of the building behind a low curtain. (Photograph courtesy of the congregation.)

THE STREATHAM SYNAGOGUE

MITCHAM LANE, SW16,

LATER ESTREHAM ROAD, SW16

Fig. 188 *Streatham Synagogue*, 15a Mitcham Lane. This building, used prior to the Synagogue in Esterham Road, is now a church. (Reproduced from the communal history.[122])

Fig. 189 *Streatham Synagogue*, Esterham Road, SW16. The interior. The Reader's Desk is against the ark and the seating is fixed, facing the ark. Stained glass windows are on either side of the ark together with prayer boards. There are tablets of the Law and probably recumbent lions on top of the ark. (Reproduced from the communal history.[122])

Fig. 190 *Streatham Synagogue*, Esterham Road, SW16. Now an Islamic centre. There are modern replacement windows over which are fairylights in the shape of onion-domes, giving at least a hint of the East.

Just down the road from Brixton, a minor wave of Jewish migration was underway to leafier Streatham. A meeting in 1945 had attracted 200 people, and 230 attended the first services in 1946, according to the history of the community written for its Silver Jubilee.[122]

A small hall was purchased in 15a Mitcham Lane (the building is now a church) and was dedicated in December 1947 (Fig. 188). Services were first taken by the Revd. J. Rockman (later at Catford), then by Rabbi M. Nemeth, and subsequently by the Revd. G. Schneider (later at West Ham). New Year services were held in the Congregational Church Hall.

In 1957 the congregation acquired a former drill hall in Estreham Road, the interior of which is shown in Fig. 189. The Almemar is located at the ark end. The 'cupboard' ark is surrounded by prayer boards and stained glass windows. The women were presumably behind the grills over the rear seats.

By 1960 there were 261 male seat holders and, in the year of its Silver Anniversary in 1970, 245 members, when it was noted that *"ideally a synagogue and community centre worthy of the joint communities* (i.e. Streatham and Brixton) *and situated in a strategically suitable place would be a most desirable thing."*[122] Rabbi P. Ginsbury, who left Streatham in 1966 to go to Brixton, is now minister of the joint community in a new building, the South London Synagogue which opened around 1985.

The building in Estreham Road is now a mosque (Fig. 190).

THE ELM PARK SYNAGOGUE

WOBURN AVENUE, ELM PARK, ESSEX

Fig. 191 *Elm Park Synagogue*. The exterior, following closure in 1999. (Courtesy of Mr. Frank Harris and Mr. Benjamin Tobin.)

I had literally just finished this book, though fully aware that further closures were in the offing, when a friend gave me an advertisement for a vacant synagogue – the Elm Park United Synagogue. This is described as a purpose-built synagogue on a rectangular site to the south of Woburn Avenue, close to Elm Park underground station. The site has a frontage of 200 feet and an area of 0.38 acres.

The photograph of the exterior (Fig. 191) shows a simple building, of brick, which displays two stained-glass windows over the door in the shape of the Tablets of the Law. How well maintained it looks and how sad to see it closed. The interior, photographed after closure (Fig. 192), shows a simple ark and Almemar.

The history of the United Synagogue[2] has no mention of it in the text, but gives the date of its admission to the United Synagogue as 1948, together with other synagogues at Dunstable, High Wycombe, Kingston, Peterborough, Watford, Welwyn Garden City and Worcester. Presumably all these congregations were started by Londoners during the evacuation and, in 1948, still had a reasonable membership.★

The Synagogue at Elm Park was probably formed around 1940 since, at that time, it had forty eight male members, rising to a peak of eighty seven in

★ My own family was evacuated to Marlow, where there was a Hebrew congregation in the house of Mr. Goldblum. There was also small orthodox congregations locally in Amersham, Chalfont and Maidenhead. Most of these ceased to function after the War, including that of Marlow.

1960. Membership declined slightly in 1982 but in 1985 still numbered sixty. By 1989 membership had dwindled to forty seven and by 1997 only thirty seven male members remained. Elm Park is an attractive area with good housing, quite a way out of London, but it never attracted Jewish residents in any significant numbers.

Other synagogues for Essex men

The *Jewish Year Book* for 1939 lists a synagogue at Beacontree, which also held Hebrew classes in Dagenham, with the Revd. N. Bergerman as the minister. Dagenham, a so-called model village, was an inter-war New Town built for East End population overspill but also to furnish labour for the local Ford car factory. Presumably a few Jews left the East End to live there along with everyone else.

The *Year Book* for 1964 lists congregations in Barking, Hainault, Harold Hill, Highams Park, Romford and Wanstead in the United Synagogue, and Leytonstone and Wanstead in the Federation, as well as Ilford and Loughton. Even the Union of Orthodox Hebrew congregations was represented in Ilford. There is a Reform Synagogue – the South West Essex Reform Synagogue – as well as a Liberal Jewish group.

Currently there are still Affiliated United Synagogues in Barking, Harold Hill, Highams Park, Romford and Wanstead, as well as Ilford. With the exception of Ilford and Wanstead, the outlying synagogues have small memberships

Fig. 192 *Elm Park Synagogue.* The interior, following closure in 1999. (Courtesy of Mr. Benjamin Tobin.)

THE FEDERATION OF SYNAGOGUES AND THE EAST END CLOSURES

The complexities of synagogue closures in the East End would have been beyond comprehension were it not for the excellent history of the Federation by Professor G. Alderman.[74]

The Federation was founded in 1887 at a meeting presided over by the Liberal MP for Whitechapel, the orthodox Samuel Montagu (the father of Lily Montagu), later Lord Swaythling. It was decided that the small or minor East End synagogues should be 'federated'. Consequently sixteen synagogues joined, with a combined membership of 1,300. The flood of immigrants from Russia and Poland greatly expanded the population of the East End, but these newcomers had little regard for the Anglicised form of Judaism presided over by the Very Reverend Dr. Hermann Adler, who allowed no-one else to use the title 'Rabbi'. The English synagogues were cathedral-like in comparison with the small rooms in which the immigrants prayed, often with people originating from their own town (*Landsmannschaften*). These small synagogues were often dingy and unsafe; many, but not all, members were extremely poor and certainly would have been unable to afford United Synagogue fees for membership and burial.

According to Alderman, the 'Federation' of the minor synagogues, supported by the wealth of Samuel Montagu, offered a way of enfranchising the poor masses in the East End and assured they would have a voice in Anglo-Jewry.

In 1889 Montagu purchased two acres of land in Edmonton from the Western Synagogue for use as a cemetery in what is now Montagu Road. The two cemeteries are side by side. J. Glasman quotes Samuel Montagu : "*The most important event in the history of the Federation was the acquisition of a burial ground. This was your great charter of liberty and independence. Without the facilities for burying your dead, you would be under the thumb of some other body and the thumbscrew might have been applied until you sacrificed your independent existence.*"[123]

Where small synagogues were considered unsatisfactory, they were refused admission to the Federation. Montagu-sponsored ones were often designed or approved by his architect, Lewis Solomon.

By 1911, with new synagogues also established outside the East End, the Federation had 6,500 male members – more than the United Synagogue, which had 3,200 male seatholders (not quite a direct comparison as not all United Synagogue members were seatholders).

The *Jewish Year Book* for 1939 lists sixty five synagogues in the Federation, most of them in the East End and ranging from the Austrian Dzikower in Dunk Street, via the Lodzer Synagogue in Davis Mansions, and the Lubiner and Lomzer in Laurence Buildings, Cannon Street Road (not to be confused with the Cannon Street Road Synagogue shown in Fig. 193), to

Fig. 193 *Cannon Street Road Synagogue*, Whitechapel. The well-known Revd. N. Halter was Hazzan here for many years.

Fig. 194 *Fulham and Kensington Synagogue* and *TalmudTorah*, 259 Lillie Road, SW6 (above right). This former Federation Synagogue is now a Seventh Day Adventist Church with no sign that it was a former Jewish house of worship.

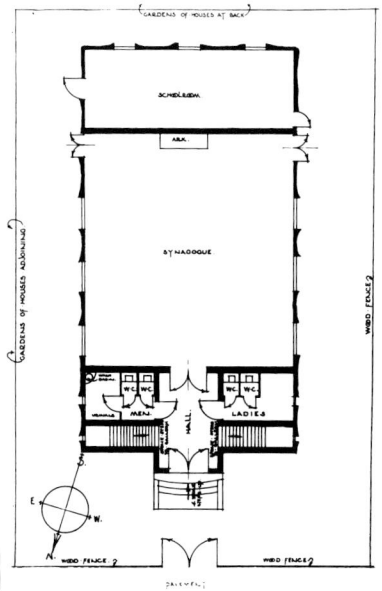

Fig. 195 *Fulham and Kensington Synagogue* (above). The interior plan of the Synagogue. (Drawing by Mr. Lewis Solomon.)

Fig. 196 *Leyton and Walthamstow New Federated Synagogue*, 79 Queens Road, E17, situated at the end of a row of rather drab terraced housing (right). The building is now an Islamic centre.

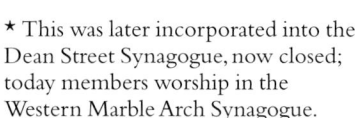

★ This was later incorporated into the Dean Street Synagogue, now closed; today members worship in the Western Marble Arch Synagogue.

the Warsaw Lodge Synagogue in Wilkes Street. Outside the East End, there were synagogues in Lambs Conduit Street in Bloomsbury;★ Lea Bridge Road in Clapton; Croydon; Forest Gate; Lillie Road (Fulham and Kensington Synagogue) (Figs. 194 and 195); Clifford Way (Gladstone Park and Neasden Synagogue, later Ahavath Shalom) (see below); Ilford, Queens Road E17 (Leyton and Walthamstow Synagogue) (Fig. 196); Notting Hill; Rouel Road (Bermondsey and Rotherhithe Synagogue, see p. 138) (see Fig.154); Poplar Grove (Shepherd's Bush Synagogue) (see below); Grove Lane in Stamford Hill; Tottenham; and Anglesea Road (Woolwich Synagogue) (see Fig. 134–137).

Other synagogues listed in the *Year Book* for 1939 include the Ezras Haim, at 2 Heneage Street (Fig. 197), the Forest Gate Federation Synagogue,

Fig. 197

Fig. 198

Fig. 199

the Lambeth (Beth Jacob) Synagogue and Lambeth Talmud Torah at 48 Kennington Road, SE1 (Fig. 198),* the Yavneh Synagogue at Ainsworth Road (Fig. 199), the Princelet Street Synagogue at 19 Princelet Street, E1 (see below) and the West Hackney Synagogue at Amhurst Road, Dalston (Fig. 200).

The Machzike Adass Synagogue

One of the most famous East End synagogues to close was the building of the Machzike Adass at the corner of Fournier Street and Brick Lane (Fig. 201). The building has had an interesting history. Originally erected in 1743 by Huguenot refugees as a Church (*Neuve Eglise*), it subsequently became, in 1819, a Wesleyan Chapel, having been a few years previously styled a 'Mission House for Converting Jews.'[124] It was consecrated as a Synagogue on Sunday, 11th September, 1898, under the name of the Spitalfields Great Synagogue

The history of this congregation has been elegantly described by Dr.

Fig. 200

Fig. 197 *Ezras Haim Synagogue*, 2 Heneage Street.

Fig. 198 *Lambeth Synagogue (Beth Jacob Synagogue and Lambeth Talmud Torah)*. This congregation appears with its own Rabbi – Rabbi S. Baumberg – in the Jewish Year Book for 1929, but there is no entry for it in that for 1939. The current photograph shows the site of the Synagogue; the original Synagogue building itself collapsed and had to be rebuilt.

Fig. 199 *Yavneh Synagogue* . North East London Beth Hamedrash, Ainsworth Road, E9, established in 1904. The interior. Its best known Rabbi was Dayan M. Fisher. (Photograph by Mr. John Brandenburger. Reproduced from *The Synagogues of London* by Paul Lindsay (1993), published by Vallentine Mitchell, London, with kind permission of the author.)

Fig. 200 *West Hackney Synagogue*, Amhurst Road, Dalston (current photograph).

* A note in the Jewish World of 2nd August 1923 describes the opening by Lord Swaythling. The Revd. H. Shoolman delivered the address. The congregation was formed in 1920; at the time of opening there were 140 members.

Fig. 201 *Spitalfields Great Synagogue (Machzike Adass)*. Formerly a Huguenot church, then a synagogue and now a mosque. (See *A Fortress in Anglo-Jewry* by Dr. B. Homa.[124])

Bernard Homa,[122] the grandson of the Rabbi there at the turn of the century, Rabbi A. Werner, who in turn was followed by two further, most distinguished Rabbis, Abraham Isaac HaCohen Kook (subsequently Chief Rabbi in Palestine) and Rabbi Yechezkiel Abramsky (subsequently a member of the Beth Din).

In part at least, the raison d'etre for the establishment of the congregation was total dissatisfaction with the perceived laxity of the then current Anglo-Jewish establishment, personified by Chief Rabbi Hermann Adler and his Dayanim. The ultimate cause of the schism was the matter of Shechita (the Jewish religious method for the killing and preparation of meat for consumption).

Rabbi Werner made certain minimum demands of Dr. Adler and the Beis Din, including (1) the prohibition of the sale of kidney suet, (2) the prohibition of the sale of unporged hindquarter meat, (3) the insistence that, when necessary, meat should be poured over with cold water and not otherwise sold, and (4) the insistence that all poultry should have a seal to show that it had been correctly slaughtered.[124]

In time, all these demands were met but not before the controversy had led to a legal action in the English courts, and great conflicts amongst European Rabbis, all of whose opinions were eagerly sought by one side or the other.

The Rabbis and the congregants of the Machzike Adass were well known for their learning, piety and devotion to prayer. It was truly a synagogue that never closed. As soon as one service had been completed, another one commenced.

The Synagogue lost its purpose when the East End became depopulated and many of the local Jewish-owned businesses closed or moved. The congregation transferred to Golders Green and the building is now a mosque.

The Princelet Street Synagogue, 19 Princelet Street, E1

In recent years many articles have appeared in the press and in journals on

Fig. 202

Fig. 203

Fig. 202 *Princelet Street Synagogue*. This Synagogue lay disused for many years and was occupied by a Jewish squatter. This interior is being restored and a Trust exists to raise funds for this.

Fig. 203 *Princelet Street Synagogue*. The interior. Photograph taken at the time of the Festival of Pentecost, when synagogues are traditionally decorated with flowers. (Photograph courtesy of Mr. S.C. Melnick.)

Fig. 204a

Fig. 204b

Fig. 204 a b *Princelet Street Synagogue*. The interior of the synagogue currently. (Photograph obtained with the kind permission of Ms Susie Symes.)

this Synagogue. It is the last, small synagogue of its type remaining in the East End, even if disused.

The first and most complete history of the Synagogue was written by Mr. Samuel Melnick,[125] grandson of Rabbi Shmuel Melnick, the Rabbi of the congregation from 1896 to 1920. This extremely detailed history is unlikely to be bettered, as the author had access to minute books and old documents.

More recently, an article by S. Paskin and J. Liddell-King described the history of the building and the curious story of its last inhabitant.[126]

The terraced house at 19 Princelet Street was built in 1719 (Fig. 202). In 1743 it became the house and also workplace of a Huguenot weaver. When the silk industry collapsed in 1826, Irish immigrants replaced the Huguenots.

In 1869, prior to the mass immigration of Jews from the Russian Empire, the building was purchased by the local United Friendly Society, who established the Synagogue, the main sanctuary measuring 16' x 40' extending into the garden.

The Ladies' Gallery on three sides of the Synagogue was reached by the internal stairs, and extended backwards into the house, over the front rooms on the ground floor. Further flights of stairs led to the upstairs flat. Painted onto the wood panels in front of the Ladies' Gallery were the names of donors to the Synagogue with the amounts they gave in pounds, shillings and pence (never done in a 'proper' synagogue, but common enough in the immigrant conventicles). The donations seem small enough today – half a guinea (52p) or a guinea (£1.05) – but the gentry, the local M.P., a Beddington, a Mocatta and a Rothschild, gave more. The last painted entry was in the mid 1950s.

The simple cupboard-type ark rests in a round, domed apse. Above the ark is the decalogue surmounted with a small painted crown. Around the platform or *Duchan,* on which the ark rests, is a wrought-iron gate. Over the apse, at one time, were painted the words "Remember before Whom you

Fig. 205 *Rabbi Schmuel Melnick*, Rabbi of the Princelet Street Synagogue. (Courtesy of his grandson, Mr. Samuel Melnick.)

stand" (Fig. 203). Today the plaster in the apse is cracking, with no sign of the painted words or stars. The interior is lit by large skylights of coloured glass (Fig. 204). The Almemar has been removed and is in storage in the front room of the house. The interior of the Synagogue, derelict and dangerous when I saw it around ten years ago, has been cleared, made safe and water-proofed. New lights and electrics are evident – a credit to the devotion of the current owner, the Spitalfields Centre Trust.

Mr. Melnick's book recounts in full and glorious detail many events in the life of this congregation, which had a 'Society for Chanting Psalms and Visiting the Sick' – a 'Chevra Tehillim'. The Synagogue was also a venue for 'cheap' or 'free' marriages for those immigrants who could not afford a wedding in a United Synagogue (which cost £3 in 1877).

Of note are two Hazzanim to the congregation. Alexander Tertis was appointed in 1878; he died in 1918. His son was Lionel Tertis, the most famous viola player of his generation. A subsequent Hazzan was the Revd. P. Fassenfeld, later of the Dalston Synagogue (see Fig. 94).

Rabbi Shmuel Melnick (Fig. 205) was born in Zakroczym, Poland, in 1862. In 1893, when the town burnt down (not an uncommon occurrence), he was forced to leave his position as Dayan and came to London, where he had friends. In 1896 he was appointed to the 'Chevra Tehillim' at the Princelet Street Synagogue. It is noted that he could – and did – preach for four or more hours on end; he was in great demand as a preacher in Yiddish in London.

In 1920 he left Princelet Street to become Rabbi of the Commercial Road Great Synagogue, a large building (the exterior of which I remember well for its massive pillared portico). Rabbi Melnick died in 1927; 20,000 people followed the hearse.

With the decline of East End Jewry after the Second World War, the Synagogue fell on hard times. Items from the Synagogue inventory were sold – two Scrolls of the Law for £70 and £75. The preacher's salary was reduced. The last accounts, for 1962, show a deficit. Rain began to pour in through the roof of the building, and services were held for a short time in the house, before the Synagogue was finally abandoned.

In a garret room lived a recluse, David Rodinsky, who was said to have 'vanished' in 1969, leaving *"the table set for dinner, a bedcover turned down with the pyjamas still on the pillow. The calendar on the wall is forever dated 1963"*.[126] A recently published book by Rachel Lichtenstein (albeit in large part autobiographical) and Ian Sinclair, is constructed around the Lichtenstein's search for Rodinsky, whose final resting place she finds in Waltham Abbey cemetery. She has arranged to place a headstone on his bare grave.[127] Subsequently it has been discovered that Rodinsky died at the age of 44 in St. Clements Psychiatric Hospital in 1969, the year of his disappearance.[128]

The Shepherd's Bush Synagogue, later the Shepherd's Bush and Fulham Synagogue, 1a Poplar Grove, W6

I was fortunate to obtain, through Mr. Morris Weintraub, two souvenir brochures, the first dated 1953 issued on the fortieth anniversary of the founding of the congregation, and the second on the Golden Jubilee.

The first meeting of the congregation was held at the home of Mr. I. Fineberg on 30th November, 1913, *"in connection with the formation of a synagogue and Talmud Torah at Shepherd's Bush, contributors to be charged 6d (2½p) per member per week."* This no doubt included membership of the Federation

Fig. 206 *Shepherd's Bush Synagogue*, 1a Poplar Grove, W6. It is now a Kingdom Hall. The Synagogue had a very distinguished series of ministers, including Rabbis Louis Rabinowitz and Morris Swift.

Fig. 207 *Shepherd's Bush Synagogue*. The interior. (Photograph by Mr. Kaufman. Courtesy of Mr. Morris Weintraub.)

Fig. 208 *Rabbi Professor Israel Abrahams*, minister at Shepherd's Bush Synagogue.

of Synagogues funeral scheme.

The first synagogue of the congregation was a hut at 61 The Lawn, Shepherd's Bush; in 1918 the congregation moved to the Park Hall, Providence Place, W12. In 1924 the ultimate home of the congregation in Poplar Grove opened as a synagogue.

The Synagogue was rebuilt in 1938-9 (Figs. 206 and 207). A communal hall was added and a flat for the minister built above this in 1962. The Synagogue was further refurbished in 1963.

The two short histories show how communities alter with time. In 1953 the community must have been flourishing. It had a Rabbi and a Hazzan, Hebrew classes and a Youth Club. It was noted that a complete Tractate of the Talmud was read every year. There were well attended daily services, morning and evening. Membership, it was noted, was constantly increasing and it was difficult to accommodate all the new members. The custom of delivering addresses in Yiddish on major Festivals was followed.

Ten years later, however, the situation was less happy. The history notes that migration was already underway from the district. In May 1959 the Synagogue merged with the neighbouring Fulham and Kensington Synagogue in Lillie Road on the closure of the latter. The two buildings are actually quite a way from each other. To walk from Lillie Road to Shepherd's Bush, you must walk past the Hammersmith Synagogue at Brook Green (if you can get across the Great West Road).

The 1963 history notes a declining membership and poor synagogue attendance, so that a Hazzan could no longer be engaged, while the *"minister can be the most brilliant speaker ever, but to what avail if the pews of the Synagogue are empty"*.

The congregation closed around 1989 when a quorum for prayer for Sabbath was no longer obtained. Mr. Weintraub told me that younger people left the district and their elderly parents would follow them to the suburbs. Looking at the names in the brochure, many of the members were shopkeepers or stall-holders associated with the local Shepherd's Bush market.

The congregation was blessed from the outset by remarkably fine Rabbis. The Revd. S.A. Michelson was the first minister, from 1914 to 1916, and was succeeded by the Revd. G. Kirsner, who went to South Africa in 1926. After him came Louis Rabinowitz (see Fig. 170), later of Cricklewood and subsequently Chief Rabbi in Johannesburg. He in turn was succeeded by Rabbi I. Abrahams (Fig. 208), subsequently Chief Rabbi of the Cape Province, and Professor of Hebrew at Cape Town University, a prolific author and historian.

In 1932 Rabbi M. Swift (see Fig. 152) was appointed and, in 1936, his brother Isaac – another outstanding preacher. Rabbi Rafael Feldman then served till 1956. He was succeeded by Rabbi I. Abrams.

Amongst the Hazzanim were the Revd. M. Brown (1915-1945), the Revd. E. Freilich, later of Hampstead Garden Suburb, and the Revd. M. Katanka, later of the beautiful Princes Road Synagogue in Liverpool.

The Neasden Federation Synagogue, Clifford Way, NW10

The Neasden Federation Synagogue had long worshipped in a former church, the long-serving minister being Rabbi I. Landau, of Czechoslovakian origin.

A brand-new large Synagogue and Community Centre was opened in 1967 but the Jewish population gradually moved away and the building is now a church (Fig. 209).

Fig. 209 *Gladstone Park and Neasden Synagogue*, Clifford Way, NW2 (above left). The modern Synagogue was erected on the site of the previous one (a converted church) and opened in 1967. Even so, it did not last long.

Fig. 210 *Ohel Shem Synagogue*, Chamberlayne Road, NW10 (above), is now a block of flats.

Fig. 211 *Shomrei Adass Federation Synagogue* (left). This building was formerly the West Hampstead Congregational Church The current state of the building shows it as a block of flats. The original windows have been replaced and there is now a front door leading to the Finchley Road. The new, small, purpose-built Synagogue can be seen in the background down the side road. The building next door was the former New College, a theological training school for non-Conformist clergy, now belonging to the Open University. It is built in a similar architectural style.

Renaming of the constituent synagogues

After the Second World War the 'constituent', as opposed to 'affiliated', synagogues of the Federation were all given Hebrew names. The first new constituent synagogue, the Shomrei Adass in West Hampstead (see below) was followed by the Ohel Shem in Chamberlayne Road, Willesden (Fig. 210), in 1946, which incorporated the Hillel House School (now also closed). These buildings are now completely unrecognisable as synagogues, having been converted into dwellings. The Emet V Shalom Synagogue in Maida Vale (1948) was in a house in Elgin Avenue; this has now also closed and the building has been demolished.

Shomrei Adass Synagogue, Finchley Road, NW3

Rabbi Kopul Rosen was appointed Principal Rabbi of the Federation of Synagogues in 1945 but, according to Alderman,[74] did not wish to live in the East End. In 1946 the Federation of Synagogues therefore purchased the former West Hampstead Congregational Church in Finchley Road for

Fig. 212 *Shomrei Adass Federation Synagogue*. The interior of the Synagogue during a wedding ceremony, showing the central Almemar and a rather simple cupboard-like ark. The lofty proportions of the building can be appreciated from this photograph. (Photograph courtesy of Mr. Phillip Stein.)

£12,500 as a seat for the Rabbi. A Reader – the Revd. Rosenberg – was also engaged. At the first High Holy day services, 250 people attended the Synagogue.

The district at that time was fairly Jewish. The Hampstead Synagogue is situated nearby in Dennington Park Road; there were Kosher butchers locally, delis and even a Jewish day school. Also in the area was a large concentration of German-speaking Liberal Jews, who had founded their own congregation.

The Shomrei Adass was a large building, in red brick and terracotta, in keeping with the surrounding buildings (Fig. 211), but had a rather austere interior (Fig. 212). There was a separate communal hall with a youth club. Next to the Synagogue was the New College for the training of Non-Conformist ministers (now Parsifal College, London headquarters of the Open University).

In his autobiography,[129] Rabbi Dr. Louis Jacobs writes that, in 1946, he was appointed by Rabbi Dr. E. Munk of the Golders Green Beth Hamedrash (whose earlier synagogue is still in use by a Sephardic congregation) to head a new Yeshiva under the aegis of his congregation. This Yeshiva, called *Shaarey Zion*, met in the hall of the Shomrei Adass Synagogue. However, the Yeshiva did not last and Rabbi Jacobs left the employment of the Beth Hamedrash.

The Synagogue has now been converted into a block of flats and the smaller congregation worships in a new purpose-built Synagogue by the side of the old building.

Fig. 213 *Rabbi Kopel Rosen.* The principal minister of the Federation of Synagogues from 1945 to 1949 and minister to the Shomrei Adass Synagogue.

Rabbi Kopul Rosen (Fig. 213)

An account of Rabbi Rosen's life can be found in Professor Cyril Domb's book *Memories of Kopul Rosen*, published in 1970.[130] Another is in Professor Alderman's history of the Federation.[74]

Kopul Rosen was born in 1913 in Notting Hill; his father was a Reader of the Prayers (*Baal Tephila*). He attended the Etz Chaim Yeshiva, taught at the Dalston Talmud Torah and preached his first sermon at the New

Fig. 214 *Bethnal Green Great Synagogue (Tifereth Israel)*, 11–15 Bethnal Green Road, E1 . Rebuilt after the Second World War, with three enormous stained glass windows, which are mainly intact, along the side of the Synagogue facing the main road.

Synagogue when aged only 16 years.

In 1934 Rabbi Rosen went to the Yeshiva at Mir in Byelorus. He returned to England before the outbreak of war, being appointed minister to the Higher Crumpsall congregation in Manchester in 1939. He remained there until 1944 when he was appointed Communal Rabbi in Glasgow, but stayed there only 18 months, returning to London in 1945 when he was inducted as Principal Rabbi of the Federation of Synagogues, with his seat at the Shomrei Adass Synagogue. In 1949 he resigned his post, sold his house and moved to set up Carmel College.

The East End Synagogues after the Second World War

The Jewish population of the East End was already in decline even by 1939; indeed, its peak was around 1910. Three congregations in Christian Street alone had closed in the 1930s. The Little Alie Street and Jubilee Street Synagogues merged, as did those of Whitechapel Road and Vine Court, Fieldgate Street Sephardish and Settles Street, The Glory of Israel and Mile End New Town, The Plotzker and Great Alie Street, and The Voice of Jacob and King Edward Street. Later, the congregations of Greenfield Road merged with Vine Court, Artillery Lane with Ezras Haim, the Romanian with Philpot Street Sephardish, and the Lubiner and Lomzer with Fieldgate Street.

Of course, many synagogues in the East End were damaged or destroyed in the War and could not be rebuilt in the immediate post-War years because of shortage of materials and planning restrictions.[74] The Local Authorities in the East End also were of the opinion that fewer, not more, synagogues were needed in the area. However, many of these synagogues, which existed in name only, were in effect independent of the central authority of the Federation and some were rebuilt, even though by then fewer Jews lived locally – the Cannon Street Road, Commercial Road Great, Fieldgate Street and Philpot Street Synagogues are examples.

The Mile End New Town Synagogue was rebuilt in 1954, using war damage compensation monies, as were the New Road, Stepney Orthodox,

Fig. 215 *New Road Synagogue*, Whitechapel, E1. Established in 1895 and rebuilt after the War, when the Revd. Kacenelenbogen was its minister.

Fig. 216 *Federation Synagogue*, 62 Montague Road, E8 (below). The building is now derelict and occupied by a squatter.

Fig. 217 *Federation Synagogue*, 62 Montague Road, E8 (far right). The interior. There was an article on this Synagogue in the *Times* of 1st August, 1998. (Photograph courtesy of Mr. Chris Harris and The Times Photo Library.)

and Bethnal Green Synagogues. They are all now closed. The Bethnal Green Synagogue was very large and could accommodate 350 men and 100 women (Fig. 214).

The Limehouse Synagogue was also rebuilt, but could not pay the monies due to the builder.

The Shadwell Synagogue amalgamated in 1959 with the Commercial Road Great Synagogue; similarly the Mile End and Bow Synagogue with the Stepney Orthodox, and the Chevrah Torah with the Bethnal Green Great Synagogue.

By 1964, the Federation included synagogues in Maida Vale, Finchley Central, Golders Green, West Hampstead (see above), Chamberlayne Road NW10 (see Fig. 210), Loughton, Edgware, Greenford and Wimbledon.

By the late 1960s, following compulsory purchase of their site, the Commercial Road Great Synagogue had amalgamated with that in Nelson Street to form the East London Central Synagogue. Funds from the closed Dzikower Synagogue in Dunk Street were used to establish a ritual bath in Ilford. The New Road Synagogue (Fig. 215), rebuilt after the War, also amalgamated with the East London Central Synagogue. The Teesdale Street congregation amalgamated with the Bethnal Green Synagogue, but this itself finally closed in 1984.

The Dalston Talmud Torah merged with the West Hackney (see Fig. 200) and Montagu Road Synagogue (Figs. 216 and 217), the funds going to Israel for charitable purposes, as did monies raised from the sale of the Synagogue in Rouel Road.

APPENDIX 1

ARCHITECTS OF THE SYNAGOGUES IN LONDON

C.H. Krinsky gives a brief list of the architects of major London synagogues and their works.[121] For a comprehensive account of the Anglo-Jewish architects in the eighteenth and nineteenth centuries, see also the chapter in *Transactions of the Jewish Historical Society of England* by E. Jamilly, who has written much on this subject.[131] For information on synagogue architecture, see the *Encyclopaedia Judaica*,[4] the thesis by Morris Joseph,[44] and the books by Krinsky[122] and by Wischnitzer.[24]

Hyman Henry Collins was responsible for the rebuilding of the Western Synagogue 1857; the Sephardic Branch Synagogue in Bryanston Street 1862 (no images available); the Borough New Synagogue 1867; North London Synagogue 1868; and the St. Johns Wood Synagogue in Abbey Road 1880. He was, notes his obituary, "*the grandson of Hyman Collins, of Cockspur Street, who founded the St. Albans Place Synagogue when it removed from Denmark Court in 1826. In this work Mr. Collins's grandfather was associated with his brother-in-law, Myer Solomon, of Pall Mall, the 'Rosh Hakahal' of the congregation in those days. Hyman Collins was Treasurer of the St. Albans Place Synagogue in 1833, his brother-in-law, Myer Solomon, being Warden at the same time, and Simeon K. Salaman (father of Charles K. Salaman) a Junior Warden.*

"*For many years, until he became a member of the Bayswater Synagogue, Mr. Collins was an active member of the St. Albans Place Synagogue. When the Western Synagogue was renovated, in 1857, the repairs were carried out under his direction and supervision. Indeed, Mr. Collins was, at one time, the principal synagogue architect in our community. Besides the buildings of the old West Ham Burial Ground, which was opened in 1856, he designed the Borough Synagogue, the North London Synagogue, the Southampton Synagogue, and several provincial places of worship. All his synagogue designs were remarkable for their gracefulness. He was also the architect of several buildings for Jewish institutions. One of the most notable erections which he planned, in connection with his son, Mr. Marcus Collins, was the Home and Hospital for Jewish Incurables at South Tottenham – a magnificent Elizabethan structure, which has elicited wide admiration. He was Honorary Architect and Surveyor of the Westminster Jews' Free School. Mr. Collins was also distinguished as an architect outside the community. He was architect of the Metropolitan Hospital in Kingsland Road, and at the time of his death he was designing the new building of the City of London Lying-in Hospital, in City Road. He was a Fellow of the Institute of British Artists, and of the Surveyors' Institution ... His eldest son, Mr. Marcus Collins, the well-known architect, is a member of the firm. Another son, Mr. Arthur Collins, is the popular manager of the Drury Lane Theatre.*"[★][132]

Barrow Emanuel (1841–1904) and his non-Jewish partner, **Henry D. Davis** (1838–1915) – the West London Synagogue, Upper Berkeley Street 1867–1870 (unfortunately, there are no comprehensive images of the

★ The film star Joan Collins and her sister, the novelist Jackie, are also his descendants.

previous synagogues of this congregation). Also the East London Synagogue (1876) and the Spanish and Portuguese Synagogue in Lauderdale Road (1896), as well as Jewish Almshouses in the East End.

Barrow Emanuel came from Portsmouth, where he had designed the local grammar school. His partnership with H.D. Davis also designed the previous City of London School on the Embankment; this building still stands today. Emanuel also designed housing on the Kidderpore Estate in Hampstead.

C.J. Eprile – Cricklewood Synagogue in Walm Lane 1930-1; the rebuilding of the West Ham Synagogue (see p. 128); Hendon Synagogue 1935. Cricklewood and Hendon Synagogues are beautiful examples in the 1930s style.

Delissa Joseph (1859-1927) – Hammersmith Synagogue 1890; Hampstead Synagogue 1892; South Hackney Synagogue 1897; Finsbury Park Synagogue 1901; South East London Synagogue 1904. He also designed the synagogue in Cardiff (1897). The son of Solomon Joseph and nephew of N.S. Joseph, he was a designer of synagogues and industrial buildings. His cousin, Ernest Joseph, was also an architect who was employed by Sir Marcus Samuel (Lord Bearsted) to design buildings for the Shell Company; he also designed several synagogues. Delissa Joseph attended Durham House School and the Jews' College, beginning his architectural practice in 1882. He also became an expert in providing superstructures over booking and lift halls of London Underground stations, for example, Moorgate Station Chambers, Coburg Court Hotel at Queensway station, Oxford Circus House and the Hyde Park Corner Hotel over their respective stations. He was also the architect for the Rembrandt Hotel in Thurloe Place, SW7. He was married to Lily Solomon, sister of the painter Solomon J. Solomon, RA; she, too, was a painter.

Nathan Solomon Joseph (1832-1909) – the Bayswater Synagogue (with Edward Salomons) 1862; the Central Synagogue 1866; Dalston Synagogue 1885. N.S. Joseph was the uncle of Delissa Joseph and the brother-in-law of Hermann Adler. He designed many working-class dwellings, as well as the extension to the largest school in England – the Jews' Free School (1883). He was a consultant to the Guinness Trust and the Four Per Cent Industrial Dwellings Company of Lord Rothschild.

Edward Salomons (1827-1906), according to Jamilly,[123] built fanciful houses with a marked French accent, including Caenwood Towers in Highgate, and Agnew's Galleries in Bond Street. With N.S. Joseph, he designed the Bayswater Synagogue in Chichester Place (1863).

Lewis Solomon (1848-1928) – Spital Square 1886; Old Castle Street 1891; New Hambro Synagogue 1899; Stoke Newington Synagogue 1903. After public school and university, he gained a Silver Medal from the Royal Institute of British Architects. He became Clerk of Works in the India Office.

Judy Glasman,[123] in her most helpful article, points out that by 1970 the United Synagogue had built some 83 synagogues. The dates of foundation give, as noted by V.D. Lipman[17] (see p. 25), a guide to Jewish migration within London.

Glasman notes that the United Synagogue structured a whole mini-economy around synagogue buildings. Central funds provided around one-third of the cost of the site and buildings, which were often larger than needed at the time of opening to allow for future increase of the congregation. Constituents of the United Synagogue had access to a wide range of central services and expertise, donations, loans and the benefit of belonging to a central community or Kehillah, but membership of the United Synagogue entailed loss of local independence.

Glasman quotes *The Builder* of 1874, in which synagogue design of the time was described as "*a blend of the Eastern and Western Schools of Art*" – a mixture of Gothic, Italian and Moorish – "*with … enough of the Eastern feeling to render it suggestive, and enough of the Western severity to make it appropriate for a street building in an English town.*"[133]

In contrast, Beatrice Webb described the conditions found in many of the small synagogues of the East End: "*It is a curious and touching sight to enter one of the poorer and more wretched of these places on a Sabbath morning. Probably the one you will choose will be situated in a small alley or narrow court, or it may be built out in a back yard. To reach the entrance you stumble over broken pavement and household debris: possibly you pick your way over the rickety bridge connecting it with the cottage property fronting the street. From the outside it appears a long wooden building surmounted by a skylight, very similar in construction to the ordinary sweater's workshop. You enter: the heat and odour convince you that the skylight is not used for ventilation. From behind the trellis of the ladies gallery you see at the far end of the room the richly curtained Ark of the Covenant.*"[134] It was these conditions Sir Samuel Montagu (later Lord Swaythling) resolved to change by founding the Federation of Minor Synagogues.

APPENDIX 2

THE BASIC DESIGN OF A SYNAGOGUE

In Western Europe the orientation of the synagogue is, whenever possible, along an east-west axis, with the ark situated at the eastern end of the synagogue. Sometimes the topography of the site does not allow this orientation, as in the current synagogue at Great Portland Street.

The ark

The ark, containing the Scrolls, is called the *Aron Hakodesh* by Ashkenazim and *Hekhal* by Sephardic Jews. The ark itself may be a simple small cupboard with doors, or large, but still in effect a chest placed against the eastern wall (however massively ornamented − as in the Sephardic Synagogue in Amsterdam, where the ark forms much of the eastern wall). If the building is small and the ark too, a simple cupboard stands on the floor, but the Scrolls are always placed in the upper part of the cupboard. Generally, however, the ark containing the Scrolls is elevated on a raised platform at the eastern end of the building ascended by three to four steps, giving the ark and the Scrolls an appropriate position of prominence, dignity and honour − they are, as it were, 'looked up to'. The platform is known as the *Duchan* − as it is from here that the Priests (Cohanim) *duchan*, that is, give their three-fold blessing.

The doors or gates of the ark are usually covered by a curtain (or *Parokhet*) of coloured fabric during the year but of white material on High Holy days; the curtain is drawn aside on the 9th of Av − the anniversary of the destruction of the Temples at Jerusalem. In some synagogues the curtain is placed *inside* the gates to the ark or is done away with altogether, but this is not current orthodox practice.

By the nineteenth century the ark had become placed in an apse, either in a cupboard built as an integral part of the apse, that is, with the doors giving access to the Scrolls flush with the curved wall, or in a chest lying against the curved wall.

When the ark lies in an apse, which may be rounded or square above, then a place exists for a choir above the ark. While this would not occur in ultraorthodox synagogues, this arrangement can be seen in many of the larger orthodox synagogues in London, the choir being screened off by grills or curtains, or both. The choir may also be placed in a gallery on the western wall, on the *Almemar* (see below) or by the ark. Occasionally, a partitioned-off portion of the Ladies' Galleries on the north or south walls is used. It was said that in the pre-War Central Synagogue, where a mixed choir sang (as was usual in those days), separate galleries were provided for men and women. When the Revd. A. A. Green was asked if they sat together, he replied, "Don't worry. They don't even sing together!"

The ornamentation of the ark and apse usually includes a suitable Hebrew text; "Remember before Whom you stand" being commonly used. Other ornaments in common use include the two tablets inscribed with Hebrew characters or numerals indicating the Ten Commandments, often surrounded by lions with or without crowns. Similar motifs may be embroidered on the curtains before the ark.

Other ornaments on the eastern wall include marble or wooden plaques engraved or painted with prayers for the Royal Family (sometimes surmounted with a crown) and for the State of Israel.

The Almemar * or Bimah**

The Scrolls are taken from the ark and placed on a desk for the Reading of the Law. The desk or *Omed* lies on a raised platform in larger synagogues or directly on the floor in small prayer halls.

The raised platform, – the *Almemar (Bimah)* – is situated centrally within the building in Ashkenazi tradition, but back against the western wall, that is, at the opposite end of the synagogue to the ark, in the Sephardic.

The Almemar is again reached by a small flight of steps so that the scrolls may be read in an elevated position. The Almemar may be square, oblong or curved. Railings of wood or metal surmount the wooden or marble base; candelabra are normally placed at each corner. In most orthodox synagogues, the prayers are recited by the Reader from the raised desk (Omed), although in ultra-orthodox synagogues a further stand or Omed is placed to the right of, and below, the ark to observe literally the verse "from the depths I called unto thee". In front of the Reader there is then a drawing or text utilising prayers, often with calligraphy making a shape, for example, of a candelabrum.

There is an enclosed row of upholstered seats for the Wardens of the congregation in front of the ark in Ashkenazi synagogues.

The Reader is the centre of attention for much of the service and generally, in orthodox services, he is in the centre of the synagogue. The fact that this lies opposite the ark is said to create a 'tension' amongst the worshippers whose attention is drawn first to the eastern ark, then to the central Almemar – a rather fanciful notion.

Seating

Originally there were few fixed seats in synagogues. A nineteenth century engraving of the interior of the Altneu in Prague shows seats attached to the sides of the Almemar. These seats were apparently for the privileged and had better illumination from the candles on the Almemar. Mobile lecterns are seen scattered about; when the Almemar is the centre of attention, they could face it and, similarly, the lectern could be moved to face the ark or the preacher. In most orthodox synagogues currently the seats lie in rows along the north and south walls, often banked, as in a theatre, for better visibility. The worshippers face the Almemar, though from the 'cheaper' seats neither the ark nor the Reader may be easily seen – a situation worsened if the galleries or roof are supported by heavy columns. Prayer books are generally stored beneath the cushioned seats, though not in ultra-orthodox synagogues. There they are generally kept in lockers secured to the back of the pew in front, an arrangement held to be more respectful to the books.

The movement to Reform

The 'Temple' in Frankfurt-on-the-Main (1810) was erected by a congregation of extreme Reform tendency. The Almemar was placed directly against the eastern wall and the appearance was that of a Protestant church.[135] The arrangement of most of the fixed benches was however as if the Almemar were still central, that is, along the north and south walls, but

* Almemar – from the Arabic *al-minbar* – platform.
** Bimah – Hebrew: elevated place.

185

now the western part of the sanctuary had pews facing the eastern wall in place of the Almemar. There was still a Ladies' Gallery with a highly ornamented facade, but no grill, so that now the women could see and be seen. The first 'Temple' in Hamburg (1818) had an entirely traditional layout, as did the West London Synagogue of British Jews in Upper Berkeley Street, which opened in 1870, both with a central Almemar (that at Upper Berkley Street was subsequently removed and replaced by transverse pews; an organ was used in services only two decades after the building was consecrated).

The Second Reform Temple (1844) in Poolstraße, Hamburg, had a circular half-domed apse with a recessed ark surrounded by two columns (a reminder of the Temple in Jerusalem). Here, the Reader's desk was on the raised Almemar at the eastern wall. All the fixed pews faced the ark; there were Ladies' Galleries but no grill.

Dr. Gotthold Salomon, styled the 'Preacher', spoke of the Temple and Hamburg as *"the centre of our new Jerusalem."*[135] Even more explicit was Israel Jacobson. On its opening, he stated that the Temple was *"the first preparation to a coming together between you and your Christian neighbours-in-faith. Now is the time to lay aside the old, now the fault for oppression is with the Jews themselves."*[135]

The redesign of the synagogue was thus directly linked to a desire to emancipate Jewry in Germany. One effect of the new position of the Almemar was to focus the attention of the worshippers to a single and elevated fixed point – as in a church – thereby eliminating any tension between ark and Almemar. More room then became available for worshippers as the pews could extend right up to the eastern end of the sanctuary.

While the officiant usually faced the ark in orthodox synagogues, the ultimate arrangement in Reform synagogues was for him to face the congregation, with his back to the ark, a practice unacceptable in most (but not all) orthodox synagogues.

Some orthodox synagogues in England in the late nineteenth century and early twentieth century did use this internal arrangement, albeit with the Reader facing the ark, sometimes because it afforded extra room in a small space (as in the last Hambro Synagogue) and perhaps also because of assimilationist tendencies in an anglicised congregation (as in the Hampstead Synagogue). On occasion, the same architect would design one synagogue with the Almemar at the eastern wall (as in the Hendon United Synagogue) but another in an equally contemporary style with it situated centrally (as in the Cricklewood United Synagogue). Presumably this was at the request of the congregations concerned and partly reflected their religious outlook, as well as a desire for extra seating. Recently, in some of these synagogues the Almemar has been resited centrally as a result of altering attitudes within centrist Orthodoxy, with mixed results – more satisfactorily at Golders Green than in Hendon, where the eastern end was altered from the original pleasant design.

Ladies' pews

In medieval synagogues, no longer existent in England, ladies were kept in separate rooms or buildings with limited visual or auditory access to the main sanctuary via small windows in masonry walls.

In the second synagogue of the Resettlement at Creechurch Lane and in the reconstructed Great Synagogue, the ladies in the Gallery sat behind latticed grills (subsequently removed in the latter) as they still do in ultra-Orthodox synagogues.

In the second Temple in Hamburg, the women sat separately in galleried pews but without a grill, as they originally did at the West London Synagogue.

In the handsome pre-War Liberal Synagogue in the Prinzregenten Strasse, Berlin, family pews were instituted, but single ladies still sat in the Gallery.

In smaller Orthodox synagogues, built without a Gallery, women may sit on the opposite side of the synagogue (as I believe was the case at Wood Green and at Chelsea United Synagogue) or on a slightly raised dais (as at Woolwich Federation), separated or not by a total or partial grill or curtain.

While mixed seating is now ubiquitous in non-orthodox synagogues, this was not always the case.

The pulpit

The idea of a sermon in the vernacular is not rooted in Jewish tradition. The Rabbi gave his major discourse on the Sabbaths before Passover and New Year. In the Great Synagogue the discourses would have been in Yiddish, if only because the earliest rabbis (with the exception of Solomon Hirschell) were foreign born, while in the Spanish and Portuguese Synagogue Portuguese was the lingua franca.

Sermons began to be given in English to mark special occasions – coronations or military victories. Modern large synagogues therefore have a pulpit as an integral part of their design. The pulpit is often situated centrally, in front of the ark, on the raised dais, often overpowering the ark and emphasising the centrality of the sermon. Some synagogues have a completely separate pulpit, reached by steps, as for instance at the East London Synagogue and currently at the West London Synagogue.

Stained glass windows

These are to be found in synagogues of all types and traditions, and reflect the tastes of their age. Those at the New West End, Hampstead and West London Synagogues are Victorian and intricate in design. Some windows contain contemporary stylised Jewish motifs (see Fig. 181). Those in the last Western Synagogue in Crawford Place are now installed in the weekday synagogue at Marble Arch and depict as well as common motifs, the tribes of Israel and Jerusalem, also Windsor Castle with a Royal Standard.

Such windows generally enhance the beauty of the synagogue and add to its interest (see inside back cover).

APPENDIX 3

Letter from John Greenhalgh to Thomas Crampton, dated 22nd April, 1662 (see p. 22)

"*Their Synagogue is like a Chapel, high built; for after the first door they go up stairs into it, and the floor is boarded; the seats are not as ours, but two long running seats on either side, as in a school: at the west end of it there is a seat as high as a pulpit, but made deskwise, wherein the two members of the Synagogue did sit veiled, as were all both priest and people. The chief Ruler was a very rich merchant, a big, black, fierce, and stern man to whom I perceive they stand in as reverential an awe as boys to a master; for when any left singing upon their books and talked, or that some were out of tune, he did call aloud with a barbarous thundering voice, and knocked upon the high desk with his fist, that all sounded again. Straight before them, at some distance but upon a seat much lower, sate (sic) the Priest. Two yards before him, on midst of the floor, stood that whereupon the Service and Law were read, being like to an high short table, with steps to it on one side as an altar, covered with a green carpet, and upon that another shorter one of blue silk; two brass candlesticks standing at either end of it; before that on the floor were three low seats whereon some boys sat, their sons, richly veiled, as gentle comely youths as one should see; who had each his Service Book in hand, in Hebrew without points, and were as ready and nimble in it, and all their postures as the men.*

"*There was brought in a pretty Boy at four years old, a child of some chief Jew, in rich coats, with black feathers in his hat, the priest himself arose and put a veil over the child's hat of pure white silk, fastening it under the hatband that he should not shake it off, and set him upon a seat among the boys; but he soon leaped off, and ran with his veil dangling up and down; once he came and looked at me, wondering perhaps that I had no veil; at length he got the inner door open and went to his mother; for they do not suffer the Women to come into the same room or into the sight of the men: but on the one side of the Synagogue there is a low, long and narrow latticed window, through which the women sitting in the next room, do hear; as the boy opened it, I saw some of their wives in their rich silks bedaubed with broad gold lace, with muffs in one hand and books in the other.*

"*At the east end of the Synagogue standeth a closet like a very high cupboard, which they call the Ark, covered below with one large hanging of blue silk; its upper half covered with several drawing curtains of blue silk; in it are the Books of the Law kept. Before it, upon the floor, stand two mighty brass candlesticks, with lighted tapers in them; from the roof, above the hangings, two great lamps of christal glass, holding each about a pottle filled up to the brim with purest oil, set within a case of four little brass pillars guilded. In the wall at either end of the Synagogue are very many draw boxes, with rings at the like those in a Grocer's Shop; and in it (as I came sooner in the morning than many or most of them) I saw that each Jew at his first entrance into the place did first bow down before the Ark wherein the Law was kept, but with his hat on, which they never do put off in this place; but a stranger must; for after a good while two Englishmen were brought in, at which I was glad, being alone before, and they were bareheaded until they were set down amongst them, which then put on their hats … Each Jew after he had bowed went straight to his box, took a little key out of his pocket, unlocked it, took out his veil and books, then threw his veil over his hat and*

*fitted it on all sides, and so went to his place and fell a tuning it upon his Hebrew
Service Book as hard and loud as he could; for all is sung with a mighty noise from first
to last, both of priest and people; saying some prayers; and all was done in the right
true Hebrew tongue, as my Rabbi affirmed to me afterwards; which, to this end, they
do industriously teach all their children from infancy, having their schoolmistresses on
purpose, especially their Service books, which they have at their finger's end. There was
none but had a book open in his hand, about the bigness of our hand Bibles.*"[13,14]

APPENDIX 4

Part of the history of the Bayswater Synagogue (see p.80)

ANOTHER "BATTLE OF TALKING"
A Sketch with a Moral

At the time of which this little history treats, there were living no great distance from each other, in one of the Western Counties, two very respectable families. They were respectively known by the names of the Bayswater Goodenoughs and the Portland Swellingtons, and the former who are chiefly connected with the events about to be narrated had settled in the county some years after the latter. Both increased yearly in numbers and prosperity. Now, after the Portland Swellingtons had resided for some considerable time in rather narrow quarters (it must be owned), they did what a great many other very worthy and prosperous families have done before them, they moved to a spacious and magnificent mansion, which they had erected at an enormous expense, and which, even though they have not since been able to afford to paint and embellish, was so costly in its simple construction, that it is not entirely paid for to this very day. Indeed, many say that it has been built on so vast a scale that it is scarcely ever adequately inhabited, excepting perhaps, during those seasons when houses in the country, and particularly those in the Western Counties, are filled to overflowing by the influx of visiting company.

All this grandeur could not belong to so near a neighbour without exciting a little feeling of envy in the hearts of the Bayswater Goodenoughs. Up to the time when the Portland Swellingtons removed to their new mansion, the Bayswater Goodenoughs had been more than delighted with their own rich and commodious dwelling, which had been erected with every consideration for the wants of a well-to-do family, whose numbers were known to be gradually increasing. The domestic economy, too, of their house had been fondly, and perhaps somewhat egotistically, believed by them to be "absolutely perfect." In the first place, there were the tutor and the governess, who were, in point of fact, the real administrators of the internal affairs of the family. These were both persons of considerable weight and experience, as well as of undoubted conscientiousness in the performance of their arduous duties. They it was who had educated their charges up to a degree of refinement which had hardly ever been previously reached by any other family in the whole county, and they had also succeeded in their capacity of managers in obtaining a very competent and efficient staff of servants for the work of the house. It is very true that the servants were paid extremely high wages, and the only mistake was that the tutor and governess were perpetually singing their praises, and this had the effect of inducing frequent applications from them for an increase in their already high wages. On the whole, however, it may be said that, taking all things into account, the Bayswater Goodenoughs were – as times go – well enough off in this matter of their servants.

The principal one was of course the cook. A more zealous and skilful person could not perhaps have been found anywhere – the food, and in particular the soup, which she put before the family, at its constant assemblies and gatherings, was of the best description; the only fault which the most fanciful among them could find was that they really did not care for soup quite so often as she gave it to them. It is true that when it came to table it was strong, nourishing, and generally full of good things, but it was only the excellence of the ingredients, and the palatable manner in which they were served up that could quite overcome the objection as to the soup which has been mentioned; however, taking it altogether, the cook was a thoroughly good servant.

The next in importance was the housemaid. She was a capital servant; active and laborious, and never found wanting in the proper performance of her duties. The only complaint that was ever known to be made of her was that she was slow, and dawdled over her work, which was thus at times unnecessarily protracted, and notably so when she took some part of the work which was more generally assigned to the under-housemaid.

The last most useful servant combined some of the minor duties of the upper housemaid with others of a superior situation, and she gave unqualified satisfaction to the whole of the Bayswater Goodenoughs. The only fault that was ever complained of in her case being that on the occasion of a contest between various members of the family (which will be referred to hereafter) she was said to have evinced a decided bias in favour of certain of the family, and this was considered by the rest as incompatible with her duties and obligations.

The family, being a well-ordered and contented one, everything went on peaceably and prosperously until a little while after the removal to their new mansion of their opulent neighbours, the Portland Swellingtons. Very soon after this event some of the brothers and sisters of Mr. and Mrs. Bayswater Goodenough, attracted by the salubrity of the locality, expressed a wish to reside in the neighbourhood. Now, it may reasonably be supposed that there was nothing in this but a cause for rejoicing, as the advent of such intimate connections of the family of the Bayswater Goodenoughs could only tend to consolidate their strength in the county and would probably promote union and harmony amongst them. And very likely this would have been the case if the new-comers could have obtained suitable residences within a moderate distance from, but not too near to, the Bayswater Goodenoughs. (Propinquity in such cases being a very different thing from proximity). But unfortunately no such residences were to be found, and fired with the ambition of rivalling their neighbours, the Portland Swellingtons, whose extensive establishment and large numbers were the theme of much comment and emulation, the tutor and governess, who, as has been before said, were the leading spirits in the family of the Bayswater Goodenoughs, were seized with the irrepressible desire of inviting their brothers and sisters with their families to reside with them, to enable them to do which, it would have been indispensable for them to enlarge their establishment, and, as a necessary consequence, to add considerably to the size of their hitherto convenient house.

It should be mentioned that the Bayswater Goodenoughs enjoyed the confidence and friendship of an influential Banking Establishment, which it had doubtless acquired from the good business which, for many years previously to the events now narrated, had been transacted between the Banking Establishment and the Bayswater Goodenoughs, the latter paying over each year to the former a handsome surplus-balance for the credit of their account; it was therefore decided by the tutor and the governess, acting as they held for the majority of the members of the family, to apply to their banking friends, whose name, by-the-bye, was the "United Company," Limited, and whose authority for so important an expenditure as they proposed, they from the nature of their joint transactions knew they would be obliged to obtain.

The dissentient members of the family at the same time represented their cause to the United Company, protesting emphatically against the projected scheme, which they denounced as extravagant and as in all respects undesirable.

The United Company now found itself on the horns of a dilemma, as any intervention between contending members of the same family leads to very unpleasant results, and frequently ends in dissatisfying both parties in any difference. On the one hand, they, in the exercise of a sound discretion, wished to encourage reasonable expenditure on the part of their "Constituents," particularly if such expenditure does not necessitate any of very large advances on the part of the United Company; on the other hand, they felt that the dissentients, who were by no means insignificant in point of numbers, had a certain amount of right on their side, and that at any rate their policy was the more prudent one.

It happened that the United Company were very fortunately situated in regard to their Board of Directors; one of whom (the vice-chairman) had rendered important and prominent services to the Company. In the difficulty in which they now found themselves, the vice-chairman suggested that himself and four of his co-directors should be appointed by the rest of the management to investigate the whole matter, and that their enquiry should embrace all the questions at issue, upon which they should frame a report for the Board of Directors.

When the Board of Directors of the United Company met for the consideration of this momentous affair, and for the transaction of their ordinary business, there was an unusually large attendance of the Board, and the contending parties were well represented by the Tutor and the Governess on one side, and by an able advocate on the part of the Bayswater Goodenoughs on the other.

After a protracted discussion of about four hours' duration, the first and only resolution of the "Inquisitorial," &c., which had been submitted to the meeting was declared to be lost, thus leaving the question which had been the cause of so much excitement in precisely the same position in which it had stood previously to its reference to the "United Company."

Thus ended a controversy which is perhaps without its parallel in point of wordy debate, and which certainly has not been, and it is to be hoped never may be rivalled in the annals of the history of the families of the Western Counties. It ended as it had begun – in talk. May the moral of its results not be without a good and permanent effect upon society, tending to restrain the aspirations of ambition and the desire to emulate the grandeur of others, and to promote the more moderate delights of contentment with one's own sufficiently good fortunes.

APPENDIX 5A

(a) Photograph of the Conference of Anglo-Jewish ministers, held between the Wars. The Conference united Jewish preachers of all denominations, orthodox and non-orthodox. (Photograph courtesy of Mrs Seymour Craig, daughter of the Revd. I. Livingstone.)

BACK ROW
1 Unknown
2 Revd A. Rose
3 Unknown
4 Revd M. Bloch
5 Unknown
6 Revd N. Goulston
7 Rabbi Dr J. Rabbinowitz
8 Revd J. Israelstam
9 Unknown

MIDDLE ROW
10 Rabbi Dr J. Newman
11 Unknown
12 Revd B. Lieberman
13 Rabbi Dr S. M. Lehrman
14 Revd S. Lipson
15 Revd M. Brown
16 Revd Dr I. K. Cosgrove
17 Unknown
18 Rabbi Dr Louis Rabinowitz
19 Unknown
20 Unknown
21 Revd J. F. Stern
22 Revd G. Levy
23 Unknown
24 Rabbi Dr M. Ginsberg
25 Unknown
26 Unknown
27 Unknown
28 Unknown

FRONT ROW
29 Dayan H. M. Lazarus
30 Unknown
31 Rabbi Salis Daiches
32 Revd I Livingstone
33 Revd A. A. Green
34 Dayan Dr Feldman
35 Chief Rabbi J. H. Hertz
36 Revd Ephraim Levene
37 Unknown
38 Unknown
39 Dyan Mendelsohn
40 Revd Vivian Simmonds
41 Dayan M. Gollop
42 Revd Arthur Barnet
43 Unknown

APPENDIX 5B

Conference of Jewish Preachers, University College, London, July 10, 1923.

Back row: Unknown; Unknown; Revd. W. Esterson; Revd. H. Goodman; Unknown; Unknown; Unknown; Unknown; Unknown.

Front row: Revd. I. Livingstone; Revd. Dr. A. Silverstone; Chief Rabbi Dr. J.H. Hertz; Revd. S. Levy; Unknown.

(b) Conference of Anglo–Jewish preachers, 1926, held at University College London. (Photograph courtesy of Dr. A. Goldberg, grandson of the Revd. W. Esterson.)

The names of the Rabbis in both of these remarkable photographs were kindly provided to me by the Revd. Dr. I. Levy, OBE, TD, to whom I am most grateful.

APPENDIX 6

(a) Map of London showing the geographical position of the synagogue buildings at their last address prior to closure.

MAP REFERENCE:
(1) Great Synagogue at Duke's Place; (2) Hambro Synagogue at Adler Street; (3) New Synagogue at Great St. Helen's; (4) Western Synagogue at Crawford Place; (5) Beth Hamedrash at Mulberry Street; (6) Borough New Synagogue at Wansey Street; (7) West London Synagogue at Margaret Street; (8) Central Synagogue at Great Portland Street; (9) Bayswater Synagogue at Andover Place; (10) North London Synagogue at Lofting Road; (11) East London Synagogue at Rectory Square; (12) Dalston Synagogue at Poet's Road; (13) Adass Yisroel at Green Lanes; (14a) New Dalton Synagogue at Birkbeck Road; (14b) Stoke Newington Synagogue at Shacklewell Lane; (15) South East London Synagogue at New Cross Road; (16) Liberal Jewish Synagogue at St. Johns Wood Road; (17) North West London Synagogue at Caversham Road; (18) Woolwich and Plumstead Synagogue at Anglesea Road; (19) West Ham (Associate) Synagogue at Earlham Grove; (20) Brondesbury Synagogue at Chevening Road; (21) East Ham and Manor Park Synagogue at Carlyle Road; (22) Brixton Synagogue at Effra Road; (23) Bermondsey and Rotherhithe Synagogue at Rouel Road; (24) Hornsey and Wood Green Synagogue at Wightman Road; (25) Muswell Hill Synagogue at Fortis Green Road; (26) South West London at Bolingbroke Green; (27) Upton Park Synagogue at Tudor Road; (28) Richmond Synagogue at Sheen Road; (29) Chelsea Synagogue at Smith Terrace; (30) Settlement Synagogue at Berners (Henriques) Street; (31) Cricklewood Synagogue at Walm Lane; (32) Willesden (District) Synagogue at College Road; (33) Mile End and Bow United Synagogue at Harley Grove; (34) West Central Liberal Synagogue at Whitfield Street; (35) Harrow Synagogue at Vaughan Road; (36) Dollis Hill Synagogue at Parkside; (37) Highgate Synagogue at Archway Road; (38) Pinner Synagogue at Cecil Park; (39) Streatham Synagogue at Estreham Road; (40) Shepherds Bush Synagogue at Poplar Grove; (41) Shomrei Adass at Finchley Road; (42) Neasden Federation Synagogue at Clifford Way; (43) Elm Park Synagogue at Woburn Avenue.

N.B. The positions of the Machzike Adass and Princelet Street Synagogue, as well as the other synagogues of the Federation in the East End, are not included on this map.

(b) Dates of the foundation of the synagogues and their closure

Map ref no.	Name of synagogue	Founded	Site	Postcode	From	To
1	Great	1690	Duke's Place	EC3	First building 1620 Second building 1722 Third building 1766 Fourth building 1790 Fifth building 1943	1958
			Adler St	E1	1958	1977
2	Hambro	1707	Fenchurch St	EC3	First building 1707 Second building 1720	1893
			Adler St	E1	1899	1936
3	New	1761	Leadenhall St	EC3	1761	1837
			Great St Helens	EC3	1838	1911
			Egerton Rd	N16	1915	still open
4	Western	?1764/5	Great Pulteney St	W1	?1764	?1765
			Denmark Court	WC2	First building 1765 Second building 1797	1797 1826
			St Alban's Place	SW1	1826	1914
			Alfred Place	WC1	1918	1941
			Crawford St	W1	1957	1991
5	Beth Hamedrash	?1782	Nr. Leadenhall St	EC3	?1782	1849
			Leadenhall St	EC3	1849	1875
			Duke's Place	EC3	1876	1905
			Mulberry St	E1	1905	?1940–1948
6	Borough (1) Borough (2) Borough New	?1800 1823 1867	Newington Causeway St George's Rd Heygate St Wansey St	SE1 SE1 SE17 SE17	?1800 1823 1867 1927	1853 1867 1927 1961
7	West London	1841	Burton St	WC1	1841	1849
			Margaret St	W1	1849	1870
			Upper Berkeley St	W1	?1867–1870	still open
8	Central	1850–1853	120 Great Portland St	W1	1855	1870
			133-141 Great Portland St	W1	First building 1870 Second building 1948 Third building 1956	1941 1956 still open
9	Bayswater	1860	Chichester Place	W2	1863	1966
			Andover Place	W2	1971-2	1984
10	North London	1863	Lofting Road	N1	1868	1958
11	East London	1873	Rectory Square (later amal. with Hackney)	E1	1873	1993
12	Dalston	1874	Mildmay Rd	N5	1876	1884
			Poet's Road	N5	1885	1967
13	Adass Yisroel	1886	Newington Green Rd	N	1886	1889
			Ferntower Rd	N	?1889	1905
			Green Lanes	N16	1905–1911	1957
14a 14b	New Dalston became Stoke Newington	1888	Birkbeck Rd Shacklewell Lane	E8 E8	1888 1903	1903 1976
15	South East London	1888	Lausanne Rd	SE15	1889	1905
			New Cross Road	SE14	First building 1905 Second building 1946 Third building 1956	1940 1956 1985
16	Liberal Jewish	1890–1902	Hill St	NW1	1911	1925
			St Johns Wood Rd	NW8	First building 1925 Second building 1991	?1990 still open
17	North West London	1890	York Rd	NW5	1890	1900
			Caversham Rd	NW5	1900	1975

Map ref no.	Name of synagogue	Founded	Site	Postcode	From	To
18	Woolwich	1892	Anglesea Rd	SE18	First building 1925 Second building 1964	1964 1996
19	West Ham	1897	Earlham Grove	E7	First building 1911 Second building 1984	1984 still open
20	Brondesbury	1900	Chevening Rd	NW6	1905	1974
21	East Ham	1902	Carlyle Rd	E12	1902	1986
22	Brixton	1905	Effra Rd	SW2	First building 1913 Second building 1921	1921 1986
23	Bermondsey & Rotherhithe	1911–1915	Jamaica Rd Rouel Rd	SE16 SE16	1915 1936	1936 1970
24	Hornsey & Wood Green	1911	Green Lanes Tottenham Lane Wightman Rd	N N N8	1911 1914 1920	1913 1920 1987
25	Muswell Hill	1911	Fortis Green Rd and 6. Methuen Park Tetherdown	N10 N10 N10	?1911 1963	1963 still open
26	South West London	1911–1915	Bolingbrooke Grove	SW11	1915	1997
27	Upton Park	1911	Tudor Rd	E6	?1920	1972
28	Richmond	1916	Parkshot Sheen Rd Litchfield Gardens	Richmond Richmond Richmond	1916 1938 1986	1938 1986 still open
29	Chelsea	1913–1916	Smith Terrace	SW3	First building 1916 Second building 1957	1957 still open
30	The Settlement	?1919	Betts St Berners (Henriques) St	E1 E1	?1919 1929	1929 1998
31	Cricklewood	1923	Walm Lane	NW2	First building 1930 Second building 1989	1989 still open
32	Willesden United Willesden Federation	1926 1933	College Road Healthfield Park	NW10 NW2	1934 First building 1934 Second building 1938	? ? 2000
33	Mile End	1927	Harley Grove	E3	1929	1977
34	West Central Liberal	1913–1928	Alfred Place Whitfield St	W1 W1	1914 1960	1941 1998
35	Harrow	1928	Sheepcote Rd Vaughan Rd	Harrow Harrow	1928 1946	1946 1972
36	Dollis Hill	1929	Parkside	NW2	1937	?1996
37	Highgate	1929	88 Archway Rd Archway Rd	N6 N6	1934 1952	1952 1976
38	Pinner	1941	Cecil Park	Pinner	First building 1950 Second building 1981	1981 still open
39	Streatham	1946	Mitcham Lane Estreham Rd	SW16 SW16	1947 1957	1957 1981
40	Shepherd's Bush (Fed)	1913	Poplar Grove	W6	1924	1989
41	Shomrei Adass (Fed)	1946	Finchley Road	NW3	1946	?1997
42	Elm Park	1948	Woburn Avenue	Elm Park	1950	1999

REFERENCES

1.   Black G. 1994 *Living Up West. Jewish Life in London's West End.* London Museum of Jewish Life, London.
2.   Newman A 1976 *The United Synagogue 1870–1970.* Routledge & Kegan Paul, London.
3.   Adler E 1930 *Jewish Communities Series: London.* Jewish Publication Society of America, Philadelphia.
4.   *Encyclopaedia Judaica* 1972. Keter Publishing House, Jerusalem.
5.   Stow J (Edited by Henry Morley in 1890) *A Survey of London.* George Routledge, London.
6.   Jacobs J 1888 The London Jewry, 1290. In: *Papers Read at the Anglo-Jewish Historical Exhibition, 1887.* Jewish Chronicle, London.
7.   Wasserzug D 1902 In: *Jewish Chronicle,* 15th August.
8.   Richardson HG 1960 *The English Jewry under the Angevin Kings.* Methuen, London.
9.   Hillaby J 1990–2 London: the thirteenth century Jewry revisited. *Transactions of the Jewish Historical Society of England,* Vol. XXXII, 89–158.
10. British Museum MSS, add., 4542
11. Burford EJ 1990 *London. The Synfulle Citie.* Robert Hale, London.
12. Margoliouth M 1851 *The History of the Jews of Great Britain.* Bentley, London.
13. Picciotto J (1875, revised 1956) (ed. J. Finestein) *Sketches of Anglo-Jewish History.* Soncino Press, London.
14. Roth C 1941 *A History of the Jews in England.* Oxford University Press, Oxford
15. Hyamson AM 1951 *The Sephardim of England.* Methuen, London.
16. Samuel W 1924 *The First London Synagogue of the Resettlement.* Spottiswode, Ballantyne & Co., London.
17. Lipman VD 1968 The Rise of Jewish Suburbia. *Transactions of the Jewish Historical Society of England,* Vol. XXI, 78–113.
18. Preface from the *Rules of the Congregation,* 1827. Published by the congregation.
19. Vigoda S 1981 *Legendary Voices.* Published by the author, New York.
20. Roth C 1950 *History of the Great Synagogue, London, 1600–1940.* Edward Goldston, London.
21. Epstein C 1996 The architecture of the Great Synagogue, Duke's Place. In: S. Kadish (ed) *Building Jerusalem. Jewish Architecture in Britain.* Valentine Mitchell, London.
22. Ackermann R 1809 *The Microcosm of London.* Repository of Arts, 101 Strand, London.
23. Summerson J 1943 *The Microcosm of London.* King Penguin, London.
24. Wischnitzer R 1964 *The Architecture of the European Synagogue.* Jewish Publication Society of America, Philadephia.
25. Newman A 1981 *The Jewish East End 1840–1939.* Jewish Historical Society of England, London.
26. Symons H 1979 *Forty Years a Chief Rabbi.* Robson, London.
27. Duschinsky C 1921 *The Rabbinate of the Great Synagogue from 1756–1842.* Oxford University Press, Oxford. Reprinted in 1971 by Gregg International Publishers, Farnborough, Hants.
28. Roth C 1942 The Chief Rabbinate of England. In: *Essays Presented to J.H. Hertz.* Edward Goldston, London.
29. Adler H 1888 The Chief Rabbis of England. In: *Papers Read at the Anglo-Jewish Historical Exhibition, 1887.* Jewish Chronicle, London.
30. Mayerowitsch H 1942 The Cantorate of the Great Synagogue. In: *Miscellanies of the Jewish Historical Society of England* Vol. IV, London.
31. Esterson W (1925) *History of the Hambro Synagogue on the Occasion of its 200th Anniversary.* Published by the congregation. (By courtesy of his daughter, Mrs. D. Lew.)
32. Samuel WS 1925 (letter) In: *Jewish Guardian,* 18th March.
33. Gollancz H (ed) 1930 *S.M. Gollancz: Biographical Sketches.* Oxford University Press, Oxford.
34. Levy AB 1960 *The 200-year-old New Synagogue.* Published by the congregation. (By courtesy of Mr. A. Rosenberg.)
35. Rosenau H 1948 *A Short History of Jewish Art.* James Clarke, London.
36. Roth C 1932 *Records of the Western Synagogue.* Edward Goldston, London.
37. Barnett A 1961 *The Western Synagogue Through Two Centuries.* Vallentine Mitchell, London.
38. Smith JT 1815 *Ancient Topography of London.* Published by the author.
39. Gordon C 1903 *Old Time Aldwych, Kingsway, and Neighbourhood.* Fisher Unwin, London.
40. London County Council 1935 *Survey of London* **18**, 126.
41. Fahrner R 1989 *The Theatre Career of Charles Dibdin the Elder (1745–1814).* Lang, New York.
42. *General Magazine and Impartial Review,* October 1791.
43. Hertz JH, Joseph M 1927 (letter). *Jewish Chronicle,* 22nd April.
44. Joseph M 1931 *Synagogue Architecture.* Thesis deposited at University of Southampton.
45. Lewis C 1965 *A Soho Address.* Victor Gollancz, London. Pp. 58–60.
46. Ornstien P 1905 *Historical Sketch of the Beth Hamedrash.* United Synagogue, London.
47. Hertzberg A. *The Beth Hamedrash.* Privately published. (Lent to me by his daughter, Elizabeth Sloam).
48. Adler H 1905 In: *Jewish Chronicle,* 15th December.
49. *Jewish Chronicle,* 8th September 1876.
50. Alderman G 1998 *Modern British Jewry,* 2nd edn. Oxford University Press, Oxford.
51. *Jewish Chronicle,* 15th December, 1905.
52. Obituary. *Jewish Chronicle ,* 3rd January 1902.
53. Burford EJ 1973 *The Orrible Synne.* Caldar & Boyars, London.
54. Rosenbaum M 1917 *History of the Borough New Synagogue.* Published by the congregation.

55.   *Illustrated London News*, 4th May, 1867.
56.   *The Graphic*, 23rd December, 1893.
57.   Obituary. *Jewish Chronicle*, 24th August 1906.
58.   Obituary. *Jewish Chronicle*, 4th May 1934
59.   *Jewish Chronicle*. 21st December, 1900.
60.   Cohen FL, Davis DM 1933 *The Voice of Prayer and Praise*, 3rd edn. The United Synagogue, London.
61.   Philipson D 1907 *The Reform Movement in Judaism*. Macmillan, New York.
62.   Rayner JD 1990 Montefiore, Montagu and Mattuck, Pioneers of Liberal Judaism. In: Anne Kershen (ed) *150 Years of Progressive Judaism in Britain*. London Museum of Jewish Life, London.
63.   Kershen AJ, Romain JA 1995 *Tradition and Change. A History of Reform Judaism in Britain 1840–1995*. Valentine Mitchell, London.
64.   Petuchowski JJ 1968 *Prayer Book Reform in Europe*. World Union for Progressive Judaism, New York.
65.   Isaacs S 1948 *History of the Central Synagogue*. Published by the congregation.
66.   Shine C 1970 *History of the Central Synagogue*. Published by the congregation.
67.   Jacob AM 1977 The Revd. A.L. Green. *Transactions of the Jewish Historical Society of England*, Vol. XXV, 87 (an exceptionally readable paper).
68.   (Author unstated) 1938 *Bayswater Synagogue 1863–1938, Origin and History*. Published by the congregation.
69.   Künzl H 1984 *Islamische Stilelemente im Synagogenbau des 19. und frühen 20. Jahrhunderts*. Peter Lange, Frankfurt-am-Main.
70.   Adler M 1939 *The Jews of Medieval England*. Jewish Historical Society of England, London.
71.   *Bristol Gazette*, 25th August, 1842 (quoted in Ref. 67 above).
72.   Obituary. *Jewish Chronicle*, 18th March 1883
73.   Philips OS and Simons HA 1963 *The Bayswater Synagogue, 1893–1963*. Privately published.
74.   Alderman G 1987 *The Federation of Synagogues, 1887–1987*. Published by the Federation, London.
75.   Lipman VD. Quoted in: Alderman G 1992 *Modern British Jewry*, 1st edn., p.119. Clarendon Press, Oxford.
76.   Gollancz H 1916 (Preached on 15th June 1912) In: *Sermons and Addresses*, Second Series. Chapman & Hall, London.
77.   N. Bergerman 1948 *The History of the North London Synagogue*. Published by the congregation.
78.   *Illustrated London News*, 3rd October, 1868.
79.   Obituary. *Jewish Chronicle*, 25th April, 1930.
80.   Joseph M 1903 *Judaism as Creed and Life*. Macmillan, London.
81.   Stern JF *Jewish Chronicle*, 6th June, 1902.
82.   Finestein I 1981 *The Jewish East End 1840–1939*. Jewish Historical Society of England, London.
83.   Obituary. *Jewish Chronicle*, 17th January, 1958.
84.   Wasserzug D 1910 *Dalston Synagogue: A Historical Sketch*. Published by the congregation.
85.   Rabbinowitz J 1935 *History of the Dalston Synagogue*. Published by the congregation.
86.   Obituary. *Jewish Chronicle*, 20th December, 1918.
87.   (Author unstated) 1936 *Adass Yisroel. The History of the Congregation on its Silver Jubilee*. Published by the congregation.
88.   Schönfeld V 1930 *Judaism as Life's Purpose*, Published by author, London.
89.   Kranzler D, Hirschler G (eds) 1982 *Solomon Schönfeld. His Place in History*. Judaica Press, New York.
90.   Grunfeld E 1980 *Shefford*. Soncino Press, London.
91.   Feldman A 1928 *A Link With The Past. Some Notes on the New Dalston Synagogue and Schools*. Women's Printing Society, London.
92.   Cohen H 1928 *Semi-Jubilee Celebration Record*. Published by the congregation.
93.   (Author unstated) 1953 *Fiftieth Anniversary Celebration Record*. Published by the congregation.
94.   Wise S 1957 *The South East London Synagogue*. Published by the congregation.
95.   Bayme S 1982 Claude Montefiore, Lily Montagu and the origins of the Jewish Religious Union. In: *Transactions of the Jewish Historical Society of England*, Vol. XXVII, 61–72.
96.   Simon O. Quoted in Philipson.[61]
97.   Cohen L 1940 *Some Recollections of Claude Goldsmid Montefiore*. Faber & Faber, London.
98.   (Author unstated) 1979 *North London Railway. A pictorial record*. HMSO. National Railway Museum, York.
99.   Lee C 1973 *The Northern Line. A brief history*. London Transport, London.
100.   Obituary. *Jewish Chronicle*, 4th July 1958.
101.   Obituary. *Jewish Chronicle*, 3rd May, 1957.
102.   Obituary. *Jewish Chronicle*, 9th April 1965.
103.   Obituary. *Jewish Chronicle*, 16th December, 1949.
104.   Bloch H 1997 *Earlham Grove Shul*. Published by the congregation.
105.   *Jewish Chronicle*, 21st March 1913.
106.   Lazarus H 1930 *History of the Brondesbury Synagogue*. Published by the congregation.
107.   Melinek A 1955 *History of the Brondesbury Synagogue*. Published by the congregation.
108.   Rosenberg S 1996 Alternative uses for "redundant" synagogues. In: S. Kadish (ed) *Building Jerusalem*. Valentine Mitchell, London.
109.   Cohen L 1958 *Fifty Golden Years: A History of the Brixton Synagogue*. Published by the congregation.
110.   Daiches-Dubens R 1953 Eighteenth century Jewry in and around Richmond. *Transactions of the Jewish Historical Soicety of England*, Vol. XVIII, 143–169.
111.   Howitt A 1930 *Richmond and Its Jewish Connections*. Published privately.
112.   (Author unstated) 1976 *History of the Richmond Synagogue*. Published by the congregation.
113.   (Author unstated) 1997 *Chelsea Shul. Fourscore Years*. Published by the congregation.

114. Rigal L 1990 The Settlement Synagogue. In: Anne Kershen (ed) *150 Years of Progressive Judaism in Britain.* London Museum of Jewish Life, London.

115. Henriques BLQ 1937 *The Indiscretions of a Warden.* Methuen, London.

116. Loewe LL 1976 *Basil Henriques. A Portrait.* Routledge & Kegan Paul, London.

117. Lieberman BB 1956 *The History of the Cricklewood Synagogue.* Published by the congregation.

118. Susser B 1994 *The Willesden and Brondesbury Synagogue 1934–1994. A Diamond Jubilee History.* Published by the congregation.

119. Rigal L 1978 *History of the West Central Liberal Synagogue.* Published by the congregation.

120. Sinclair R (undated) *Historical Wanderings of Harrow and Pinner.* Published by the Pinner congregation.

121. Krinsky CH 1985 *Synagogues of Europe.* MIT Press, Cambridge, Mass.

122. Content H, Aarons L 1970 *A History of the Streatham Synagogue.* Published by the congregation.

123. Glasman J 1987 Architecture and anglicization: London synagogue building 1870–1900. *Jewish Quarterly* **34** (2) 16–21.

124. Homa B 1953 *A Fortress in Anglo-Jewry. The Story of the Machzike Hadath.* Shapiro Vallentine, London.

125. Melnick SC 1994 *A Giant Amongst Giants.* Pentland Press, Bishop Auckland.

126. Paskin S, Liddell-King J 1998/9 Standing still: still standing. The Synagogue at 19 Princelet Street. *Jewish Quarterly* **45**(4), 21–25.

127. Lichtenstein R, Sinclair I 1999 *Rodinsky's Room.* Granta, London.

128. Letter. *Evening Standard*, 4th June, 1999.

129. Jacobs L 1989 *Helping with Enquiries.* Vallentine Mitchell, London.

130. Domb C 1970 In: *Memories of Kopul Rosen.* Published by Carmel College, Sussex

131. Jamilly E 1956 Anglo-Jewish architects and architecture in the 18th and 19th centuries. *Transactions of the Jewish Historical Society of England*, Vol. XVIII, 127–141.

132. Obituary. *Jewish Chronicle*, 15th December, 1905.

133. *The Builder,* 12th September 1874

134. Webb B, interview, 13th December 1897, recorded in Charles Booth's unpublished Notebook 27, p.63 (preserved at the London School of Economics). Quoted in Glasman.[123]

135. Hammer-Schenk H 1978 *Hamburgs Synagogen des 19. und fruehen 20. Jahrhunderts.* Hower, Hamburg.

GLOSSARY

Adon Olam	The concluding prayer at the end of the morning service on the Sabbath.
Almemar	The platform in the synagogue from which the *Seipher Torah* is read. The Almemar is centrally placed in most Ashkenazi synagogues, though it may be against the western wall in some synagogues adhering to the Eastern rite. With the movement to reform, the Reader's desk was transported to the eastern end of the synagogue.
Amidah	A standing prayer, said in silence.
Arba Minnim	The four species (see *Lulaf*).
Aron-hakodesh	The ark.
Ashkenazim	Jews originating in Germany, Poland and Russia.
Asoro Batlonim	The ten poor men who are paid to make up the quorum.
Austrittsgemeinde	A congregation separating itself from the main community, originally in Germany, usually ultra-Orthodox, but also of the Reform movement.
Baal Koré	The Reader from the *Seipher Torah*.
Baal Tephila	Literally, 'master of the prayer', that is, the *Hazzan*.
Baale-Batim	Members of the congregation.
Barmitzvah	The attainment of religious majority by a boy at the age of thirteen.
Bayis Shalom	Literally, 'house of peace'.
Bimah	Another word for *Almemar*.
Cheder	Literally, 'a room', where young children are taught the essentials of Judaism.
Chevra	Brotherhood.
Chupah	The canopy beneath which the bride and groom stand at the wedding.
Conventicle	A small hall or room where services are held, as opposed to a large or major syngaogue. Also known as a *Shtiebl*.
Dayan	Religious judge.
Decalogue	The Ten Commandments.
Derashot	Lectures on a religious topic (singular: *Deresha*).
Derech Eretz	Literally, 'way of the earth', taken to mean 'respect'.
Duchen	The platform before the ark upon which those of priestly descent *duchen*, that is, bless the congregation. In Reform congregations, the priestly blessing is no longer given and the Reader's desk, or *Omed*, is placed upon this platform, facing the congregation.
Frum	Yiddish for 'religious'.
Gemara	Aramaic for 'learning' which, together with the *Mishnah*, makes the entire *Talmud*.
Haggadah	The book read in the home on the first two nights of Passover, discussing the exodus of the Jews from Egypt.

Haham	The Chief Rabbi of the Spanish and Portuguese Synagogue.
Hassidim	Followers of the Jewish revivalist movement of the seventeenth century.
Hazzan	The Cantor, Precentor or Reader – the officiant, paid or otherwise, who leads the prayers in the synagogue.
Hazzanut	The art of the *Hazzan* or Cantor.
Hebra Kadisha	The holy brotherhood or burial society responsible for performing the last rites.
Herem	Excommunication.
Ilui	A teenage prodigy.
Jahrzeit	The anniversary of a person's death.
Kaddish	The prayer recited by mourners at all services.
Kashrut	Food which may be eaten by an obervant Jew. (Adj. *Kosher*)
Kehillah	A congregation.
Kosher	The adjective for *Kashrut* (see above).
Landsmannschaften	A group of men from the same town worshipping together.
Lomzer	Someone from Lomza, Lithuania.
Lubliner	Someone from Lublin, Poland.
Lulaf	One of the four species of plant taken in the hand on the Festival of Tabernacles. The four species are the palm branch, the citron, the myrtle and the willow.
Maariv	The morning service.
Machzor	A prayer book for use on Festivals.
Mahamad	The governing body of the Spanish and Portuguese Synagogue.
Menorah	The candelabrum lit on the Feast of Lights.
Mikveh	A ritual bath filled with rain water, which removes impurity.
Mincha	The afternoon service.
Minhag Polin	Prayers according to the Polish rite.
Minyan	The quorum of ten males necessary to say certain prayers.
Mishnah	see *Talmud*.
Neilah	The concluding service on the most solemn day of the Jewish year, the Day of Atonement.
Olenu	A prayer said at the end of morning, afternoon and evening services.
Omed	The desk from which the *Hazzan* reads the prayers. This may be situated on the Almemar or may be below and to the right of the ark.
Parokhet	The curtain placed before the ark.
Piyutim	Additional poems, often of medieval origin, expanding upon the original prayers.
Praga'er	Originating from Prague.
Rashi	Rabbi Solomon Yitzchaki (1040-1105), the great medieval French commentator on the Bible and *Talmud*.
Rav, Reb or Rebbe	Rabbi.
Seipher Torah	The hand written scroll containing the five books of

	Moses.
Seipher	Hebrew book.
Selichos	Prayers said before, during and after the New Year and on the Day of Atonement.
Sephardim	Jews originally from Spain. The term now also includes those from North Africa, Baghdad and other countries in the Middle and Far East.
Shabbes Goy	A Gentile employed in the ghetto for lighting fires, etc., on the Sabbath.
Shabbat Behaloscho	The five books of Moses are divided into weekly portions, so that they may all be read within a year. Each portion takes its name from its initial word or phrase.
Shabbat Hagadol	The Great Sabbath - the Sabbath before the Feast of Passover.
Shabbat Shuva	The Sabbath between the New Year and the Day of Atonement. On these the Rabbi would typically give a *Derasha*, often on an obscure topic, to demonstrate his mastery of the Holy texts.
Shamash	The Beadle in the synagogue.
Shammes	See *Shamash*.
Shechita	The Jewish method of slaughter for meat.
Shiur	A discourse given by the Rabbi.
Shomer	Religious supervisor responsible for ensuring the acceptability of food for religious Jews.
Shtiebl	See *Conventicle*.
Siddur	Prayer book.
Simchas Torah	'Rejoicing of the Law'. The end and beginning of the annual cycle of reading of the five books of Moses.
Succah	The temporary dwelling or tabernacle which is lived in during the Feast of Tabernacles.
Tahara	The ceremony of purifying the dead by washing.
Takkanos	Rule books.
Tallit	A prayer shawl, attached to which are fringes. Worn during the morning service by adult males. The fringes are a visible reminder of the Divine commandments.
Talmud Shiurim	Lectures on the *Talmud*. (Singular: *Shiur*).
Talmud Torah	Jewish religion classes.
Talmud	Compilation of the *Mishnah* and *Gemara*. The *Mishnah* was a work in 63 volumes, compiled around the year 200 and containing commentaries by the Rabbis on the Divine Laws in the Bible.
Tephilin	Boxes worn on the arm and on the forehead. Worn at morning prayers during the week. They contain small scrolls of parchment upon which are written Biblical passages; their wearing is ordained by Scripture.
Teva or *Teba*	Desk.
Torah	The five books of Moses.
Tosephot	Additional commentaries upon the *Talmud*.

INDEX

Page numbers in **bold** indicate main entries

Aaron the Scribe of Dublin	36
Abrahams, Rabbi Israel	112, 176
Abrams, I.	176
Abramsky, Rabbi (Dayan) Yechezkiel	61, 100, 172
Adass Yisroel	**100**
Tahara House, Burma Road	102
Adelphi Theatre	51
Adler House	62
Adler Street	61
Great Synagogue in	35
Hambro Synagogue in	41
Adler, Cyril (architect)	147
Adler, Dr. Hermann	36, 59, 68, **80**, 87, 96, 112, 116, 118, 169, 172, 182
Adler, M.	75
Adler, Nathan Marcus	31, 36, 37, 42, 43, 59, 62, 68, 82
Adler, Woolf	147
Adolph Tuck Hall, Woburn House	75
Aggas' map of London	19
Ahavath Shalom, see *Gladstone Park and Neasden Synagogue*	
Ainsworth Road, synagogue in	171
Almemar	**184**
Amhurst Road, synagogue in	171
Anekstein, Revd. S.	138
Anglesea Road	
St. Andrew's Presbyterian Church in	124
synagogue in	124, 170
Anglo-Jewish Historical Exhibition of 1887	19
Another "Battle of Talking"	80, 190
Architects of the synagogues of London	**181**
Ark, siting of	184, 185
Arnold, Solomon	59
Aron, Harold	80
Artillery Lane Synagogue	179
Ascher, Simon, of Groningen	37
Assembly Hall, Woolwich New Road	123
Assembly Passage, Mile End Road, *Minyan* in	90
Athenaeum, Muswell Hill	140
Attias, Rabbi Moses	21
Avigdor School, Stoke Newington	102
Bakewell Hall	19, 20
Bakewell, Thomas	20
Balham and Tooting congregation	142, 143
Balham High Road, synagogue in	143
Balls Pond Road, cemetery in	71
Bancroft Road, Mile End, cemetery	52
Barnett Raingold Communal Hall	67
Barnett, Revd. Arthur	48, 88, 193
Barnsbury, migration to	25
Basevi, George	46
Bayswater Synagogue	25, 73, **79**, 96, 116, 118, 121, 182
Another "Battle of Talking"	190
in Andover Place	80, 83
in Chichester Place	27, 79–82
Bayswater, migration to	25
Bearsted, Lord, see *Samuel, Sir Marcus*	
Bearsted, Viscount	75, 78, 148
Bentham, Jeremiah	21
Beresford Street, Drill Hall in	124
Bergerman, Revd. Nathan	85, 86, 94, 168
Bermondsey and Rotherhithe Synagogue	**138**, 143, 170, 180
Bermondsey, poverty in	148
Berners Street, Settlement in	149
Bernhard Baron St. George's Jewish Settlement	149, 150
Beth Hamedrash	**58**
of the Sephardim	58
in Booker's Gardens (Sussex Place)	58
in Golders Green	103, 178
in Highbury New Park	101
in Leadenhall Street	59
in Mulberry Street, opening of	61
in Muswell Hill Synagogue	141
in Newington Green Road	100
in North London	100
in Willesden Green	156
pre-expulsion	58
Bethnal Green Great Synagogue	179, 180
Betts Street, girls' club in	148
Bevis Marks, synagogue in	21, 26, 32, 44, 71, 145
Bimah, see *Almemar*	
Bloch, M.	69, 193
Bolingbroke Grove, congregation at	142
Bornstein, Revd. H.	110, 121, 122
Borough Jewish School	**67**
Borough New Synagogue	**63**, 108, 134, 136, 143, 181
ark of	57
in Heygate Street	65
in Wansey Street	27, 66
memorial candelabrum	75, 110
Borough, Jewish settlement in	26
Boundaries Road, congregation at	142
Boyers, Revd. G.	56
Brady Street, burial ground in	44
Braham, John	37
Branch Synagogue of Great Synagogue, see *Central Synagogue*	
Branch Synagogue, Wigmore Street	71
Brewer Street	
in West End, congregation at	51
in Woolwich, services in	124
Bricklayers' Hall	44, 45
British Jews, opening of synagogue of	71
see also *West London Synagogue of British Jews*	
Brixton	66
transport lines to	26
Brixton Synagogue	67, **134**, 143, 166
Hebrew classes in	135
Brompton, Western Synagogue cemetery in	52
Brondesbury Synagogue	**131**
Brondesbury, Jewish settlement in	25
Brown, Revd. Mendel	121, 176, 193
Bryanston Street, synagogue in	181
Bucklers' Hall, see *Bricklayers' Hall*	
Bueno de Mesquita, D.	88
Burma Road, Addas Yisroel, building used for *Tahara* in	102
Canning Town	126
Cannon Lane, Pinner, services in	165
Cannon Street Road Synagogue	169, 179
Cannon Street Road	
boys' club in	148
synagogue in Laurence Buildings in	169
Canonbury, migration to	25
Cantorate of the Great Synagogue	**37**
Carlton Hall, Turnstall Road	134
Carmel College	179
Carter, E.	86
Castello, M.N.	23
Cateaton Street, see *Gresham Street*	
Catte Street, see *Gresham Street*	
Cecil Park, synagogue in	165
Central Hall, Parkshot, services in	146
Central Synagogue	25, 27, 38, 41, 54, 55, **73**, 76, 79, 110, 118, 182
first building	74
memorial candelabrum	75, 78, 110

memorial plaque	75
second building	75
stained glass windows of	153
third building	78
Chamberlayne Road, synagogue in	177, 180
Chanukah Military Service	69
Chasidim	47
Chelsea Synagogue	**147,** 187
Cheltenham Synagogue	45, 46
Chevra Mekor Chayim, Newington Green Road	100
Chevrah Torah Synagogue	180
Chief Rabbi	
duties of	31
title of	80
Choir, siting of	184
Christian Street, synagogues in	179
Circular candelabrum	
at Borough Synagogue	110
at Central Synagogue	110
at South East London Synagogue	110
City of London, location of synagogues in	26
Clapham, transport lines to	26
Clarence House, Tottenham Lane, services in	139
Clephane Road, services at	95
Clifford Way, synagogue in	170, 176
Clifton Hall	117
Cofnas, Rabbi	165
Cohen, Revd. Francis Lyon	66, **68,** 89
Cohen, Harriet	69
Cohen, Rabbi Harris	106
Cohen, Revd. Isaac	160
Cohen, Revd. J.M.	100
Cohen, Judah Loeb	35
Cohen, Revd. P.	75
Coleman Street, synagogue in	20
College Road, synagogue in, see *Willesden (District) Synagogue*	
Collins, Hyman Henry	54, 65, 85, **181**
Colveston House, Birkbeck Road, services in	95
Commercial Road Great Synagogue	174, 179
Congregational Church, Rouel Road	138
Constituent synagogues, renaming of	**177**
Copperman, Revd. P.	57
Cosgrove, Revd. Dr. I.K.	94, 193
Cree Church Lane, see *Creechurch Lane*	
Cree Church, Leadenhall Street	44
Creechurch Lane	
synagogue in	21-23
second synagogue in	186
Crewe, B.	127, 128
Cricklewood Synagogue	25, 128, **151,** 176, 182, 186
Croydon, synagogue in	170
Daiches, Salis	193
Dalston Synagogue	25, 59, 84, 86, **95,** 104, 131, 174, 182
secession from	96
Dalston Talmud Torah Synagogue	180
Dance, George, Snr.	32
Davidson, M.	138, 143
Davies, Revd. Coleman	105, 107
Davies, J.	46
Davis Mansions, synagogue in	169
Davis, D.M.	89, 93, 118
Davis, Henry D.	92, **181**
de Banquelle, John	20
de Medina, Solomon	145
de Rothschild, Sir Anthony	75
Dean Street synagogue, see *Western Synagogue*	
Denmark Court, synagogue in	181
Dennington Park Road, synagogue in	178
Design, basic, of synagogue	**184**
Dibdin, Charles	50
Dollinger, Revd. J.	56
Dollis Hill Synagogue	25, **162**
Domus Conversorum	63
Drill Hall, Beresford Street	123
Drukker, Revd. E.	121
Drury Lane	49
Duchan	**184**
Duke	
of Cambridge	33
of Cumberland	33
of Sussex	33
Duke's Place, synagogue in, see *Great Synagogue*	
Dunk Street, synagogues in	157, 169, 179, 180
Dzikower Synagogue	169, 180
Ealing, synagogue in	25
East End Synagogues	
after WWII	**179**
closures of	**169**
East Ham and Manor Park Synagogue	**130**
East London Central Synagogue	180
East London Synagogue	88, **90,** 107, 121, 182, 187
Edgar, Rabbi	159
Edgware	
synagogue in	180
transport lines to	26
Edmonton	
railway to	25
Western Syn cemetery in	55, 56
prayer hall of	55
Eger, R. Akiba	42
Egerton Road, synagogue in, see *New Synagogue*	
Einhorn, Revd. S.	106
Elfand, Revd. S.	133
Elias, Binom, of Darmstadt	37
Elm Park Synagogue	**167**
Emancipation of Jewry, Germany	186
Emanuel, Barrow	92, **181**
Emden, Schlomo	40
Emet V Shalom Synagogue	177
Eprile, C.J.	128, **182,** 151
Essex synagogues	**168**
Esterson, Revd. Woolf	42, 118, 194
Ezra, Abraham Ibn	17
Ezras Haim Synagogue	170, 171, 179
Faigenblum, Revd. P.	153
Fassenfeld, Revd. P.	174
Federation of Synagogues	55, 104, 155, 156, 157, 158, **169,** 177, 179, 183
Feldman, Dayan Asher	59, 61, 88, 104, 105, 193
Feldman, Rabbi Rafael	176
Fenchurch Street, synagogue in, see *Hambro Synagogue*	
Fieldgate Street Sephardism Synagogue	179
Finchley Central, synagogue in	180
Finsbury Park Synagogue	98, 125, 182
Forest Gate	126
Forest Gate Federation Synagogue	170
Forscher, Hazzan	38
Franks families	145
Freilich, Revd. E.	176
French Chapel Royal, off Portman Square	56
Friars of St. Anthony	20
Friars of the Sack	18
Friedlander, Revd. Gerald	56
Friedlander, Revd. J.	118
Fulham and Kensington Synagogue	170, 176
Games, Abraham	141
Gaster, Dr.	23, 88
Gestetner, Alice	102
Gingold, Revd. M.	125
Ginsberg, Rabbi Dr. M.	88, 146, 193
Ginsbury, Rabbi P.	166
Gladstone Park and Neasden Synagogue, see *Neasden Federation Synagogue*	
Glory of Israel Synagogue	179
Goldblum's Synagogue	98, 101, 167
Golders Green	
Beth Hamedrash	103

Synagogue 35, 180, 186
transport lines to 26
Goldsmid, Benjamin 145
Goldston, Revd. N. 88, 108, 110
Gollancz, Samuel Marcus 41, **42**, 84
Gollancz, Sir Hermann 42, 43, 80, 83, **84**, 96, 116
Gollop, Dayan M. 84, 88, 193
Goodman, H. 139, 194
Goodman, Tobias 51
Gordon, Abraham 37, 38
Gordon, Lord George 41
Goulston, N. 193
Graeditz, Solomon 52
Great Alie Street Synagogue 179
Great Central Hotel, Marylebone Station 113
Great Portland Street, synagogue in, see *Central Synagogue*
Great Synagogue (pre-expulsion) 20
Great Synagogue 27, 39, 41, 42, 44, **30**, 51, 62, 69, 70, 73, 76, 95, 106, 107, 145, 186, 187
ark of 36
Cantorate of **37**
choir of 106
destruction of 35
interior of 32
plaques of 46
Rabbinate of **35**
Rules of the Congregation, 1827 30
Green Lanes, congregation in 100
Green Lanes, synagogue at Queen's Parade in 139
Green, Revd. A.A. 78, 85, 113, 184, 193
Green, Revd. Aaron Levy 38, 73, **75**
Greenfield Road Synagogue 179
Greenford synagogue in 180
Greenhalgh, John 21, 188
Gresham Street, synagogue in 18, 19, 20
Grosnass, Dayan 61
Grotian Hall, Wigmore Street 56
Grove Lane, synagogue in 170
Grunewald, Rabbi 165
Hackney Synagogue 107, 160
HaCohen Kook, Rabbi Abraham Isaac 172
Haines, Revd. Marcus 54, 118
Halter, N. 169
Hambro Synagogue **39**, 47, 73, 84, 90, 118, 182, 186
amalgamation with Great Synagogue 42
in Adler Street 41, 42
in Magpie Alley, Fenchurch Street 27, 39-41
property deposited in Central Synagogue 41
proposed amalgamation with Great Synagogue 41
Hamburger, Marcus 39
Hammersmith Synagogue 25, 38, 121, 125, 176, 182
Hampstead Garden Suburb Synagogue 122, 176
stained glass windows of 153
Hampstead Synagogue 131, 178, 182, 186
stained glass windows of 187
Hampstead Town Hall, services at 87, 112
Hanway Place, Westminster Jews' Free School in 54
Harlesden Hebrew congregation 155
Harris, Revd. John 88
Harris, Revd. Samuel 83
Harrow (Kenton and District) Hebrew Congregation **160**
Hart, Aaron 36, 39
Hart, Moses 30, 145
Harwood, J. 33
Hasmonean School, Hendon 102
Hass, Revd. S. 75
Hast, Marcus, of Breslau 37, 38, 69
Heathfield Park, synagogue in, see *Willesden (District) Synagogue)*
Hendon Reform Synagogue, stained glass windows of 153
Hendon United Synagogue 128, 151, 154, 182, 186
Heneage Street, synagogue in 170
Henriques Street, see *Berners Street*
Henriques, Basil 148, 149

Henriques, Jacob 148
Henry, Nathan 63
Hertz, Dr. JH. 35, 36, 55, 88, 103, 134, 193, 194
Hertz, Samuel, of Schwersenz 37
High Wycombe, congregation in 137
Highbury, Jewish settlement in 25
Highgate Synagogue **164**
Hillel House School 177
Hillman, David 153
Hillman, Dayan 61
Hirschell, Rabbi Solomon 30, 35, 36, 37, 40, 44, 58, 187
Hoffman, Revd. 101
Homa, Bernard 102
Home and Hospital for Jewish Incurables 181
Home for Aged Jews Nightingale Lane 143
Hooker, Revd. 160
Hornsey and Wood Green Synagogue **139**
Howard, Thomas, Duke of Norfolk 21
Howitt, Arthur 146
Hyamson, Revd. M. 59, 96, 100
Ilford
ritual bath in 180
synagogue in 170
Immigration, Jewish population increase due to **24**, 83
Ironmonger Lane, synagogue in 20
Isaacs, Revd. Simeon 110
Israelstam, J. 193
Jacob, Moses 44
Jacobs, Joseph 19
Jacobs, Rabbi Louis 178
Jacobson, Israel 186
Jakobovits, Dayan I. 36, 61, 93, 111, 133
Jamaica Road, see *Union Road*
Jehuda Leib ben Moses of Lissa 37
Jessel, Sir George 75
Jewish Lads' Brigade 69
Jewish life in Stoke Newington 101
Jewish Literary and Scientific Institution 46
Jewish Museum 146
Jewish population
increase due to immigration **24**, 83
of London at end of nineteenth century 24
Jewish Religious Union 94, 116, 158
foundation of 112
Jewish Secondary Schools movement **102**
Jewish traders in Kentish Town Road 118
Jewish Year Book, founding of 19
Jews' College 24, 59, 68
Jews' College School 68
Jews' Free School 35
Jews' Free School, East End 64
Joseph, Cantor of the Great Synagogue 37
Joseph, Revd. David 86
Joseph, Delissa 41, 110, **182**
Joseph, M. (architect) 114
Joseph, Revd. Morris 52, 72, **86**, 89, 112, 113, 116, 127, 131
Joseph, Nathan Solomon 73, 83, 95, **182**
Jubilee Street Synagogue 179
Kaddish, Laws regarding 31
Katanka, Revd. M. 176
Katherine Road, synagogue in 144
Katz, Revd. Abraham 37, 38
Katz, Rabbi 165
Keizer, Moses, of the Hague 38
Kennington Road, synagogue in 171
Kentish Town Road, Jewish traders in 118
Kenton Synagogue 154, 160
Kilburn, Jewish settlement in 25
King Edward Street Synagogue 179
Kirsner, Revd. G. 176
Kisch, Simon 51
Kishor, Ish 104
Klein, B.D. see *Klien, B.D.*

Klien, Rabbi B.D.	121, 122
Kusevitsky, Revd. J.	98
Kusevitsky, Revd. Simcha	35, 36, 37, 38, 106, 107
Ladies' pews	**186**
Lambeth (Beth Jacob) Synagogue and Lambeth Talmud Torah	171
Lambs Conduit Street, conventicle in	55, 170
Landau, Rabbi I.	176
Landauer, F.	156
Landmark Hotel, see *Great Central Hotel*	
Landy, Rabbi M.	153
Lauderdale Road, synagogue in	182
Beth Hamedrash at	58
Laurence Buildings, synagogue in	169
Lazarus, Dayan Harris	88, 131, 133, 193
Lea Bridge Road, synagogue in	170
Lea Valley, furniture industry in	25
Leadenhall Street, synagogue in, see *New Synagogue*	
Lehrmann, B.	193
Leighton Court Road, synagogue in	136
Lesser, Revd. J.	95
Levene, Ephraim	193
Levi, David	24
Levin, Revd. Walter	84, 86, 118, 121
Levine, David	35
Levine, E.	88
Levy, Dayan Aaron	59
Levy, G.	193
Levy, Revd. Dr. Isaac	84
Levy, Judith	30, 145
Levy, Revd. Solomon	47, 88, 127, 194
Lew, Rabbi J.	157
Lew, Dayan M.	106, 107, 157
Lew, Rabbi Maurice	157, 164
Lew, Myer	118
Lewin, Hirsch, see *Lyon, Hart*	
Lewis, Revd. A.	110
Leyton and Walthamstow Synagogue	170
Liberal Jewish Synagogue	**112**
in Hill Street	113, 114, 116
in St. John's Wood Road	114, 115
Liberal Synagogue, Berlin	187
Lichtigfeld, Rabbi Isaac	153
Lieberman, B.	193
Liepman, Wolf	48
Lillie Road, synagogue in, see *Fulham and Kensington Synagogue*	
Limehouse Synagogue	180
Lipson, Revd. S.	121, 193
Litchfield Gardens, synagogue in	146
Little Alie Street Synagogue	179
Livingstone, I.	88, 193, 194
Lodzer Synagogue	169
Loebel, Hirsch, see *Lyon, Hart*	
Loewe, Rose	148
Lomza	89
London Jewish Hospital	94
London Jewish Male Voice Choir	153
Lothbury (Lothburie)	17
Loughton, synagogue in	180
Löwy, Revd. Dr. A.	118, 131
Lubiner and Lomzer Synagogue	169, 179
Lunzer, R.	102
Lyon, Hart	36
Machzike Adass Synagogue	100, **171**, 172
Machzor by David Levi	24
Magna scola	20, 58
Magpie Alley, Fenchurch Street, synagogue in, see *Hambro Synagogue*	
Maida Vale,	
migration to	25
synagogue in	180
Maiden Lane Synagogue	27, 50, **51**, 54, 71, 86, 118
cemetery of	52
closure of	51
Manette Street, conventicle in	55
Manné, Revd. S.	104, 105
Manor Park	126
Marble Arch, synagogue at, see under *Western Synagogue*	
Marks, Revd. Prof. David Woolf	54, **71**
Marks, F.W.	131
Marrano merchants	21
Mary Ward Settlement, service in	158
Mattuck, Rabbi Israel Isadore	88, 114, **116**
Mayerowitsch, Revd. H.	31, 35, 37
Melinek, A.	106, 133
Melnick, Shmuel	173, 174
Memorial plaque, Central Synagogue	75
Mendel, Menachem	37
Mendelsohn, Dayan Louis	127, **128**, 129, 193
Mendleson, J.	141
Methuen Park, services in	140
Metropolitan Line	25, 165
Metropolitan railway	131
Metz, Myer, of Offenbach	37
Michelson, Revd. B.	121
Michelson, Revd. S.A.	176
Microcosm of London	32
Mikveh, Essex Road	100
Mildmay Road, synagogue at	95
Mile End and Bow United Synagogue	**157**, 180
Mile End New Town Synagogue, Dunk Street	157, 179
Miller, Rabbi	147
Minyanim in Stepney	90
Mishcon, Rabbi A.	88, 134, 136
Mocatta, David	46
Mombach, J.L.	37, 69
Montagu Road	
synagogue in	180
cemetery in	169
Montagu, Lily	113, **116**, 158, 159, 169
Montagu, Marian	158
Montagu, Sir Samuel, see *Swaythling, Lord*	
Montefiore, Claude Goldsmid	56, 112, **115**, 148, 150,
Montefiore, Sir Moses	43, 73, 148
Morein, Revd. Woolf	86
Morris, Revd. E.	106
Mulberry Street	61
Munk, Rabbi E.	103, 178
Munz, Revd. S.	89
Muswell Hill Synagogue	**140**
Myers, Moses	36, 44, 95
National Organisations of Girls' Clubs	159
Neasden Federation Synagogue	170, **176**, 177
Neasden Mission Hall, services in	162
Nelken, Julius	147
Nelson Street, synagogue in	180
Nemeth, Rabbi E.	75, 164, 166
'Nemo'	76
New Christian merchants	21
New Dalston Synagogue	**104**
New Road Synagogue	179, 180
New South London Synagogue	143
New Synagogue	39, **44**, 73, 84, 178,
choir of	127
closure of	47
in Egerton Road	47, 104
in Great St. Helen's	27, 44, 46, 47
in Leadenhall Street	44
New West End Synagogue	25, 54, 68, 89, 96, 112, 118
stained glass windows in	187
Newman, J.	193
North London railway	25, 85, 117
North London Synagogue	52, 84, **85**, 94, 95, 181
closure of	98
in John Street West	27
in Lofting Road	27, 104, 118, 119
North West London Reform Synagogue, Alyth Gardens	75
North West London Synagogue	84, **117**

in Caversham Road	110, 118
in York Road	117
Northern Line	117
extension of	67
Notting Hill Federation Synagogue	137, 170
Notting Hill, migration to	25
Nunes, Isaac	145
Ohel Rachel Synagogue, Shanghai	121
Ohel Shem Synagogue	177
Old Castle Street Synagogue	182
Old Jewry, synagogue in	17, 18, 20
Old Kent Road, synagogue in	138
Omed	**185**
Ornstein, Nathan	64
Ornstein, Philip	132
Ostroff, Revd. I.	142
Oxford and St. George's Boys Club	148
Park Hall, Providence Place, services in	176
Parokhet	**184**
Parsifal College	178
Parsons Hill, services in Welsh Chapel in	124
Peckar, Revd. N.	106, 133
Philpot Street Sephardish Synagogue	179
Pinner Synagogue	**165**
Plashet Grove, East Ham, synagogue in	144
Plashet, cemetery at	128
Plotzker Synagogue	179
Plumstead Road, services in	124
Polak, Revd. Isaac, of Holland	37
Pond Square, services in	164
Poplar Grove, synagogue in	170, 176
Prager, Wolf	40
Pre-expulsion synagogues	**17**
Price, H.L.	88
Princelet Street Synagogue	171, **172**
Prospect Place, synagogue in	63, 64
Pugin, Charles	32
Pulpit, siting of	**187**
Queen's Parade, Green Lanes, synagogue in	139
Queens Road, synagogue in	170
Rabbi, title of	68, 169
Rabbinate of the Great Synagogue	**35**
Rabbinowitz, Revd. Dr. J.	96, 193
Rabinowitz, Rabbi Louis	153, 176, 193
Rapaport, Rabbi Dr. I.	106
Rappaport, Revd. S.	131
Rashi's commentary, English translation of	69
Readmission of the Jews	**21**
Red House, Smith Terrace	147
Redesign of the synagogue	186
Reform Cemetery, Hoop Lane	88, 148
Reform Synagogue	54, 65, 70, 82, 112, 118, 148, 150
design of	186
Reform movement	**185**
Reinhart, Rabbi	82, 94
Reinowitz, Rabbi	100
Reverend, title of	68
Richmond Synagogue	**145**
Rivilis, Revd. Jacob	31, 37, 38
Robles, Antonio	21
Rockman, Revd. J.	166
Rodinsky David	174
Roeg, Revd. I.	57
Romanian Synagogue	179
Rose, A.	193
Rosen, Rabbi Kopul	**177**
Rosenbaum, Revd. Morris	63, **69**
Rosenberg, Rabbi Gottlieb	**125**
Rosenberg, Louis	122, 125
Rosenberg, Revd.	178
Rosenberg, Revd. L.	122
Rosenblatt, Joseph	31
Rosenthal, Revd. G.	127, 128, 129
Roth, Cecil	102
Rothschild family	35, 61, 75, 92
donations from	64
memorial bookplate	93
Rouel Road, synagogue in, see *Bermondsey and Rotherhithe Synagogue*	
Rowlandson, Thomas	32
Saatchi Synagogue	80
Sabbath afternoon services	87, 112
Salomon, Dr. Gotthold	186
Salomons, Edward	**182**
Samuel, Revd. Isaac	83
Samuel, Mr.	80
Samuel, Sir Marcus	118, 182
Sandringham Road, *Minyan* in	96
Sans Souci Theatre	50
Savage, Marjorie	110
Schiff, Rabbi David Tevele	36, 37, 44
Schneider, Revd. G.	128, 166
Schönfeld, Rabbi Solomon	**103**
Schönfeld, Rabbi Victor	100, **102**
Schonfield, A.	118
Schwartz, Revd. M.	143
Seating in synagogues	**185**
Secession from Dalston Synagogue	96
Second Reform Temple, Hamburg	186, 187
Sephardic Branch Synagogue, Bryanston Street	181
Sermons, use of vernacular for	187
Settlement Synagogue	**148**
Settlement, Mary Ward	158
Settles Street Synagogue	179
Shaarey Zion Yeshiva	178
Shadwell Synagogue	180
Shechter, Revd. A.	153
Shechtman, Revd. M.	140
Sheen Road, synagogue in	146
Shefford, school in	103
Shepherd's Bush and Fulham Synagogue	137, 170, **174**, 175
Shepherd, T.H.	47
Shine, Rabbi C.	75
Shomrei Adass Synagogue	**177**, 178
Shoolman, H.	171
Silbermann, Rabbi M.	69
Simmonds, Vivian	193
Singer, Revd. Simeon	**68**, 94, 113, 166
Slavinsky, Revd. A.	89
Slum clearance, post-War	26
Smiths Buildings, Leadenhall Street	59
Soffe, Hazzan	101
Soho Square, conventicle in	55
Solomon, Lewis	42, 104, 124, 169, **182**
Solomon, Nathan, of Groningen	37
South East London Synagogue	**108**, 122, 182
destruction of	111
South Hackney Synagogue	182
South London Synagogue	143, 166
South West Essex Reform Synagogue	150
South West London Synagogue	67, **142**
Southwark, Jewish settlement in	63
Spanish and Portuguese Synagogue	23, 26, 41, 70, 71
in Bevis Marks	21, 26, 32, 44, 71, 145
in Creechurch Lane	187
in Lauderdale Road	182
Spiers, Bernard	59, **62**
Spiller brothers	32
Spital Square Synagogue	182
Spitalfields Great Synagogue, see *Machzike Adass Synagogue*	
St. Alban's Place, synagogue in, see *Western Synagogue*	
St. Anthony's Hospital	18
St. Anthony, Friars of	20
St. Gabriel's Hall, services in	151
St. George's, boys' club in	148
St. Johns Wood Synagogue	181
stained glass windows of	153

St. Mary Axe 58
St. Stephen's Church 20
Stained glass windows **187**
    in Central Synagogue 153
    in Hampstead Garden Suburb Synagogue 153
    in Hampstead Synagogue 187
    in Hendon Reform Synagogue 153
    in New West End Synagogue 187
    in St. John's Wood Synagogue 153
    in West London Synagogue of British Jews 187
    in Western Marble Arch Synagogue 187
    in Western Synagogue, Crawford Place 187
St. Mary Axe 58
Stamford Hill 47
Steinberg, Dayan Meyer **137**
Stepney Jewish School 92
Stepney Orthodox Synagogue 92, 179, 180
Stepney, small *Minyanim* in 90
Stern, Revd. Joseph Frederick 88, 90, **93**, 113, 127, 193
Stoke Newington Synagogue 25, 59, 96, 98, 99, **104**, 133, 182
Stoke Newington, Jewish life in 101
Stow, John, *Survey of London* 17
Strand Palace Hotel 49
Stratford 126
Streatham Synagogue 136, **166**
Streatham, transport lines to 26
Suburbia, opening up of 26
Super, Revd. A. 137
Surrey Tabernacle 66, 67, 143
Swaythling, Lord 47, 116, 158, 171, 183
Swift, Rabbi Isaac 176
Swift, Morris 128, 136, **137**, 176
Synagogues
    basic design of **184**
    redesign of 186
    small, of the East End, conditions of 182
Taube, Revd. S. 98
Teesdale Street, synagogue in 180
Temple, Frankfurt-on-the-Main 185
Temple, Hamburg 185
Tertis, Revd. Alexander 174
Tertis, Lionel 174
Tetherdown, synagogue in 141
Threadneedle Street, synagogue in 18, 20
Tottenham Lane, services in Clarence House in 139
Tottenham, synagogue in 170
Toynbee Hall 148
Tuck
    Adolph 86
        Hall 75
        pulpit donated by 89
    Gustave 106
        Hall 106
        pulpit donated by 106
    Hermann 86
    Raphael 86
Tudor Road, synagogue in 144
Turner, Revd. R. 137
Turnstall Road, services in Carlton Hall in 134
Union Road, synagogue in 138
United Synagogue 27, 47, 57, 59, 61, 64, 66, 68, 73,
    80, 87, 90, 92, 93, 95, 98, 104, 110, 121, 131,
    134, 139, 143, 146, 155, 156, 161, 164, 167, 169, 173, 182
    music handbook of 88
University College 24
University College London, Chair of Hebrew at 84
Upper Berkeley Street, synagogue in,
    see *West London Synagogue of British Jews*
Upton Park Synagogue 130, **144**
Venitt, Revd. S. 125
Victoria and Chelsea Synagogue **147**
Vigoda, Samuel 31, 88
Vilna 89
Vine Court Synagogue 179

Voice of Jacob Synagogue 179
Waley-Cohen
    Hall 164
    Sir Robert 164
Walm Lane, synagogue in, see *Cricklewood Synagogue*
Walthamstow, railway to 25
Walworth, Jewish settlement in 26
Wandsworth and Balham congregation 142
Wandsworth and Battersea congregation 142
Warsaw Lodge Synagogue 170
Warshaw, Rabbi 165
Wasserzug, Revd. David 96, 98, **99**, 127, 131
Wasserzug, Revd. Haim 86, 87, **88**, 98
Welsh Chapel in Parsons Hill 124
Werner, Rabbi A. 172
West Central Jewish Girls' Club 158
West Central Liberal Synagogue **158**
West Hackney Synagogue 171, 180
West Ham (Associate) Synagogue **126**, 130, 144, 166, 182
West Ham Burial Ground 181
West Hampstead, synagogue in 177, 180
West London Synagogue of British Jews 27, 51, 52, 54, **70**,
    87, 94, 112, 113, 127, 131, 186, 187, 181
    stained glass windows in 187
West Willesden (United) Synagogue, College Road 155
Western Marble Arch Synagogue, see under *Western Synagogue*
Western Synagogue **48**, 64, 71, 79, 96, 118, 146, 169, 181
    at Marble Arch 57, 67, 170
        stained glass windows in 187
    Burial Society of 134
    cemetery of 52, 55, 56
    Dean Street congregation 51, 57, 164, 170
    Girls' Club adjacent to 158
    in Alfred Place 54
    in Crawford Place 56, 57, 67
        stained glass windows in 187
    in Denmark Court 48, 49
    in Great Pulteney Street 48
    in St. Alban's Place 27, 52-54, 181
    Maiden Lane, secession of 51
    membership of 51
    move to Central Synagogue 56
    Sans Souci Theatre 50
Westminster Jews' Free School **52**, 181
Whetstone 150
Whitechapel Art Gallery, services in 149
Whitechapel Road Synagogue 179
Whitfield Tabernacle 158
Wightman Road, synagogue in 139
Wigmore Street, synagogue in 71
Wilkes Street, synagogue in 170
Willesden (District) Synagogue 25, **155**
Willesden Cemetery 75
Willesden Green (Federation) Synagogue, Heathfield Park 155, 156
    Beth Hamedrash in 156
Willesden Green and Cricklewood congregation 151
Willesden, Jewish settlement in 25
Williams, Sir Owen 163
Wimbledon Synagogue 143, 180
Woburn House 62
Wood Green Synagogue 139, 187
Woodside Park Synagogue 75, 111
Woolwich and Plumstead Synagogue **123**, 170
Woolwich Federation Synagogue 187
World Union for Progressive Judaism 159
Yavneh Synagogue 171
York Road, Wandsworth, congregation at 142
Zeffertt, Revd. Mendel 88, **94**